William Whitaker, Francis James Bennett

The Geology of the Country Around Ipswich, Hadleigh, and Felixstow

William Whitaker, Francis James Bennett

The Geology of the Country Around Ipswich, Hadleigh, and Felixstow

ISBN/EAN: 9783337184964

Printed in Europe, USA, Canada, Australia, Japan

Cover: Foto ©Andreas Hilbeck / pixelio.de

More available books at **www.hansebooks.com**

MEMOIRS OF THE GEOLOGICAL SURVEY.

ENGLAND AND WALES.

THE GEOLOGY OF

THE COUNTRY AROUND

IPSWICH, HADLEIGH, AND FELIXSTOW

(EXPLANATION OF QUARTER-SHEETS 48 N.W. AND N.E.)

BY

W. WHITAKER, B.A., F.G.S., Assoc. Inst. C.E.,

(With Notes by W. H. DALTON, F.G.S., and F. J. BENNETT, F.G.S.)

PUBLISHED BY ORDER OF THE LORDS COMMISSIONERS OF HER MAJESTY'S TREASURY.

LONDON:
PRINTED FOR HER MAJESTY'S STATIONERY OFFICE,

AND SOLD BY

LONGMANS & Co., Paternoster Row; TRÜBNER & Co., Ludgate Hill;
LETTS, SON, & Co., Limited, 33, King William Street;
EDWARD STANFORD, 55, Charing Cross; J. WYLD, 12, Charing Cross;
B. QUARITCH, 15, Piccadilly; and T. J. DAY, Market Street, Manchester;

ALSO BY

Messrs. W. and A. K. JOHNSTON, Edinburgh;
HODGES, FIGGIS, & Co., 104, Grafton Street, and ALEXANDER THOM & Co.,
Limited, Abbey Street, Dublin.

1885.

Price Two Shillings.

NOTICE.

The two Quarter-Sheets which are described in the present Memoir include the chief area occupied by the Red Crag of England. The most interesting and important part of the Memoir, therefore, is that which deals with the Red Crag in Chapters IV., V., and VI. Some small tracts of the Coralline Crag are also included, but as the main district in which that subdivision of the Pliocene series is developed lies to the north of the area embraced by the present Memoir, the full account of the Coralline Crag will be given in the Memoir descriptive of Sheets 50 S.E. and 49 S. The whole of the Pliocene deposits of the East of England having now been completely surveyed and published, it is intended to prepare a Stratigraphical Monograph illustrative of them.

From the thickness and extent of the various Drift deposits, the areas occupied by the Crag and underlying formations cannot be satisfactorily determined. The Crag is seen at intervals along the coast, capping the Eocene beds, also along the bottoms and slopes of the valleys in the interior. In similar situations the Lower Eocene clay and sand are laid bare below the Crag, while in two or three places the erosion of the main valleys has exposed the Chalk. Only one edition of the Maps, that showing the distribution of the superficial deposits, can therefore be published.

Arch. Geikie,
Director General.

Geological Survey Office,
  6th March, 1885.

NOTICE.

As the town of Ipswich is partly in Sheet 48 N.W. of the Geological Survey Map, and partly in Sheet 48 N.E., it has been thought best to have a joint Memoir for the two maps, the chief town of Suffolk being then practically the central spot of the district described.

Sheet 48 N.W. was chiefly surveyed by Mr. F. J. BENNETT; but the survey of the southern (Essex) part was made by Mr. W. H. DALTON, and the eastern border by Mr. W. WHITAKER.

Sheet 48 N.E. was chiefly mapped by Mr. WHITAKER, the N.E. part however (beyond the rivers Finn and the Deben) is almost wholly the work of Mr. DALTON.

The whole was carried out under Mr. WHITAKER'S superintendence; and he has also prepared this Memoir, using the notes of his colleagues (though the greater part is from his own notes), the tract mapped by him being that in which most of the chief sections occur.

Both Maps were published in December 1882; the price of each is three shillings.

The small part of Essex in Sheet 48 N.E. (about 5 miles westward from Harwich) has been already described in the short Memoir, by Mr. WHITAKER, on the tract to the south (48 S.E.), to which therefore the reader is referred.

H. W. BRISTOW,
Senior Director.

Geological Survey Office,
March, 1885.

CONTENTS.

	PAGE
Notice by Director-General	iii
Notice by Director	iv

CHAP. I. Introduction.—Area. Rivers. Geological Formations. Shape of the Ground. By W. W. ... 1

CHAP. II. Cretaceous and Eocene (Lower London Tertiaries).—Chalk (Valley of the Stour. Valley of the Brett. Gipping Valley). Thanet Beds (Valley of the Brett. Valley of the Gipping). Reading Beds (Valley of the Stour. Valley of the Brett. Valley of the Gipping). Oldhaven Beds. By W. W. and F. J. B. ... 5

CHAP. III. Eocene and Pliocene.—London Clay (South of the Stour. North of the Stour, above the Brett. North of the Stour, below the Brett. Valley of the Orwell. Valley of the Deben). Coralline Crag (Tattingstone, Sutton, Ramsholt, Boyton Marshes). By W. W., W. H. D., and F. J. B. ... 17

CHAP. IV. Red Crag.—General Description (The Nodule Bed. Fossils. Rate of Deposit). Literature. By W. W. ... 29

CHAP. V. Red Crag, continued. Details (South of the Stour, Essex. Between the Stour and the Brett. Valley of the Brett. Valley of the Stour, between the Brett and the Orwell. Valley of the Orwell, up the Right Side. Valley of the Orwell, down the Left Side. Felixstow Cliffs and Pits.) By W. W., W. H. D., F. J. B. ... 44

CHAP. VI. Red Crag, continued. Details (Valley of the Deben, up the Right Side, to the Brightwell Valley. Brightwell Valley. Valley of the Deben, up the Right Side, between the Brightwell and Finn Valleys. Valley of the Finn. Valley of the Deben, down the Left Side. Bawdsey Cliffs. Valley of the Ore.) By W. W., and W. H. D. ... 58

CHAP. VII. Glacial Drift.—General Remarks. Gravel and Sand (South of the Stour, Essex. Valley of Stour, Left Side, above the Boxford Valley. Boxford Valley. Valley of the Brett. Valley of the Stour and Tributaries, between the Brett and the Orwell. Valley of the Orwell, and Tributaries. Valley of the Deben, and Tributaries.) By W. W., W. H. D., F. J. B. ... 72

CHAP. VIII. Glacial Drift, continued.—Brickearth or Loam. (South of the Stour, Essex. Between the Stour and the Orwell. East of the Orwell). Boulder Clay. (South of the Stour, Essex. Between the Stour and the Orwell. Between the Orwell and the Deben. East of the Deben.) By W. W., W. H. D., F. J. B. ... 83

		PAGE
CHAP. IX. Post Glacial Beds.—High Level Gravel. River or Valley Drift. 1. Gravel (Valley of the Stour and Tributaries. Valley of the Orwell. Valley of the Deben). 2. Loam or Brickearth. List of Fossils from Stutton. Recent Beds. 1. Alluvium. 2. Coast Deposits (Shingle, Blown Sand). By W. W., W. H. D., and F. J. B.		92
CHAP. X. Miscellaneous.—Disturbances. Economics (Building Materials, etc. Mineral Manures, with Analyses of Phosphatic Nodules. Water). By W. W.		100

APPENDIX A.—Well-sections. 1. Essex. 2. Suffolk. By W. W. and F. J. B. — 106

APPENDIX B.—Borings. By W. W. — 126

APPENDIX C.—Supplementary Notes to other Memoirs.—1. Sections at Sudbury (Sheet 47).—2. Analyses of Septaria from Colchester (Sheet 48 S.W.). By W. W. and W. H. D. — 132

APPENDIX D.—List of Works on the Geology and Palæontology of Suffolk. By W. W. (and in part W. H. D.) — 134

POSTSCRIPT. Well-section at Bradfield — 152

INDEX. By W. W. — 153

PARTS BY THE VARIOUS AUTHORS.

W. WHITAKER, Pages 1–19, 21–70, 72, 73, 76–90, 92–156.

W. H. DALTON, Pages 17, 18, 26–28, 44, 45, 67, 70, 71, 73, 82, 83, 87, 90–92, 95, 98, 99, 109, 148–150.

F. J. BENNETT, Pages 5, 6, 18–22, 45, 46, 73–78, 83, 84, 88, 92, 93, 111–116, 120–122, 124.

LIST OF ILLUSTRATIONS.

	PAGE
Fig. 1.—Section in a Pit South-westward of Bramford Church. (W. W.)	7
,, 2.—Section in Stoke Brickyard, Ipswich. (W. W.)	11
,, 3.—General Section at the Chalk Pit, nearly a mile Northward of Bramford Station. (W. W.)	14
,, 4.—Cliff-Section on the Right Bank of the Stour, Wrabness. (W. W.)	18
,, 5.—Section at Boxford Tile Kiln. (F. J. B.)	19
,, 6.—General Section at Aldham Brickyard. (F. J. B.)	20
,, 7.—Section at Hadleigh Brickyard, showing Disturbance. (W. W.)	21
,, 8.—Section of the Southern Side of the Brickyard at Whitton Leys. (W. W.)	24
,, 9.—Section in Chalk Pit, Monks' Eleigh. (W. W.)	45
* ,, 10.—Section in a Pit at Park Farm, Tattingstone. (PRESTWICH.)	47
,, 11.—Section in a New Road-cutting, just N. of the Convalescent Home, Felixstowe. (S. V. WOOD.)	57
* ,, 12.—Section in a Coprolite Pit by Foxhall Hall. (WOOD.)	63
* ,, 13.— * ,, 14.— } Sections in a Pit South of Martlesham. (WOOD.)	65
* ,, 15.— * ,, 16.— } Sections at Sutton. (PRESTWICH.) * ,, 17.—	68
* ,, 18.—Section in Red Crag at Ramsholt. (PRESTWICH.)	69
,, 19.—Section in Drift at Cosford Union House. (F. J. B.)	74
,, 20.—Section South of Semer Church. (F. J. B.)	75
,, 21.—Section East of Hadleigh Railway Station. (F. J. B.)	75
,, 22.—Section in a Gravel Pit near Hintlesham Priory. (F. J. B.)	77
,, 23.—Diagram-Section at Kirton Kiln. (W. W.)	86
,, 24.—Section in an old Pit westward of Layham Church. (W. W.)	88
,, 25.—Section in the Cutting on the Felixstow Railway, northward of Albion Mills, Woodbridge Road, Ipswich. (W. W.)	89
,, 26.—Section on the Railway S.E. of Playford Hall. (W. W.)	90
,, 27.—Plan of Borings at the S. End of Ipswich Dock	126
,, 28.—Section in the Chalk Pit at Sudbury Waterworks. (W.W.)	132

* These figures are from *Quart. Journ. Geol. Soc.*, vols. xxvii., xxxiii.

THE GEOLOGY OF

THE COUNTRY AROUND

IPSWICH, HADLEIGH, AND FELIXSTOW.

CHAPTER I.—INTRODUCTION.

Area.

The two northern quarters of Sheet 48 of the Geological Survey Map represent an area of over 330 square miles, which consists chiefly of the extreme southern part of *Suffolk* (with the towns Hadleigh, Ipswich, Nayland, and the southern end of Woodbridge), but includes also the neighbouring border of *Essex* (Harwich and Manningtree). This tract is wholly in the geological district known as the London Basin; and comprises some 18 miles of coast, from a little south of Harwich to a little south of Orford (in Sheet 50, S.E.).

A small part of this area, the neighbourhood of Harwich, has already been described in the Geological Survey Memoir on 48, S.E.,* with which Map this particular part of 48, N.E. (S. of the Stour) is naturally joined.

Rivers.

The *Stour*, which is the county-boundary, runs through our district from La Marsh, on the west, to Harwich, on the east, where it meets the Orwell, the combined rivers then reaching the sea in about a mile. It is tidal to above Manningtree and navigable throughout. The length of this river is 61¾ miles, and the area of its basin 420 square miles, its two chief tributaries having a combined length of 34 miles.† On the south the Stour receives only a set of small brooks; but on the north it has the following tributaries :—1. Below Bures the small stream rising near Assington, from the Drift beds overlying the London Clay. 2. The *Boxford River*, starting in the Boulder Clay country of Little and Great Waldingfield and Groton, flowing south-eastward, through the lower beds of the Drift, and the Red Crag, and over the London Clay, and joining the Stour more than three miles

---

* The Geology of the Eastern End of Essex (Walton Naze and Harwich). 1877.
† Report from the Select Committee of the House of Lords on Conservancy Boards, &c., 1877.

below Nayland. 3. The *Brett*, which rises north of our district,* enters it westward of Monks' Eleigh, whence it flows, at first eastward, through Drift and occasionally Chalk, and then southward, through Drift and London Clay, with Red Crag between on the south, to the Stour at Higham, about half a mile below the Boxford stream. 4. The stream rising from the Drift north of Capel, with a branch from the Red Crag at Bentley, which joins the Stour at Stutton New Mill. 5. The stream rising from Drift and Red Crag W.S.W. of Belstead, and flowing thence south-eastward to the main river just below Stutton.

The *Orwell* or *Gipping*. This river, known as the Gipping in its non-tidal part, above Ipswich, but as the Orwell in its tidal estuary, below that town, rises north of our district,* through which it flows south-eastward from the north of Bramford to the sea at Harwich, just after receiving the Stour. On the right the Orwell is joined, just below Ipswich, by the stream rising in the Drift near Elmsett and flowing thence E.S.E.; but on the left it has only very short streams.

The *Deben*, which, rising to the north,* has its tidal estuary in our district, from Woodbridge S.S.E. to the sea at Bawdsey Haven. On the right it receives two tributaries:—1. The *Finn* some 10 miles long, which, rising to the north, enters our district at Tuddenham and flows eastward, through Drift, Red Crag and London Clay, to the Deben at Martlesham. 2. The brook that rises in the Red Crag east of Ipswich and flows eastward through that bed to the London Clay, joining the Deben just below Hemley. On the left are only short streams, the brook from the Red Crag east of Sutton being the only notable one.

The *Ore* or *Alde* reaches the coast at Aldborough, about four miles north of our district; but it is there turned southward by a bank of shingle, which, turning south-westward as it enters the N.E. corner of our district, continues some six miles further, dividing the river from the sea until just east of Hollesley. The *Butley River*, which rises a little north, joins the Ore about two miles above this.

The short Hollesley brook discharges itself into Bowman's Creek, which, though now flowing, by one arm, direct to the sea, may be regarded as a tributary of the Ore, into the mouth of which its other arm flows.

---

* See " The Geology of the Neighbourhood of Stowmarket," *Geological Survey Memoir*, 1881.

GEOLOGICAL FORMATIONS.

The beds that occur at the surface in our district are shown in the following table, in which the right-hand column gives the divisions that are shown by colour, etc. on the Geological Survey Map :—

Recent
- Blown Sand.
- Shingle.
- Alluvium.

Valley Drift, Post-Glacial.
- Loam or Brickearth.
- Gravel.

High Level Gravel (of doubtful age).

Glacial Drift
- Boulder Clay.
- Gravel and Sand.
- Loam or Brickearth.

Pliocene
- Red Crag.
- Coralline Crag.

Eocene
- London Clay.
- Woolwich and Reading Beds, including a little of the Oldhaven Beds, above (Ipswich), and a little of the Thanet Beds, below. These three forming together the Lower London Tertiaries.

Cretaceous - Chalk.

For a notice of the beds found beneath the Chalk in the boring at Harwich, see Memoir on Quarter-Sheet 48 S.E., p. 23. (1877.) This adds the following to the formations proved to occur in our district, though not at the surface :—

Cretaceous
- Upper Greensand?
- Gault.

Palæozoic - Lower Carboniferous.

The *Chalk*, whilst forming the basement-rock of the whole, and occurring as such throughout the district, and far beyond it on every side, is yet very rarely to be seen at the surface, in the bottom of some of the main valleys. The *Reading Beds*, too, crop out only to a slight extent in the same valleys; but the *London Clay*, though almost wholly confined in its outcrop to the valleys, plays a more important part in them, forming great part of their flanks. Were the district bared of Crag and Drift it would show, in its western half, a band of Chalk on the north, varying in width from about five miles to nothing, followed by a comparatively narrow belt of the Reading Beds; whilst to the south, as well as over the whole of the eastern part of the district, there would be London Clay. The *Coralline Crag*, is a very local bed, and there are but three outcrops of it. The *Red Crag*, on the other hand, occurs over a large part of the district, generally with a narrow outcrop at the higher part of the valley-flanks. The various beds of *Glacial Drift* occur over nearly the whole of the area; indeed it is for the most part in the valleys only that other beds are to be seen, whether those underlying ones already noted, or those newer deposits which are essentially of valley-formation The shore accumulation of shingle is well represented, especially on the north-east.

Shape of the Ground.

The physical features of the district are simple. We have to deal with part of a low, wide-spread plateau of Glacial Drift (from about 50 to 200 feet above the sea), which was once continuous, but is now more or less divided by the valleys that have been cut through it. On the west and north-west this plateau is formed by the Boulder Clay; whilst in the other parts, which on the whole are at a lower level, the underlying gravel and sand form the flat tops of the low hills.

W. W.

CHAPTER II.—CRETACEOUS AND EOCENE (LOWER LONDON TERTIARIES).

CHALK.

WE have only to do with the top part of the Upper Chalk. Of the formation as a whole, it is enough to say that at Harwich its thickness has been proved to be 890 feet.

Valley of the Stour.

In the valley southward of Chilton Church, at the western edge of the map, there is a small outcrop, the easterly end of that at Sudbury, already described in the Geological Survey Memoir on Sheet 47.*

Brett Valley.

At Monks' Eleigh there is a small outcrop, and the Chalk is shown in section beneath Crag and Drift (see Fig. 9, p. 45).   W. W.

At Chelsworth is another outcrop, with a large old pit, marked on the Map, about half-mile S.E. of the church. This pit is now almost abandoned and overgrown, showing only about 12 feet of soft jointed bedded chalk, with very few flints. To the north-east, across the stream, is another pit, also almost abandoned, between the road and the windmill.

There is a very small exposure along an old river-cliff about half-a-mile N.E. of Cosford Bridge, with a pit (see p. 6), and at Kersey Mill, just below, is another, also in a river-cliff, at the base of which the Chalk is just visible, whilst it can be clearly seen in the bed of the mill-stream.
           F. J. B.

Valley of the Gipping.

The outcrop of the Chalk along this valley in the tract just to the north (50 S.W.) continues for about half-a-mile into our district on the right side, and about a mile on the left, to near Bramford Station.

At the old chalk-pit, marked on the Map, about 1¼ miles N.N.W. of Bramford Church, there is some gravel, and apparently some Boulder Clay, over the Chalk. At one spot there was a black mass in the Chalk, tending to go off into a thin layer, and at another (freshly cut) there was a black smudging, chiefly along two irregular layers of chalk. This, perhaps due to manganese, is like what has been noticed in a neighbouring pit, in 50 S.W.†

On the left side of the river there are good exposures in the two large pits described at pp. 14, 15, and the Chalk is also shown in the large old overgrown pit in the wood to the south, and in the small pit eastward of Bramford Station (see p. 88).

South of Bramford the Chalk has a very narrow outcrop along the steep bank on the left side (Hazel Wood, see p. 6). At the northern part of the wood is a large old pit, quite overgrown and hidden, where Chalk was probably got; at the bottom at all events: at the top there is gravel.

On the south of Ipswich the Chalk seems to have been brought up, by a disturbance of the beds, near or to the surface. It is shown in an old pit on the southern side of the farm, about a quarter of a mile S. of Stoke Rectory, and on the southern side of the side-stream, just W. of the Ostrich Inn, it seems also to have been found, judging by the occurrence of green-coated flints (from the base of the Tertiary beds) on the site of a pit, now ploughed over.

---

* The Geology of the N.W. Part of Essex and the N.E. Part of Herts. with Parts of Cambridgeshire and Suffolk. 1878.
† The Geology of the Neighbourhood of Stowmarket, p. 4. *Geological Survey Memoir*, 1881.

THANET BEDS.

The occurrence of the lowest division of the Lower London Tertiaries at the western border of Suffolk has already been noticed in a Geological Survey Memoir,* and from the district therein described the division seems to reach eastward to Ipswich, where, however, it is thinner than at Sudbury, being represented only by the clayey greenish bed that forms its base. It is, of course, far too thin to be mappable, and therefore, as in Sheet 47, has been included with the Reading Beds.

Valley of the Brett.

The clayey base-bed was shown in a pit less than a quarter of a mile south of Semer Church (see p. 75). W. W.

At the old chalk-pit, marked on the Map, about half-a-mile north-eastward of Cosford Bridge, the following section was seen:—

Boulder Clay, at one part.

Thanet Beds
- Pinkish clayey sand, firm, bedded, passing into the bed below.
- Dark green clayey sand. A foot.
- Light-grey clayey sand, with green grains, blocky and jointed, the interstices filled with a white incrustation, forming in one place a hard calcareous nodule. 4½ feet.
- Layer of green-coated flints.

Chalk, rather hard, with few flints. Slight dip to S.E.

At Kersey Mill a like section was shown in the river-cliff, the beds being as follows:—

Boulder Clay, in part, cutting across the next two beds.

Reading Beds.—A wedge-shaped piece of green sand.

Thanet Beds
- Fine buff bedded clayey sand, firm, blocky and jointed. The bottom part pinkish and passing into the bed below. 6 feet.
- Rather clayey bedded green sand.

The junction with the Chalk was hidden by talus.

F. J. B.

Valley of the Gipping.

North of Rogers-field Grove, at the very edge of the map, there seems to be a trace of the base-bed, between the Drift sand and the Chalk.

At the two large pits northward of Bramford Station the layers of green sand and grey clay next above the Chalk may belong to the Thanet Beds (see p. 14).

In the ditch running westward from the western corner of Hazel Wood, south of Bramford, and close to the marsh, there was at the bottom some very chalky clay (? reconstructed or decomposed Chalk) and some clayey green sand (of the base-bed) mixed up; showing the proximity of the junction of the Thanet Beds and the Chalk. Just within the wood is an old overgrown chalk-pit, with a little clay at top in parts.

---

* The Geology of the N.W. Part of Essex, etc. (Sheet 47), pp. 13, 15-17. (1878).

Fig. 1.

Section in a Pit three quarters of a mile South-westward of Bramford Church. 1872.

S.E.   N.W.

Scale, horizontal and vertical, 40 feet to an inch.

a. Brown soil, or wash, in hollow (derived from Boulder Clay).
b. Valley Drift. Loam, sand, and gravel, false-bedded ; a hole in the bottom of the pit showed sharp false-bedded sand, with shells, mostly broken (*Cyclas?, Helix?, Planorbis*) ; 12 feet seen. Where it ends off the lines of bedding seem to have been sharply overturned. A wash of Boulder Clay (*c'''*) spreads some way over.
c. Light-buff Boulder Clay, resting evenly on the bed below ; ? re-arranged at *c'*, nearly 15 feet.
d. ? Base of Thanet Beds; over 5 feet.
  { Dark clayey green sand, in places red at top, with a few green-coated flints ; up to a foot or more.
  Greenish-grey sandy marl, the cracks ironstained; much like the Thanet marl of East Kent; about 16 inches.
  Greenish-grey clayey sand, with a few green-coated flints ; about 9 inches ; passing into—
  Pale grey clayey sand, with a few green-coated flints, about a foot ; passing into—
  Buff more clayey bed (? with allophane?) ; about 6 inches.
  Greensand with green-coated flints, up to a foot, or perhaps more (in another part of the pit).
e. Chalk with flints. A layer of large flints at or near the top ; about 4 feet shown.

The slight hollow in the central part may be the remains of an old shallow pit.

A pit about half a mile to the south east gives the clearest section of the Thanet Beds in this neighbourhood (Fig. 1), showing the thin reddish bed that occurs so universally above the green sand around Sudbury (Sheet 47). The evenness with which both the Boulder Clay comes on above the Thanet base-bed, and the latter above the Chalk is noteworthy.

In the Ipswich Museum there are some casts of shells (a large *Nucula, Cardium*, &c.) which Dr. J. E. Taylor told me that he had found in this pit, and which he thought might have come from the Reading Beds. This, however, is unlikely, though they might belong to the basement-bed of the London Clay; but as no other part than the very base of the Eocene series is to be seen in the pit, I am inclined to think that the specimens must have come from some transported mass.

Reading Beds.

Although but little seen at the surface, by reason of the wide spread of Drift, there can be no doubt of the universal presence of this varying set of sands and clays beneath the London Clay, as may be inferred from the sections of wells sunk through the last (see Appendix A). In thickness the Reading Beds, as we may call them, the shelly Woolwich conditions being absent in our district, seem to vary from about 20 to 50 feet; but it is doubtful in most cases whether the clayey green sand at the base may not rather belong to the Thanet Beds.

In Prof. Prestwich's paper on this Series,* which gives so full an account of other districts, very little is said of Suffolk (pp. 92, 93), the author clearly not having seen such good sections as were open to us. The statement that "it appears that the space of 30 or 40 feet between the London clay and the chalk is occupied by sands only," will be seen not to hold good, as the characteristic mottled plastic clays also occur.

It will be convenient in describing the sections to work from west to east.

Valley of the Stour.

On the left bank of the Stour there is an outcrop south of Chilton; but the bottom of the series is hidden by the deposit of loam and gravel in the lower part of the valley. The outcrop seems to begin near Kiln Farm, and thence runs north-westward along the flank of the valley for about a mile†.

At the pottery nearly a mile east of south from Chilton Church the pit just by the kiln (western and lower edge of the yard), gave the following section (1873):—

	Feet.
Surface-earth, loam, &c.	up to 3
Drift. Fine soft brownish rather clayey sand, with layers of clay	up to 3
London Clay, bluish when freshly cut but getting darker and brown by weathering, with vertical cracks in part, causing it to split off in great irregularly columnar masses. No basement-bed	up to 8

---

* *Quart. Journ. Geol. Soc.*, vol. x., p. 75.
† See also the Memoir on Sheet 47. (1878.)

LOWER LONDON TERTIARIES.

		FEET.
Reading Beds	Sharp loose light-coloured sand - from 0 to over 1	
	Dark grey firm fine sand, compacted, passing into the next - - - - - from 0 to nearly 1	
	Dark grey sandy clay, partly ironshot, passing into the next - - - - - - 1 or more	
	Pale greenish fine sandy clay and clayey sand, mottled with red at the bottom part - - 3 or 4	
	Pale greenish and light coloured fine sand, with two marked layers of pipe-clay, shown to over 4	

The top bed of the Reading Series passes over the second one and then rests on the third, soon, however, ending off, when the London Clay rests on the last.

A pit just north of the corner of the road north-west of the Pottery gave the following section (1873), partly derived from information, the lower part not being visible:—

Coarse bright-coloured sand, with a little ironstone; the upper part rather clayey, the lower false-bedded; about 10 feet. Though mapped with the Drift this very likely belongs to the Crag.

London Clay, the top 3 feet clean, the rest with "malms" (=race), about 10 feet.

Reading Beds { Sharp sand, nearly white, 3 feet (=the 1 foot bed at the pottery).
Reddish clay said to occur below.

From this short outcrop, at the western edge of our district, the Reading Beds are not again seen for more than seven miles. We will, however, leave the northern outcrop to notice a small isolated protrusion of this series, due to local disturbance, at a still more unexpected place than Shelly (noted below).

The low cliff of the Stour from nearly half a mile below Stutton Mill eastward is overgrown and tumbled. At first there is some gravel, but this soon ends, and the London Clay may be seen, sandy and like basement-bed at the bottom in parts. A trifle further, in the very slight hollow in the shore due south of Stutton Hall, there was (in 1872) at the bottom, in a tumbled mass, some reddish mottled clay, like the plastic clay of the Reading Beds, and close by fine light-coloured sand, with some pieces of sandstone, occurs beneath this clay. (A block of greywether-sandstone and some smaller pieces that were lying about may have come from this.) At the top was a little gravel, but nowhere any clear section. The sandy London Clay comes on again directly, so that there would seem to be merely a very small (unmappable) boss of the beds below.

Valley of the Brett.

On the right bank of the valley there seems to be an outcrop from Semer to Kersey (up the side-valley) and also up the next side-valley to Kersey Hole.

A mere trace has been noted at Kersey Mill, on the left bank of the Brett (see p. 6).

Just north-eastward of Hadleigh there is a narrow outcrop along a side-valley, and at the brickyard nearly three quarters of a mile S.W. of Aldham, the mottled clay and sand is worked beneath London Clay, (see p. 20).

The Reading Beds seem also to have been touched in the brickyards, lower down the valley, at Hadleigh and Layham (pp. 19, 21).

Still further down the valley, at Shelly, there seems to be some local rise of the beds, by which the Reading Beds have been brought to the surface. However, when the Geological Survey of that part was carried out by MR. BENNETT, he was unable to findany sign of an outcrop, the pit, noted by the REV. W. B. CLARKE many years before, being filled in. As far as we could make out it must have been just west of the church, where there were traces of a small hole. I can, therefore, do no more than give MR. CLARKE's account:—*

---

* *Trans. Geol. Soc.*, ser. 2, vol. v., p. 373. (1840.)

Pit near Shelly Church (W. side of ravine).

		Ft.	Ins.
Mould	. . . .	5	0
[Reading Beds, or partly so]	Chalky clay (? with race) . . .	1	0
	White clay	1	8
	Ochreous yellow clay	2	0
	Greenish clay, with fullers' earth . .	4	0
	Reddish loam	2	0
	Hard bluish clay, with green particles and pebbles [flints?]	2	6
Chalk with large flints, to the level of the river	. .	1	0
		19	2

All the beds of the Reading series were curved up to the N.W.

In all probability this outcrop is of very small extent. We were obliged to neglect it.

From the Valley of the Brett, at Aldham, we have to go five miles eastward before again seeing the Reading Beds.

Valley of the Gipping.

On the right bank of the Gipping above Ipswich the Reading Beds seem to be masked by Drift, except just westward of Grindle Farm, N.W. of Sproughton, where the occurrence of the loam and pebbles of the basement-bed of the London Clay a little way up the slope shows the outcrop of the beds below, and it is possible that this outcrop may run higher up the little valley westward of Thornbush Farm than has been shown on the map; but there were no sections to be seen.

Below Sproughton I was obliged to colour the London Clay as reaching down to the river-level, though it is quite possible that there may be a narrow outcrop of the Reading Beds here.

On reaching Ipswich Railway Station we find that the beds begin to rise eastward, so that whilst at the bridge the London Clay seems to go down to the river, immediately to the east there is evidence of the occurrence of the Oldhaven Beds (see p. 16), which are at once succeeded by the Reading Beds. Mottled plastic clay occurs along the river north of Burrell Street, and there must have been a good section in the old brickyard, now a garden, between this and Willoughby Road.

The outcrop continues southward through the parish of Stoke, though much hidden by Valley Gravel, and a good section is given by the large brickyard just S. of the church.

In 1875 the clearest and most interesting part of this section was in the S.W. corner of the yard, directly S. from the kiln for about 25 yards, which showed the London Clay in apparent conformity with a hollow of Glacial Drift and cutting sharply into the beds below, as in Fig. 2, a most unusual thing, and such as I had never seen before to nearly so great extent.

On the other side of the kiln, that is at a distance of only 12 yards, the base of the London Clay was shown at about the level ×, which is much the same as that of the base of the kiln, and the clay is underlain by a thin pebble-bed and a sand, which I had little doubt represented the Oldhaven Beds, a division of the Lower London Tertiaries that had not before been noticed in Suffolk (see p. 15).

Between the kiln and the cottages to the west (and close to the section in Fig. 2), the gravel (b) is somewhat thicker and, as before, with the Boulder Clay (c) beneath it. The latter would seem not to belong to the great mass that forms the upper part of the Glacial Drift, but to be a local bed connected with the sand and gravel.

South of Stoke Brickyard the Valley Gravel sweeps inwards for a short way, hiding the outcrop, but the Reading Beds soon show again. On the southern side of the farm south of Stoke Rectory there is London Clay on the west, whilst in the old overgrown chalk-pit on the east red mottled

LOWER LONDON TERTIARIES. 11

Fig. 2.

Section in Stoke Brickyard, Ipswich, 1875.

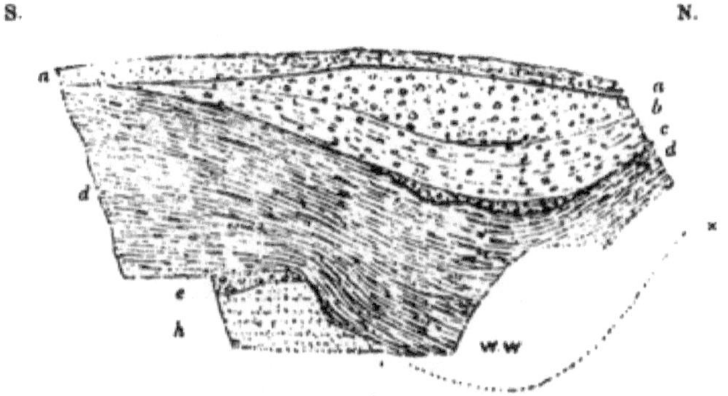

S.   N.

[figure]

For convenience of reference the letters to the various beds are made the same as in the general section below.

                                                                                          FEET.

a. Sandy soil - - - - - - about 2

Glacial Drift { *b.* Sand and gravel - - - nearly 10
c. Boulder Clay. At the bottom a layer of sand and stones (? = Red Crag. Phosphatic nodules have been found in it) - - - up to about 11

d. Bedded sandy London Clay - - - - - 20 or more.

e. ? Oldhaven Beds. Sandy gravel, with broken shells - - up to 2

h. Reading Beds. Light-grey sand, a little mottled (green and red) at top.

The curved broken line draws the probable continuation to the point *x*, near where the base of the London Clay was again seen.

The following general section of the Oldhaven and the Reading Beds here is made from observations in the various parts of the yard where the section was at all clear:—

d. London Clay, nearly flat at the western and higher part of the yard: at the bottom a sandy pebble-bed up to 6 inches thick, with a few broken shells, which may belong to the underlying series (= *e*).

f. Oldhaven Beds? Fine buff sand, with some grey clayey layers (partly ferruginous), in places hardened into stone; 6 feet or more.

Reading Beds {
g. Grey and red-mottled plastic clay, blackish at the very top, greenish at bottom, shows something of a passage into the bed below (? from staining it), with a little race: about 4 or 5 feet.

h. Sand, brown and grey or irregularly mottled red, and sometimes rather clayey, at top, the rest light-coloured, sometimes very pale green; several feet, bottom not seen.
}

clay over sand were seen at top on the eastern side. There must be some fault or other disturbance to bring up the Chalk here, and it is unfortunate that no clear section could be seen.

The short shallow railway-cutting about three-quarters of a mile S.S.E. of Ipswich Station, just south of where the line forks (Halifax Junction), is overgrown; but I was able to make out something on the western (deeper) side. The northern end was quite hidden; but further on there is brown clay, loam, and fine clayey sand, from below which, seemingly, mottled plastic clay has been turned up (by the signal-post at the fork).

At about the middle there seems to be Boulder Clay beneath the gravel, and at one spot the following order of beds was to be seen, the top of the cutting, however, being hidden :—

Glacial Drift { A little Boulder Clay.
Brown clay and sandy clay; about 18 inches.
A little gravel.

Red-mottled clay (Reading Beds) at bottom.

On the south there is a little gravel, perhaps in pipes, over red-mottled plastic clay.

The outcrop seems to extend to the side-valley south of the house in Stoke Park, where there is some mottled clayey sand, and to the other side of that valley just west of the Ostrich Inn (see p. 5).

From a cesspit, about 10½ feet deep, in front of some new cottages (1875) close to, and west of, Gusford Hall, yellowish sand was turned out, and I was told that this was capped by clay and stone, the upper half of the pit being in clay, the lower in sand. Probably we have here London Clay and Reading Beds, though there is no sign of the outcrop of the latter.

Crossing the Orwell the Reading Beds come to the surface at the base of the left bank, N.E. of The Ostrich. A good section was made here some time after the Geological Survey was done, the whole cliff having been cut back in making the outfall-sewer from Ipswich. I saw this cutting in June 1882, and though somewhat hidden, the following succession could be made out. The beds rise northwards at first, but seem to fall slightly in that direction at last :—

Brown London Clay, the lower part sandy and with a layer of pebbles at the bottom.

Reading Beds {
Brown and grey mottled clay, with small lumps of race; about 3 feet. Where this crops out, at the northern part of the section, it has weathered until much like London Clay, for which at first I mistook it.
Buff fine sand, about 2 feet. This has some blocks of sandstone in it, one about 8 feet long and up to 18 inches thick. It is like the Oldhaven sand, and passes down into—
Buff and greyish fine loam and clayey sand; about 3 feet.
Grey clay, crimson-mottled lower down; up to 4 feet.
Pale green and red mottled sandy clay; about 5 feet.

At the southern part there is a hollow of gravel, south of which the Eocene beds come up again suddenly (perpendicularly or even slightly overhanging) and the buff sand is represented only by some small blocks of sandstone, about 6 inches thick, which soon die out, when, however, the sand seems to come on again. At the extreme south gravel comes on, at first with great layers and masses of mottled clay in it.

The outcrop runs a little way up the side-valley east of Greenwich Farm, and the low cliff just south of the Cliff Brewery again shows plastic clay; but northwards the narrow outcrop is soon hidden under Valley Gravel, again to reappear, however, in the midst of the town, for a little, when the Reading Beds seem to be finally hidden through the rest of the town, first by a covering of gravel and then probably also through a local westerly dip, carrying them downwards.

At Trinity brickyard, just S.E. of the church, the beds are as follows:—

London Clay
- Brown bedded clay; up to about 12 feet.
- Basement-bed. Brown loam and clayey sand with green grains; about 6 feet shown, hidden by water below, but said to be 1½ feet more.

? Oldhaven Beds.—Sand, with a few pebbles at top. Some lying about was fine, grey, and much like that of the Oldhaven Beds elsewhere. Said to be 6 feet.

Reading Beds.—Hard dark earth said to occur below, probably plastic clay.

St. Helen's Pottery and the Back Hamlet Brick and Tile Work, just N. of Trinity Church, are practically one for our purpose, the pits joining, and the following is the succession of the beds, the account of those below the London Clay being from information on the spot:—

A little Boulder Clay over Red Crag, on the N.E.

London Clay
- Bedded clay, partly sandy, with a marked layer of cement-stone and other light-coloured layers; for the most part brown, but at bottom dark grey (at the deepest part); up to more than 20 feet.
- Basement-bed. Dark grey loam (brown where near the surface) with a few shells at top, and a layer of pyrites; about 5 feet seen, said to be 2 feet more.

Oldhaven Beds. Fine buff sand (I saw some of this lying about); about 3 or 3½ feet.

Reading Beds
- Green and red mottled plastic clay, 5 or 6 feet; but in a little pit at W. edge of yard; 8 to 9 feet.
- Brown loamy bed; 1½ or 2 feet.
- Sand, with water.

A boring in a well close to the kiln, already 24 feet deep, and therefore below the last bed, passed through:—

Dark earth, 2 or 3 feet.
Green sand, 2 or 3 feet.
Clay, 3 or 4 feet.
Mixed beds (clayey).
Total, to chalk, from the surface, about 40 feet.

The section given by the REV. W. B. CLARKE, of brick-pits at St. Helen's * probably refers to these; but it errs, like others of his sections, in making some of the beds much too thick, the London Clay being made 42 feet, at a time when it could not have been cut back into nearly as much as now: perhaps, however, this division has been carried too low in that account.

The foreman of the Trinity Brickyard told me (in 1875) that at a brickyard in what is now Argyll Street (Woodbridge Road) where he had worked for 50 years, there was at top 30 feet of clay, like that at Trinity Brickyard (London Clay) for the most part, then sand, which was dug to a depth of 20 feet, and bored 30 feet more in a well, when Chalk was touched, and bored into some depth, plenty of water being got.

The Reading Beds rise again on the N.W. of Ipswich, and sand is found beneath the London Clay in the brickyard N.W. of Brook's Hall (see p. 23). There is a small outcrop just north, by the railway.

In the brickyard at Whitton Leys sand occurs beneath London Clay (fig. 8, p. 24), and two little diggings at the lower (western) end of the common bearing that name on the Map seemed also to show London Clay over light-coloured sand. There are flint-pebbles lying about, a sign of the basement-bed of the London Clay.

Hence northward there is a narrow outcrop along the sharp slope of the valley for about a mile, when it turns eastward along the side-valley to Akenham.† It is in this part of the left bank of the Gipping that

---

* *Trans. Geol. Soc.*, ser. 2, vol. v., p. 382.
† See the Geology of the Neighbourhood of Stowmarket (Explanation of Quarter Sheet 50 S.W.), p. 4. (1881).

B 2

14

FIG. 3.
General Section at the Chalk Pit nearly a mile Northward of Bramford Station.
Scale 8 feet to an inch.

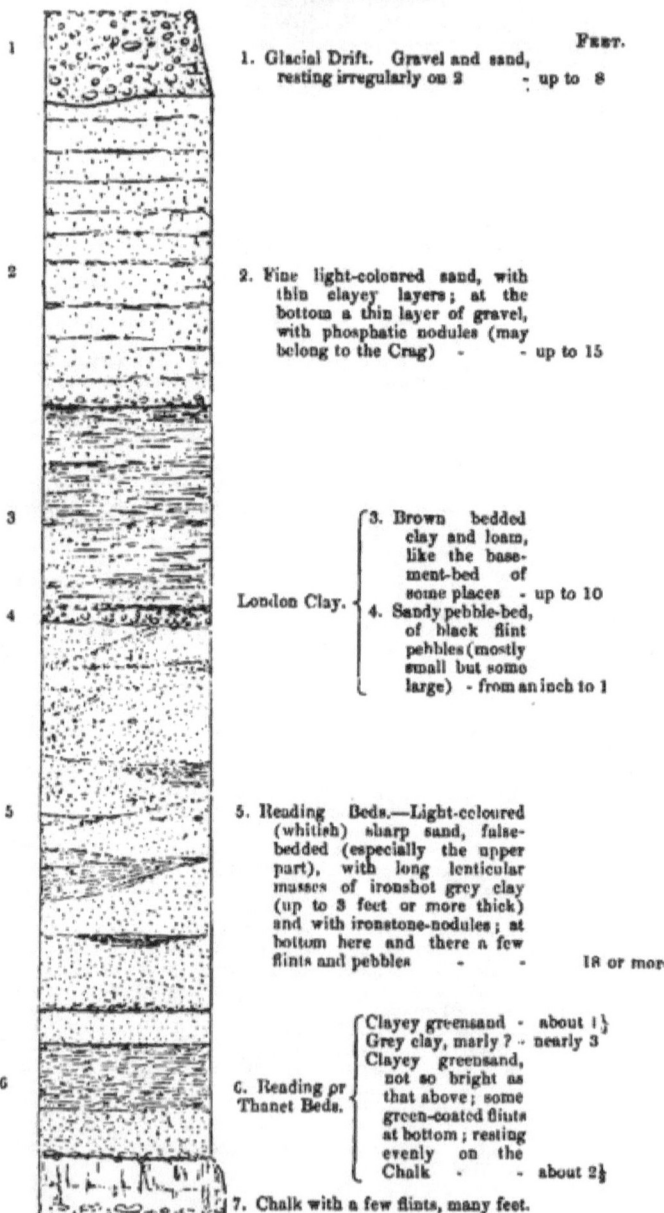

FEET.
1. Glacial Drift. Gravel and sand, resting irregularly on 2 - up to 8

2. Fine light-coloured sand, with thin clayey layers; at the bottom a thin layer of gravel, with phosphatic nodules (may belong to the Crag) - - up to 15

London Clay.
{ 3. Brown bedded clay and loam, like the basement-bed of some places - up to 10
4. Sandy pebble-bed, of black flint pebbles (mostly small but some large) - from an inch to 1

5. Reading Beds.—Light-coloured (whitish) sharp sand, false-bedded (especially the upper part), with long lenticular masses of ironshot grey clay (up to 3 feet or more thick) and with ironstone-nodules; at bottom here and there a few flints and pebbles - - 18 or more.

6. Reading or Thanet Beds.
{ Clayey greensand - about 1½
Grey clay, marly ? - nearly 3
Clayey greensand, not so bright as that above; some green-coated flints at bottom; resting evenly on the Chalk - - about 2½

7. Chalk with a few flints, many feet.

occur two of the finest sections in our district. These are given by the large chalk-pits northward of Bramford, and in describing them the same index-figures will be used for both, so that comparison may be easy. The southern of the two was the clearer and better section, all the beds being accessible. It is marked "Chalk pit" on the Map, and is less than a mile northward of Bramford Station. Here the London Clay comes on above the Reading Beds, so that we have the full thickness of the latter, the fine section being as in Fig. 3 (1875–77).

The northern pit is about a quarter of a mile further up the valley, east of the Paper Mill of the Map. Touching it, and to the north, on the higher ground, was a small sand-pit, which showed the following beds:—

? 1 & 2. False-bedded sand; with a gravelly layer, half a foot thick, at the bottom, chiefly of flint-pebbles, but with some flints and phosphatic nodules; resting irregularly on 5.
5. Sand, with a lenticular mass of grey clay. (Reading Beds.)

At the clearest part of the large pit the section was—

1. Glacial Drift. Gravel and sand, false-bedded; up to 8 feet thick resting somewhat unevenly on 2.
2. Buff and brown sand, with thin ferruginous layers: at the bottom a gravelly layer, with phosphatic nodules; up to 8 feet.
5. Reading Beds. Sand, with clay; hidden, but apparently like that in the small pit; some feet thick.
6. Reading or Thanet Beds? (partly inaccessible). Clayey green sand, grey clay, and again clayey green sand (with green-coated flints); some feet, resting evenly on the Chalk.
7. Bedded chalk with very few flints; many feet.

Although bed No. 2 has been mapped with the Drift (from which it could hardly be separated except in sections), I am inclined to think that it may perhaps belong rather to the Crag, as in the tract to the north.*

In the springy hollow N.W. of Whitton Church a shallow drain showed clay, some like London Clay, but some (at the bottom) red-mottled and probably belonging to the Reading Beds. There would seem, therefore, to be a small outcrop of these two clays (too small to be shown on a one-inch map) in the midst of the Drift.

At Tuddenham Kiln there is some mottled sandy clay (see p. 25), not, however, at the surface, and this is the last seen of the Reading Beds in our district.

Oldhaven Beds.

The occurrence of this uppermost division of the Lower London Tertiaries in the town of Ipswich, and apparently nowhere else, is peculiar; indeed its occurrence anywhere in Suffolk was not to be expected. It is the most local of the three divisions, being confined in the southern part of the London Basin to the eastern part of Surrey, parts of Kent, and a small part of S. Essex, and not having been before noticed along the whole of the northern edge of that Basin, except for a possible wee patch (of pebbles) at the border of Essex (with Suffolk).† It consists essentially of fine light-coloured sand, often with flint pebbles. In East Kent this sand sometimes contains hardened masses, which seem to have been the parent bed of many of the blocks of greywether-sandstone scattered over the surface of that part. Now in Ipswich, where this sand seems present, it is singular that many blocks of like stone have been met with.

---

* See Memoir on Sheet 50 S.W., p. 5.
† The Geology of the N.W. Part of Essex . . . etc. (*Geological Survey Memoir on Sheet 47*), p. 24. (1878.)

Some of these masses of sandstone occur on the bank of the river, near the railway-station, just where the outcrop of the sand would be expected.

In June 1882, after the above was written, the widening of the railway (S.W. side) at the station showed the junction with the London Clay. Near the tunnel there was clay; then the loamy bottom part of the clay rose up, with a layer of pebbles at the base, and then fine light-coloured sand. Opposite the centre of the station there seemed to be loam again, but I could not tell whether it was in place or slipped.

The best section is at the Stoke Brickyard (see p. 11), and the sand also occurs at the bottom of the railway-cutting, up to the tunnel-mouth, on the S.W., beyond which nothing has been seen of it on this side of the river.

In the wood, on the site of an old brickyard, just south of the house in Stoke Park, there are many greywethers. Some of these came from the old brickyard at Willoughby Road, Stoke, and would seem, therefore, to belong to the Oldhaven Beds; some are of concretionary structure and partly soft. If any came from the brickyard at the spot they would lead one to infer a local outcrop of the Oldhaven Beds.

On the left side of the Orwell the sand has been found beneath the London Clay at Trinity Brickyard and at St. Helen's Pottery (see p. 13).

Of course the outcrop of so thin a bed is too narrow to be shown on the one-inch Map, and it has, therefore, been included with that of the Reading Beds.

In the well at Landguard Fort pieces of stone, like greywether-sandstone were found.

In concluding this chapter, I may express a hope that the older Tertiary beds of Suffolk may in future have more attention from geologists than they have had in past years. The marvellous accumulations of fossils in the Crags seem so to have fascinated observers as to have led them to pass by unnoticed the really fine sections of the older beds that have been open for many years.

I may remark also, though the matter is one referring to the district to the N.E., that the evidence of well-sections has shown us that the usually accepted notion of the ending off of these older Tertiary beds in Suffolk is quite wrong. They seem to extend, under Crag and Drift, along the whole of the eastern border of the county, as MR. DALTON has shown in a short note on the subject.*

W. W.

---

* *Rep. Brit. Assoc.* for 1880, p. 375, and *Geol. Mag.* dec. 2, vol. vii., p. 518.

CHAPTER III.—EOCENE AND PLIOCENE.

LONDON CLAY.

THIS formation has its usual character, and consists, where seen at the surface, of a brown clay, rather sandy towards the bottom, and with layers of septaria, or concretionary masses of clayey limestone, at intervals. The brown colour is, however, due to oxidation, and when a section shows the clay at some depth from the surface it is usually found to be dark bluish-grey, unless where it is covered only by permeable deposits, when the topmost part has turned brown.

In our district we are far from having the whole thickness of this clay, the greater part of which has been carried away, by denudation, before the deposition of any of the overlying beds: indeed, we have only the lower part, which here in great measure is somewhat sandy and often rather well-bedded, the bedding being shown by the comparatively frequent calcareous layers, which sometimes form continuous beds of cement-stone.

The bottom part, generally very sandy, and often with a layer of flint-pebbles, is so distinctive as to have acquired the name of basement-bed.

The London Clay is almost unfossiliferous here, the only notable fossils being the remains of turtles, which were found on the coast when the cement-stones were dredged for the manufacture of Roman cement, a byegone industry, and the great number of pyritized plant-remains that occur on the beach at Felixstow: so plentiful are these latter that I have sometimes seen patches of scanty beach, on the clay foreshore, almost wholly formed of them.

W. W.

South of the Stour, Essex.

On the right bank of the Stour the London Clay occurs in continuous exposure from La Marsh to Harwich. In most sections it is seen to be somewhat sandy and regularly bedded.

It may be seen on the road about a third of a mile southward of La Marsh Church and in the railway-cutting at Bures Hill.

It is worked at the kiln on the west of the railway at Bures Station. The top part is brown and stiff, then comes brown bedded clay, then brown sandy clay, and then dark grey clay has been found. Clay is said to have been dug to a depth of about 30 feet, when quicksand (Reading Beds) was found. At the lowest part of the pit there is a wash of London Clay, with flints; and in some parts gravel seems to cut into the clay.

Between Bures and Dedham the clay is often shown in temporary sections, but no large pits occur. At Dedham and Manningtree four brickyards are worked in it. The cutting on the main line S.E. of

Dedham is in London Clay, as also are the cuttings on the Harwich Branch Railway (with or without a capping of Drift). The clay is well seen in the cliffs east of Mistley Quay. In a brickyard on the quay the bottom part is very sandy. Septaria occur at Nether Hall in a low cliff-section.
W. H. D. (and W. W.)

In the river-cliff north of Low Farm, Wrabness, a fault may be seen with an eastern downthrow, but of indeterminable amount, in a slight arch of London Clay, the bedding being well marked by continuous calcareous layers, and by septaria, as shown in Fig. 4.

Fig. 4.

Cliff-Section on the Right Bank of the Stour, Wrabness.

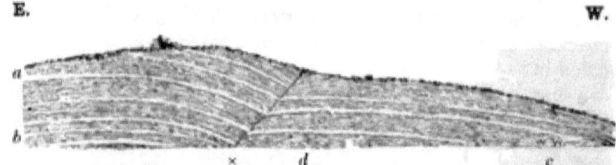

a. Clay with a few calcareous layers.
b. Clay with calcareous layers near together.
c. Clay with calcareous layers and septaria.
d. Grey clay (at bottom).
× Fault.

The London Clay from Wrabness to Harwich has already been described in the Geological Survey Memoir on the Eastern End of Essex (48, S.E.); but since our mapping was done the works for the new landing-place, station, etc., at Ramsay Ray gave a fine section, and I quote the following from Dr. J. E. Taylor's note thereon:—"In many places the London Clay is . . thrown into a series of very gentle folds. At . . nine places in the section small faults are as plainly visible as in a geological diagram, owing to the banded character of the strata. With one exception all the faults have an angle of about fifty degrees, the exceptional fault . . being nearly vertical. . . The largest . . measures upwards of twelve feet."* When I saw these works, at a later date, the section was mostly inaccessible, from wet; but they bid fair to destroy the outlier of gravel that I had mapped on the hill-top.

North of the Stour above the Brett.

Along the Suffolk side of the Stour the London Clay also crops out from beneath the Drift, as well as up the side-valleys to Assington and Leadenheath, and up that of Boxford as far as Groton.

The junction with the Reading Beds was shown at the Pottery south of Chilton and with possible Crag sand at a pit close by (see pp. 8, 9).
W. W.

At the tile-kiln, marked on the Map, at Boxford, N.E. of the village, the section showed a disturbance affecting alike the Glacial Drift and the London Clay, as in Fig. 5.

---

* *Geol. Mag.*, dec. ii., vol. vi., p. 383. (1879.)

LONDON CLAY.

FIG. 5.

Section at the Tile Kiln N.E. of Boxford.

Scale 16 feet to an inch.

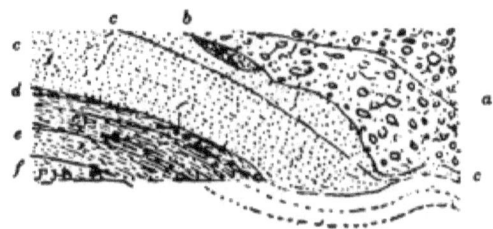

Glacial Drift.
- *a.* Boulder Clay (brown at top, blue below) at one part.
- *b.* Lenticular mass of loam.
- *c.* Rather fine, bedded and false-bedded, reddish-yellow, sand, with a ferruginious layer (*c'*) in the upper part.

London Clay (bottom part).
- *d.* Rather stiff sandy clay, bedded, the upper half greenish, the rest reddish; 3 inches to 2 feet.
- *e.* Rather stiff brown clay, with sand-partings; 2 feet.
- *f.* Brown sandy clay; 5 feet seen. I was told that this went 9 feet further down, and was succeeded by sand and then pebbles, showing the base of the formation.

Valley of the Brett.

In this valley there are some good sections of the bottom part of the London Clay, the most northerly being at Aldham Brickyard (marked on the Map), about a mile N.E. of Hadleigh Church, where the beds dip slightly S.E., and show the succession described in Fig. 6 (p. 20).

F. J. B.

The section described by PROF. PRESTWICH as on a hill a mile E.N.E. of Hadleigh refers to this brickyard, E.N.E. having been printed for N.N.E.* As when he saw the section it differed somewhat from what MR. BENNETT and myself saw, I give the earlier account (condensed):—

London Clay, brown, passing down into grey and sandy, with a few shells and teeth of *Lamna*.
Flint pebbles in sand and clay, with teeth of *Lamna*.
Reading Beds.—Light-coloured sands.

It serves to show the varying nature of the Reading Beds, the 5 feet of mottled clays of Mr. Bennett's section, between the basement-bed of the London Clay and the sand, not having been touched.   W. W.

At the Hadleigh Brickyard (also marked on the Map), W.N.W. of the church, the general section of the London Clay is as follows:—

			FEET.
London Clay.	{ Stiff chocolate-coloured clay, with septaria		12
	Basement-bed. { Brown sandy clay		9
	Dark ash-coloured clay, tough though rather sandy		4
	Brown sandy clay		14
	Dark brown sand with sharks' teeth		2
	Pebbles said to occur below, and then a hard bed with crushed shells.		

Reading Beds.—Yellow sand, said to occur beneath.

F. J. B.

---

* *Quart. Journ. Geol. Soc.,* vol. vi., p. 271. (1850.)

Fig. 6.
General Section at Aldham Brickyard.
Scale 8 feet to an inch.

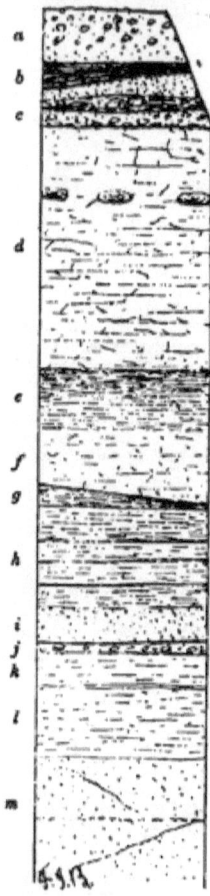

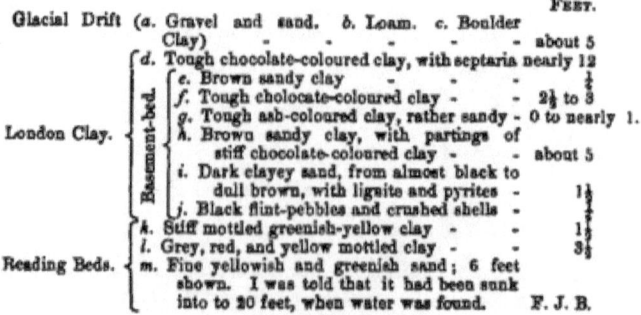

			FEET.
Glacial Drift	(*a.* Gravel and sand. *b.* Loam. *c.* Boulder Clay)		about 5
London Clay.	Basement-bed.	*d.* Tough chocolate-coloured clay, with septaria	nearly 12
		e. Brown sandy clay	½
		f. Tough chocolate-coloured clay	2½ to 3
		g. Tough ash-coloured clay, rather sandy	0 to nearly 1.
		h. Brown sandy clay, with partings of stiff chocolate-coloured clay	about 5
		i. Dark clayey sand, from almost black to dull brown, with lignite and pyrites	1½
		j. Black flint-pebbles and crushed shells	⅓
Reading Beds.		*k.* Stiff mottled greenish-yellow clay	1½
		l. Grey, red, and yellow mottled clay	3½
		m. Fine yellowish and greenish sand; 6 feet shown. I was told that it had been sunk into to 20 feet, when water was found.	

F. J. B.

The pit shows a disturbance, affecting both the London Clay and the Drift, of the same kind as those seen in the valleys to the west at Sudbury* and Boxford (p. 19). The section was as in Fig. 7.

Fig. 7.

Section at Hadleigh Brickyard, showing Disturbance.

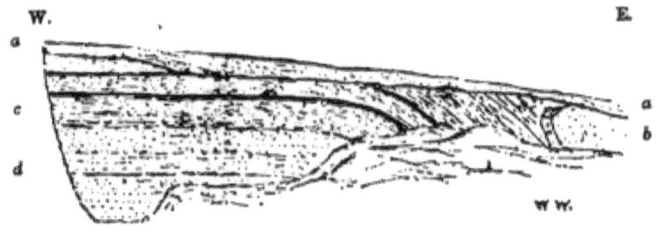

a. Soil.
b. Glacial Drift.—Gravel and sand. A bed of gravel at the base (against the London Clay) contains some phosphatic nodules, and may represent the Crag.

London Clay
{ c. Clay, distinctly bedded, with two marked layers of cement-stone; 8 feet or more (12 feet or more in another part of the pit).
d. Basement-bed.—Loam with layers of clay; 15 feet or more, not bottomed.

Some of the London Clay goes *over* the Drift sand at the vertical junction.
W. W.

The next good section is at Layham Brickyard, on the hill E.N.E. of the church (as marked on the Map), where the following succession of beds was seen, though partly hidden by slips:—

	FEET.
Glacial Drift.—Coarse sand with a little gravel about	3
Red Crag.—Current-bedded coarse ferruginous sand, with layers of ironstone-nodules containing casts of shells, the commonest being the Crag species *Cardium angustatum*†	8
London Clay (? including Basement-bed). { Layers of brown, grey, and rusty clay	3
Stiff chocolate-brown clay, with septaria	5
Brown and black sandy clay	4
Brown sandy clay	6
Black clay, rather sandy	4
Brown clay said to occur beneath.	

F. J. B.

It would seem as if lower beds had been laid open here in Mr. Clarke's time, his account being as follows:—‡
Gravel.
Blue London Clay, with pyrites, wood, septaria, crumbling shells and sharks' teeth; 60 feet.
[Reading Beds?]—Sand, 3 feet; blue clay, 4–7 feet; and sand.

There must be some mistake, however, in the great thickness given to the London Clay. Now, from the pit being cut back further into the hill more of the beds above the London Clay are shown than formerly.
W. W.

---

* The Geology of the N.W. Part of Essex, etc. *Geological Survey Memoir* (on Sheet 47), pp. 53, 55. (1878.)
† W. Whitaker, *Quart. Journ. Geol. Soc.*, vol. xxx., pp. 404, 405. (1874.)
‡ *Trans. Geol. Soc.*, ser. 2, vol. v., p. 374.

Our next section is at the brickyard marked on the Map, at Higham, close to the bridge over the river, where the following beds were seen:—

		FEET.
Soil		2
London Clay, including Basement-bed.	Stiff chocolate-coloured clay, with septaria	11
	Brown and grey clay, with sandy partings and septaria	7
	Dark grey clay, rather sandy	4
	Brown sandy clay, with sharks' teeth	14
	Stiff dark-grey clay	1
	Dull brown sand	7
	Thin layer of pebbles.	

F. J. B.

Here again MR. CLARKE seems to have recorded a deeper section, into sands. As it is hard to identify some of the beds in both sections, it is better to give the earlier one, which is as follows*:—

		FEET.
Earth [soil]		4
[London Clay.]	Thick clay with limestone (septaria?)	7
	Brownish clay with clay nodules and vegetable impressions	29
[Reading Beds?]	Very fine white sand with clayey flakes	2 to 6
	Black clay	2
	Sand	2 to 4
	Brown clay with ochreous concretions; depth unknown.	

A few pebbles are said to occur in the lower beds, which are here classified with doubt.

North of the Stour below the Brett.

The narrow outcrop of the London Clay continues along the main valley, and also up the forked side-valleys to Capel and Bentley, to Tattingstone and north of Holbrook, and to the shorter one round Harkstead; but along this course few good sections were seen.

In this lower part of the Stour the London Clay is probably cut through in the deepest parts of the river-bed, as also may be the case along the valley of the Orwell.

At the brickyard on the eastern side of the road near Potash Farm, and over a mile north of Holbrook Church, the section was as follows (1872):—

> Irregular brown washy loam.
> Irregular gravel and sand.
> Bluish-grey London Clay, which seemed to be laminated.

The pit of the brickyard on the Holbrook stream close to its junction with the Stour, west of Harkstead, is in brown bedded London Clay, with a layer of cement-stone. At the western end there was shown (in 1872) a few feet of fine light-coloured clayey sand, apparently abutting against and overlying the clay, and probably belonging to the Valley Drift.

At the cliff S.E. of Holton Green there are signs of a very loamy bed (? near the bottom of the clay), and the next cliff, westward of Nether Hall, shows traces of gravel over bedded clay, with a layer of cement-stone, again loamy and sandy at the bottom.

At the brickyard less than half a mile north of Harkstead Church the small pits showed traces of sand and gravel over brown and grey bedded London Clay.

Valley of the Orwell.

The London Clay crops out on the banks of this valley to some way above Ipswich, and also up the side-valley of Washbrook to above Burstall. Below the junction with this side-valley there were no notable

---

* *Trans. Geol. Soc.*, ser. 2, vol. v., pp. 372, 373.

sections on the right bank at the time the Geological Survey was made; but there is now a large brickyard near Shotley, where this clay must be worked.

In the little wood on the left bank of the side stream, S.S.W. of the house in Stoke Park, there is a sort of low cliff, which, though overgrown, shows at the bottom grey London Clay, the lowest part being sandy, and with green grains, like the basement-bed.

Some sections in and near Ipswich that show the junction with the beds below have been already described (pp. 10-14), as also the outcrop of the pebbly basement-bed near Sproughton (p. 10).

On the left bank of the valley a fine section of the junction with the Reading Beds was noted at the brickyard which is marked on the Map at Whitton Leys, a mile W.S.W. of Whitton Church. The pit reached (in 1875) to within a few yards of the lane, and the beds were as shown in Fig. 8 (p. 24). At the S.W. corner of the yard there was nothing but Boulder Clay, and the foreman told me that at the farm (Lovetoft's Hall) close by to the south, in making a well, the same kind of clay was found to a depth of 60 feet without getting to the bottom of the deposit.

At the Old Brick-kiln, about halfway between Bramford and Whitton Churches, the pits have been filled in. At the top there is a trace of Boulder Clay (which continues above) over gravel and sand (? in the Boulder Clay). In the lower part London Clay seems to have been worked. Fortunately, however, this section has been observed and recorded by PROF. PRESTWICH, whose account of it is substantially as follows*:—

Mixed clay and gravel; up to about 4 feet.

London Clay.
- Brown and occasionally light-bluish-grey clay, with a few small ferruginous concretions; up to about 9 feet; passing down into—
- Slightly micaceous brown clay, laminated with ochreous and yellow sand; nearly 8 feet.
- Flint pebbles, up to 10 inches in diameter, in ochreous sand and brown clay, with teeth of *Lamna*; about a foot.

Reading Beds.—Light-coloured sand, with a few small clayey concretions; over 16 feet shown.

The still earlier account by the REV. W. B. CLARKE, of Whitton Brick-kiln, 2½ miles N.W. by N. of Ipswich, probably refers to this, and differs in showing less of the upper beds, but more of the lowest, the sand being given as 20 feet.†

South-eastward from this small outcrop, which extends from the Bramford Pits to Whitton Leys, the London Clay is hidden by Drift for about a mile, when there is another northwards from Brook's Hall (Ipswich), whilst just to the south of this begins the narrow outcrop that continues to the sea.

At the brickyard N.W. of Brook's Hall the following section was noted, in 1877 :—

London Clay.
- Clay, more or less bedded as far as could be seen (the top 15 or 20 feet mostly hidden by fallen masses), loamy in parts. The lowest part, where freshly cut (to about 6 feet) dark grey, bedded, and evenly divided by a rusty line from the underlying—

Basement Bed.
- Grey and brown loam, with a few clayey layers; nearly 7 feet.
- Flint pebbles in a sandy or loamy matrix; from a few up to 15 inches.

Fine buff sharp sand (Reading Beds).

In another spot, where the lowest part of the London Clay came to the surface, it was of course brown instead of grey from discolouration. The pebble-bed comes up to the bottom of the ditch by the entrance.

---

* *Quart. Journ. Geol. Soc.*, vol. vi., p. 272. (1850.)
† *Trans. Geol. Soc.*, ser. 2, vol. v., p. 379. (1840.)

Fig. 8.

Section of the Southern Side of the Brickyard at Whitton Leys, 1875.

Scale 60 feet to an inch.

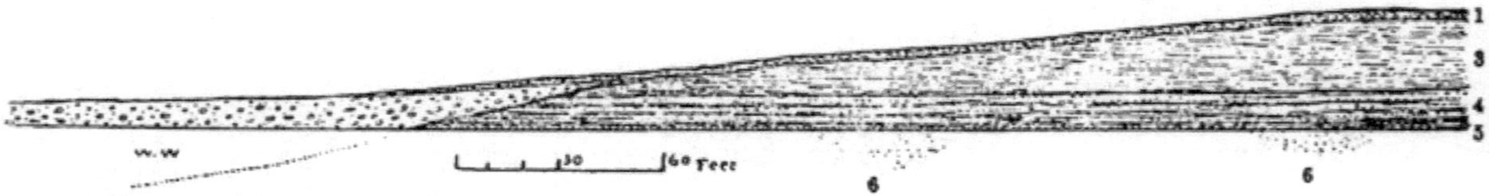

1. A little wash, with a little Boulder Clay in parts.
2. Boulder Clay. The broken line shows its deepening towards the lower ground.
3. Bedded brown and grey clay; up to 18 feet (with the soil).

London Clay. Basement Bed. { 4. Brown bedded loam; 7 feet.
5. Sandy pebble-bed; black flint pebbles (I saw an ironstone nodule and a subangular flint) about a foot, but varying from 3 to 18 inches.

6. Reading Beds.—Buff false-bedded sand; the upper part with some lenticular patches of clay (and clay galls?) just as in the large Chalk Pit to the north (see p. 14); over 13 feet seen. This was exposed only in places, and the bottom part of the basement-bed of the London Clay was hidden in parts by fallen earth.

At Woodside, a large house on the hill-top north of the hospital, I was told that a well was sunk about 90 feet deep, through sand, iron-sandstone, and Crag. In the little valley on the north London Clay is got, and at the house just west (lower) that clay occurs high up the valley-flank, close to the house; so that the top of the London Clay would seem to be very uneven here.

In the excavations for the viaduct of the Felixstow Railway across Spring Road, the following beds were passed through :—

    Soil and boggy earth (springs).
    London Clay, with loam at the bottom.
    Pebbles and sand, bored down to.

Below Ipswich there are cliff-sections, thus, at the western end of Orwell Park sandy London Clay may be seen at the foot of the river-cliff; and again, along the shore at Great Wood, where the cliff is not hidden by slips, as is much the case.

At the brickyard (? abandoned), about a third of a mile E.S.E. of Nacton Church, there is London Clay, and, just above, a small pit showed coarse ferruginous sand (Crag without shells), with some gravelly patches at top.

The short railway-cutting close to the Ordnance Hotel, Felixstow, is in London Clay, with a small hollow of sand and gravel at the northern end. The clay of the coast-section will be noted further on (pp. 54–56).

Valley of the Deben.

On the right side of this valley there is a nearly continuous outcrop, except where patches of Valley Gravel reach up to the Crag. The clay also crops out up the side-valley to Bucklesham, and along that of the larger tributary, the Finn, to a little north of our district. On the left side of both the Finn and the Deben the continuity of the outcrop is broken by the descent of the Red Crag to the river-level.

At the kiln, by the edge of the marsh, a mile N.N.E. of Walton Church, a large but shallow old pit showed (in 1874) brown London Clay, covered by a wash of sand down the northerly slope, which sand hid the clay at the northern end, where the pit turned westward. A new pit, just south, on the other side of the hedge, also showed a loamy wash down the westerly slope.

There is a brickyard over a quarter of a mile south of Hemley Church, and another on the river-bank north-east of Waldringfield Church. At the cement-works close by I was told that the well was sunk through 20 feet of London Clay. No noteworthy section, however, was seen along the right bank of the streams until reaching our northern limit, where, in the Finn Valley, at Tuddenham Kiln, north of the church, the upper pit showed the section to the top of the London Clay, and the lower pit continued it downwards. The lowest beds I did not see, however in 1876; but got my information from the foreman.

Mr. S. V. Wood, Junr., saw this section in 1881, and has kindly shown me his notes, from which the remarks in square brackets in the following account have been taken :—

    Gravelly soil; up to 3 or 4 feet.

Glacial Drift (and Crag ?) { [Bedded gravel; from about 2 to 7 feet.]
Light-coloured and brown false-bedded sand, with some small clay layers; at the bottom a thin layer of flints and phosphatic nodules (Crag ?); about 18 feet. [Mr. Wood describes as sandy brickearth, with tougher layers, up to 8 feet at most, passing down into bedded sand, about 12 feet.]

London Clay. { Sandy clay (upper pit).
Dark grey clay, with iron-pyrites; 12 or 15 feet seen, and said to have been dug 5 feet deeper.
Grey clay; about a foot.

Reading Beds.—Brown earth, etc. Lying about was some greenish and reddish mottled sandy clay.

                                                                      W. W.

On the left side of the Finn the deserted brickfield, five-eighths of a mile N.E. of Little Bealings, was worked in the London Clay and overlying Crag sand.

The same clay forms the floor of the railway-cutting at Whin Hill, northward of Martlesham, and the following section was exposed in 1839 at the brickyard at Kingston, or Kyson, Quay, now closed, but showing the upper beds in a weathered face :—

London Clay
- Brown clay with traces of fossils; 12 or 13 feet.
- Flint pebbles in yellow sand. Teeth of *Lamna* common. Here also were found *Didelphys colchesteri*, Charlesworth, *Hyracotherium cuniculus*, Owen (first called *Macacus eocenus*), and Cheiroptera. Crops out on the level of the river [? mean tide-level]; a foot.

Reading Beds (?).—Light-coloured sands. Large oyster-shells said to occur in concretions in the upper part, not bottomed; 8 feet shown.

Mr. Wood's original note* of the discovery of the *Didelphys* is not accompanied with any section, but it states that the remains were found in the sand immediately below the clay. Sir C. Lyell's note† of further discoveries does not notice the pebble-bed, but masses it with the sand, yellow and white, 12 feet, not bottomed. The complete section is given by Prof. Prestwich,‡ from whose paper the above details are taken.

The London Clay, with septarian bands, is exposed in an old Crag pit at Ferry Farm, opposite Kingston Quay, and it was worked for brickmaking at Methersgate Dock.

Between Shottisham and the Deben it rises to a considerable height, probably owing to the protecting influence of the patch of Coralline Crag rock, which, before the formation of the Red Crag, occupied a larger area than now. W. H. D.

The clay is shown along the bottom part of Bawdsey Cliff (see pp. 69, 70), and northwards there is a narrow outcrop along the remaining (right) side of the Ore valley, and along the Boyton tributary.

According to Dr. Voelcker,§ the clay of Bawdsey Cliff contains 1·68 *per cent.* of iron, mostly as protoxide, but with traces of protosulphate and of basic sulphate, and 1·031 *per cent.* of bisulphide of iron.

Coralline Crag.

As the chief mass of the older division of the Crag is north of our district (in Sheets 50, S.E. and 49, S.), the general account of that division will be left for the Memoir on those Maps; it will be enough here to describe the three small separate exposures of Tattingstone, of Sutton, and of Ramsholt, leaving the spur at Gedgrave, which forms part of the chief mass to the north, to be described therewith.

Tattingstone.

At Tattingstone Hall, on the left side of the stream, there is a small outcrop of Coralline Crag, little more than a quarter of a mile along the bottom of the valley from north to south, and only an eighth of a mile wide at most. It is bounded westward by the narrow alluvium, on the other side of which London Clay crops out, and elsewhere by Red Crag, which comes on above, and the underground extent of the older Crag is probably small.

The section given by the two pits here (almost touching each other) was as follows, in 1877, when the southern one was given up and its lower part filled in, so that the Coralline Crag could not then be seen. I had, however, seen it there better and to a greater depth than in the other pit :—

---

* *Mag. Nat. Hist.*, ser. 2, vol. iii., pp. 444, 445. (1839.)
† *Ann. Nat. Hist.*, vol. iv., pp. 189, 190. (1840.)
‡ *Quart. Journ. Geol. Soc.*, vol. vi., pp. 272, 273. (1850.)
§ *Quart. Journ. Geol. Soc.* vol. xxiv., p. 356.

Glacial Drift.—Ferruginous sand, with gravel, much like, but resting irregularly on, the Crag sand; up to 8 feet.

Red Crag.—Ferruginous shell-less sand, with loamy layers and ironstone, passing down into false-bedded shelly Crag, with unfossiliferous loamy layers and phosphatic nodules. In the lower part lenticular masses of nearly white sand. At the base some phosphatic nodules, flint pebbles, and flints; up to about 20 feet thick, resting tolerably evenly, but irregularly on—

Coralline Crag.—Evenly bedded, firm, made up of finely broken shells, mostly buff, hardened into stony lumps in discontinuous layers; about 5 feet, but has been deeper. (See also p. 47.)

At the back of the buildings between the pits brown shell-less Red Crag sand overlies the Coralline Crag.

The section in this small mass of Coralline Crag has been described by MR. CHARLESWORTH,* by SIR C. LYELL,† apparently by the REV. W. B. CLARKE,‡ and by PROF. PRESTWICH.§ SIR C. LYELL speaks of the Coralline Crag as consisting "chiefly of greenish marl, with only a few stony beds;" and again he says, "I caused a pit about seven feet deep to be sunk in the yard at Tattingstone Hall farm, piercing the lowest part there exposed of the coralline crag, through green marls, with intervening layers of flaggy limestone, two or three inches thick. At the bottom of this pit I found marl of the same character, containing a large *Nucula*, *Venus ovata*, and some other shells; when the workmen were stopped by the quantity of water which flowed in. One of the flaggy beds of limestone was almost of a brick red colour, and consisted chiefly of comminuted shells, like the green marl." May not the green of the so-called marl have been owing to damp? W. W.

Sutton.

The outcrop here, on rising ground south of Pettistree Hall and close to the Deben, is only about a third of a mile across, from N.E. to S.W., and about a quarter of a mile from N.W. to S.E.

The bed of phosphatic nodules at the base of the Coralline Crag was once worked here, in a pit about 770 yards due south of the Hall, which has been filled in for years: luckily, however, not before it had been carefully noted by PROF. PRESTWICH, from whose paper the following description is condensed‖:—

Soil (thin).

Coralline Crag, about 22 feet.
- White marly sands with seams of *Cyprina*; about 7 feet.
- White marly sands; *Anomia*, *Astarte*, *Cardita*, *Diplodonta*, and Foraminifera common in the upper part; *Mya*, *Cyprina*, and Bryozoa common in the lower part; about 10 feet.
- Comminuted shells, with single valves of *Cyprina*, *Mactra*, and *Pecten*, *Terebra*, *Turritella*, and *Cellepora*; about 4 feet.
- Phosphatic nodules, mammalian (chiefly cetacean) bones and teeth (highly mineralized, rolled, and of the same species as those in the bed at the base of the Red Crag), rolled London Clay crustacea, sharks' teeth, a Jurassic saurian vertebra, blocks of London Clay septaria (bored by molluscs), balls of sandstone often containing a cast of a shell [= "box-stones"], small pebbles of quartz and of flint, large pebbles of sandstone, and a rounded boulder of dark red porphyry, weighing about a quarter of a ton; 12 to 15 inches.

London Clay; (8 feet above high-water level of the Deben).

---

* *Phil. Mag.*, ser. 3, vol. vii., pp. 83, 84. (1835.)
† *Mag. Nat. Hist.*, ser. 2, vol. iii., p. 314 ? (1839.)
‡ *Trans. Geol. Soc.*, ser. 2, vol. v., p. 381. (1840.)
§ *Quart. Journ. Geol. Soc.*, vol. xxvii., p. 349. (1871.)
‖ *Quart. Journ. Geol. Soc.*, vol. xxvii., pp. 116–118. (1871.)

The quarry, near by the last, and on the western side of the hill-top, is still worked. The following account, also condensed from Prof. Prestwich's,* shows three kinds of Crag under a thin soil:—

> Soft dark ferruginous rock, of comminuted shells and fragments of Bryozoa and entire Bryozoa, with a few entire shells; partly false-bedded. Soft white calcareous veins run through from the top; 11 feet.
>
> Fine sand and grit, comminuted shells, many small perfect shells, and some Bryozoa, with finely laminated hard irregular seams of yellow marl or limestone, and dark green grains; partly false-bedded; 5 to 8 feet.
>
> Fine compact sand, with small shells, and Bryozoa (mostly in the position of growth, and sometimes in regular beds); 4 feet.

Prof. Prestwich regards the beds here shown to be higher than those of the foregoing section. The lowest bed here is 12 feet thick at the Bullock-yard Pit, on the N.E. side of the hill, three eighths of a mile S.S.E. of Pettistree Hall, where the overlying sand and grit is also seen, as well as Red Crag. The top bed of the quarry belongs to the Upper Division of Prof. Prestwich, the rest of the beds to the Lower Division; the thickness of which, "as proved at Sutton, is about 47 feet;" but, from the levels given by him † would seem to be less (? 35 feet), for the surface at the site of the old coprolite-pit is 43 feet above low water, and therefore the London Clay floor must be 20 feet, and the top of the quarry is 65·6 feet, so that the base of the upper division there must be 54½ feet.

The figures of these pits are reproduced on p. 68.

Ramsholt.

The exposure here cannot be coloured on the map, being confined to the small river-cliff south of Shottisham Creek, where Coralline Crag occurs to a thickness of 7 feet, overlain by 4 feet of Red Crag,‡ and a small pit near here yielded many rare and well-preserved fossils, Prof. Prestwich remarking that "Many species were more abundant at Ramsholt than in any other locality, and were generally in a very fine state of preservation, the bivalves often with both valves."§

Boyton Marshes

Near Caldwell Hall Coralline Crag phosphate is worked, below the alluvium, and therefore generally under water, which is kept down by pumping. Only "about 18 inches of Coralline Crag are overlain by Red Crag, and . . . in working the labourers mix the two together."∥

The Gedgrave spur, with its capping of Red Crag, will be described in the Memoir on Sheet 50, S.E.

W. H. D. (and W. W.)

---

* *Quart. Journ. Geol. Soc.*, vol. xxvii., pp. 119, 120.
† *Quart. Journ. Geol. Soc.*, vol. xxvii., pl. vi.
‡ Charlesworth. *Phil. Mag.*, ser. 3, vol. vii., p. 81.
§ *Quart. Journ. Geol. Soc.*, vol. xxvii., p. 118.
∥ [A.] Bell quoted by S. V. Wood. *Quart. Journ. Geol. Soc.*, vol. xxxiii., p. 120. (1877.)

CHAPTER IV.—RED CRAG.

General Description.

The Red Crag is essentially a sand, generally coarse, strongly coloured by iron-peroxide, showing well-marked oblique or false bedding, and in great part crowded with marine shells, sometimes to such an extent as to be chiefly made up of these. The shells are mostly broken up; but there is an abundance of perfect, or nearly perfect, specimens, the great variety of which has made this deposit so interesting to geologists and collectors: even one who is well accustomed to see it can hardly stop himself from collecting shells in a Crag pit.

Here and there loamy layers occur, and also beds of a gravelly character, with small pebbles of flint and quartz, rolled pieces of flint, and phosphatic nodules. The ferruginous matter is often abundant enough to cement the whole into a firm mass, and it also occurs segregated into bands or nodules. The redness is probably not original; but caused by peroxidation of iron, which seems to occur as a protosalt where the Crag is protected from surface-actions, as in some deep wells in the district to the north, in which the bed is not red.

As might be expected from the permeable character of the Red Crag, its shells have to some extent been dissolved away by the percolation of acidulated water, and sometimes the calcic carbonate thus taken away from upper beds has been deposited, as a whitish marl, along small more or less vertical fissures in lower beds. In many parts the shells seem to have wholly disappeared, though leaving their mark in the form of casts and impressions in the firm iron-sandstones and ironstones. Often, however, especially on the outskirts, not even this trace is left, and we find only an unfossiliferous sand which an observer would at first hardly believe to be merely the decalcified state of the wonderfully shelly deposit usually understood by the term Red Crag. It is only by tracing these sands along their outcrop, by the examination of their relation to the beds above, and by noting their lithological character, that one is enabled to make out what they are, and in some cases this can hardly be done with certainty.

As we should expect, the process of decalcification of the Crag sand has often been very irregular; so that the upper shell-less part is divided from the shelly part in a very uneven way, and this has given rise to the impression of there being an eroded surface between the two. This, however, is not really the case, and we have only an example of an occurrence common in permeable and especially in calcareous beds, for a detailed account of which the reader cannot do better than read the Memoir of M. E. Vanden Broeck,* which refers largely to beds of a like character to our Crag, in Belgium.

In our district the thickness of the Red Crag ranges up to about 40 feet, but that amount is rarely reached: nor is a greater

---

* Sur les Phénomènes d'Altération des Dépôts superficiels par l'Infiltration des Eaux météoriques. *Mém. couronnés*, etc. (*Ac. R. Belg.*), t. xliv. (1881.)

thickness ever seen at the surface, though wells, in other parts, seem to pass through more.

The Nodule Bed.

The most interesting part of the deposit is perhaps the thin layer at the bottom, which has been so much worked for the phosphatic nodules, of which it often so largely consists. This bed is one of the same kind as those at the base of the Chalk, and in the Lower Greensand, in Cambridgeshire, Bedfordshire, etc., all of them being of a conglomeratic or gravelly character, and containing so-called "coprolites," or fossils and nodules composed chiefly of phosphate of lime.

In our case the nodule-bed contains the usual shells of the Red Crag, together with a miscellaneous collection of various rocks, in small waterworn pieces and in larger blocks. Amongst these flint and flint-pebbles are the most plentiful, many of the former being unworn and partly covered with the shells of a *Balanus*; quartz and quartzite also occur, and pieces of sandstone (Carboniferous and Greywether), of various Jurassic and Cretaceous beds, of granite and other igneous rocks, and of London Clay septaria (sometimes large). The most peculiar of the rock-contents are, however, the "box-stones," so called from the fact that many of them contain the cast of a shell. These are irregular rounded lumps of a tough, brownish sandstone, shown, by the contained fossils, to be of comparatively late Tertiary age, though older than the Coralline Crag, and lithologically unlike any English Tertiary bed. These are indeed the only record in our country of their age. They are the remnants of beds that once existed either where the Crag sea reached beyond our island, or in parts from which these beds have been wholly swept away, and they have their present representatives in the Diestian of Belgium.

Besides the phosphatic nodules, which are rolled pebbles of London Clay septaria or of hardened phosphatized clay, there are great numbers of phosphatized fossils, which, like the rocks, are of various ages. In the collection of Mr. W. Crowfoot, of Beccles, I have seen rolled pieces of *Ammonites*, probably *A. biplex* (Kimeridgian), of like character to the phosphatized remains found in the Lower Greensand of Bedfordshire, etc., from which they may have been derived ; and, in the same collection, there were some true coprolites. The great majority, however, consist of sharks' teeth and other remains from the London Clay, of teeth of many land mammals (pig, rhinoceros, mastodon, tapir, deer, horse, bear, etc.), that have been derived from some older Pliocene beds, and of many bones and teeth of marine mammals of like age, pieces of the ribs of whales being indeed amongst the most common things to be seen on the phosphate heaps, and the ear-bones being not uncommon.

Prof. E. R. Lankester has described the strange derivative fauna of this bed, and in his paper of 1870 (see p. 39) there is a list of the mammalian remains, as well as one of the fossils from the box-stones, to the number of 5 vertebrata and 35 mollusca. A fine collection both of the mammals and of the box-stones may be seen in the Ipswich Museum. It is needless to treat of this bed at greater length, as an account of the published researches on it is given a few pages further on.

Fossils.

Long lists of the shells of the Red Crag have been given by Prof. Prestwich* and by Mr. S. V. Wood,† the latter of whom noted the occurrence of the species by groups of localities, and it is needless to reproduce these lists, or those of Mr. Bell ;‡ enough here to draw attention to the general character of the fauna, as shown by the mollusca.

As would be expected, from the late geologic date of the deposit, the great majority of the non-derivative fossils are of still existing species. Authorities, however, unfortunately differ much as to the proportion of extinct forms, probably from the different value attached to certain characters as specific or only varietal. Thus whilst Prestwich (? on the authority of Jeffreys) gives 7·7 as the per-centage of extinct species in the Red Crag of Suffolk,§ Wood gives 50 out of 148 in the case of the Walton Naze, or older Red Crag, and 55 out of 199 in that of the rest of the Red Crag,|| or as much as 33·7 and 27·6 per cent. respectively.

With regard to the distribution of the living forms I cannot probably do better than reproduce the statements of the above authors, which are as follows, with the per-centages added, in order to reduce them to a common denominator, as they differ with regard to the total number of species.

Geographical Distribution of 216 living Species of Red Crag Mollusca : Prestwich.

Mediterranean	167 =	over 77·3 per cent.
British	157 =	nearly 72·7 ,,
West European	156 =	over 72·2 ,,
Scandinavian	135 =	,, 62·5 ,,
Atlantic	84 =	nearly 38·9 ,,
Arctic	40 =	over 18·5 ,,
North American	17 =	,, 7·8 ,,
Various others	7 =	,, 3·2 ,,

Geographical Distribution of Red Crag Mollusca : Wood.

—	Walton Naze, or older Red Crag.	Rest of the Red Crag (not including the Scrobicularia beds).
British (not Mediterranean)	13 = nearly 8·8 per cent.	30 = over 15 per cent.
British and Mediterranean	61 = over 41·2 ,,	78 = nearly 39·2 ,,
Mediterranean (not British)	14 = ,, 9·4 ,,	14 = over 7 per cent.
Not British or Mediterranean	10 = ,, 6·7 ,,	22 = ,, 11 ,,

It follows, therefore, that Wood makes 50 per cent. of British species and about 50·7 of Mediterranean species in the Walton Naze Crag, whilst his figures are about 54·2 and 46·2 for the rest of the Red Crag; much less in all cases than Prestwich's figures.

---

* *Quart. Journ. Geol. Soc.*, vol. xxvii., pp. 480–494.
† Supplement to the Crag Mollusca, 1874 (pp. 203–218), 1879 (pp. 54, 55), 1882 (pp. 14–17).
‡ *Proc. Geol. Assoc.*, vol. ii., pp. 208–215.
§ *Quart. Journ. Geol. Soc.*, vol. xxvii., p. 473. (1871.)
|| Supplement to the Crag Mollusca, Part ii., p. 219. (1874.)

There is one point at which the Red Crag stands at the head of British formations (save perhaps the Drift): that is in the great number of derived fossils that it contains, which have chiefly come from the destruction of the Coralline Crag, as far as Mollusca are concerned, though there are many from the London Clay.

Rate of Deposit.

Whilst acknowledging that there is evidence of some change from the Red Crag of our district to the more regularly bedded Crag to the north (which has been named Fluvio-marine, Norwich, and Mammaliferous), I cannot see that we have good evidence of distinct upward succession, though the latter Crag seems to be somewhat newer than part, at all events, of the former. What we have is rather a slight change of conditions, and the whole of the small set of deposits between the Chillesford Clay and the Coralline Crag seems to have been formed in so short a time (a mere geologic second) that such a term as the Red Crag Period is beside the mark; these sands being apparently such as would be accumulated in a very short time: a heaping up of no great thickness of loose materials on or near a shore being all that was done. I think, therefore, that compared with such deposits as our Glacial Drift, or our River Gravels, with their various terraces, the Red Crag is a small thing, so far as time is concerned, and I doubt whether it is not so in comparison even with the alluvium, or marsh-deposits, of our rivers. Were it not for the number of its fossils the Red Crag would probably have been almost unnoticed by geologists, as of no greater importance than some of the sandy beds of the Drift.

LITERATURE.

As our district contains the chief part of the Red Crag, it may be useful to make a summary of what has been written on the subject, in the order of the dates (or years of publication), so as to give a history of the views of geologists thereon. In doing this one may pass over some of the earlier notices, which amount to little more than notes of the occurrence of shells, &c., and do not really bear on the question of the stratigraphy or origin of the Crag, with which we are here concerned. Purely palæontological works, such as consist only of descriptions of fossils, are also omitted; but all are noted in Appendix C. Conspicuous among original observers are CHARLESWORTH, WOOD, PRESTWICH, S. V. WOOD, JUN., and E. R. LANKESTER.

The first paper that seems to call for notice appeared in 1811, when J. PARKINSON[*] noticed the occurrence of shells, partly of extinct species, in the Crag, which, however, he does not call by that name, regarding it as the upper part of his Sand and Gravel Series; and he also noted the occurrence of rolled bones.

In 1822, the REV. W. D. CONYBEARE and W. PHILLIPS, in their remarkable work,[†] described the Crag, noticed that the greater number of its shells seem not to differ specifically from those of neighbouring seas, and

---

[*] *Trans. Geol. Soc.*, vol. i., pp. 330, &c.
[†] Outlines of the Geology of England and Wales, pp. 10-13.

concluded that it is probably the newest bed of the Upper Marine formation, or in other words, newer than the Bagshot and Isle of Wight beds.

In 1824 R. C. TAYLOR* noticed the occurrence of shelly Crag in Suffolk, and that many of the shells approach those of our shores in character, whilst others are of extinct species; but he refers chiefly to the Norwich Crag.

In 1827 the same author† referred to the connexion of the Suffolk Crag with that of Norfolk, concluding that they are parts of one contemporaneous formation, and noticed rapid local variations in the Crag, in which perhaps he includes some of the Drift, however.

In 1833 SIR C. LYELL‡ paralleled the Crag with the Subapennine deposits (as containing remains of many recent species, and as resting on beds that contain very few such); classed it as older Pliocene; described its structure (including in the Crag, though with some doubt, much that we now class with the Drift); and compared it with the Faluns of the Loire, concluding that these two are not contemporaneous, but merely formed under similar geographical conditions at different periods. In the Appendix (pp. 47–49, 51) the per-centage of living and extinct species found in the Crag is referred to (? for the first time).

These remarks have of course reappeared, with many changes, in the various editions of Sir C. Lyell's works, to the last of which only perhaps need further notice be drawn.

In 1835, E. CHARLESWORTH,§ to whom belongs the credit of making out the divisions in the Crag, which had before been treated as one mass, described the Crag deposits. He pointed out that the Crag consists of two well-defined beds, the upper marked by its ferruginous colouring, the lower by its corals (Polyzoa); proposed the names Red Crag and Coralline Crag for these; quoted a letter by MR. S. V. WOOD, showing that he had been for many years aware of the existence of the two beds, and thought that the upper had been formed from the ruin of the lower; noted the occurrence of teeth of London Clay fish in the Red Crag; noticed differences in the fossils of the two Crags; concluded that they were deposited under different conditions, at different periods; and regarded the Norfolk Crag as agreeing with the Red Crag.

In another paper ‖ he controverted the criticisms of WOODWARD (see below) on the foregoing paper; to this WOODWARD made a rejoinder in vol. viii., pp. 138, 139 (1836); but the contents are purely controversial.

S. WOODWARD,¶ said that the Red Crag is diluvium or disrupted crag, objected to the name Coralline, and concluded that the Norfolk Crag is newer than the Red.

In 1836 CHARLESWORTH** supported his division of the Crag into Red and Coralline, discussed the fossil contents of the Crag, disputed the founding of a classification on the proportion of extinct Mollusca, and noticed how organic remains of different periods may be mixed in one deposit.

In 1837 he returned to the same subjects†† and, in another paper,‡‡ said that the Mammaliferous (Norfolk) Crag is not an extension of the Red Crag, but a distinct deposit newer than the latter. He also referred again elsewhere to the mixing of shells of different ages in the Crag.§§

In the same year DESNOYERS‖‖ criticised the principle of the determination of the age of beds by the number of existing species in them,

---

* *Trans. Geol. Soc.*, ser. 2, vol. i., p. 371.
† *Phil. Mag.* ser. 2, vol. ii., pp. 329, 330.
‡ Principles of Geology, vol. iii., pp. 19–21, 61, 171–182, 203–206.
§ *Phil. Mag.*, ser. 3, vol. vii., pp. 81–94. Abstract in *Proc. Geol. Soc.*, vol. ii., no. 41, pp. 195, 196.
‖ *Phil. Mag.*, ser. 3, vol. vii., pp. 464–470.
¶ *Phil. Mag.* ser. 3, vol. vii., pp. 353–355.
** *Phil. Mag.*, ser. 3, vol. viii., pp. 529–588, and *Mag. Nat. Hist.*, vol. ix., pp. 537–542.
†† *Phil. Mag.*, ser. 3, vol. x., pp. 1–9.
‡‡ *Rep. Brit. Assoc.* for 1836, *Sections* pp. 84–86, and in *Mag. Nat. Hist.* n. ser., vol. ii., pp. 40–43. (1838.)
§§ *Mag. Nat. Hist.* n. ser. vol. i., pp. 42, 96, 97.
‖‖ *Bull. Soc. Géol. France*, t. viii., pp. 203–211. Partly translated in *Mag. Nat. Hist.*, n. ser., vol. ii., pp. 111–120. (1838.)

referring especially to the Crag and to the Faluns of the Loire. He thinks that the division of the Crag into two by Charlesworth (1835) is inadmissible, the union of the two [as regards fossils?] being so intimate. CHARLESWORTH added a long note to the translation, criticising some of DESNOYERS' conclusions.

In 1838, the REV. W. B. CLARKE* referred to the presumed occurrence of bones of terrestrial Mammalia in the Crag; but CHARLESWORTH added a note showing that there is not evidence enough to make it clear that these came from Crag, which is virtually allowed (in most cases) in the second letter. The third letter criticises LYELL's view (1833) of the impossibility of drawing a line of separation between Crag and Drift, an opinion given up in later editions of LYELL's work.

In 1839 SIR C. LYELL† followed Charlesworth as to the superposition of the Red on the Coralline Crag, the former resting on a denuded surface of the latter; and described the junction of the two at Sutton, where the Coralline Crag has been perforated by *Pholas*, and in parts forms a low buried cliff against which the Red Crag rests. He described the so-called Fluvio-marine Crag of Southwold, but seems to include therein the overlying pebbly sands at Easton Bavent cliff, and treated of the Norwich Crag at greater length. He accepted the opinion of DESNOYERS that the Red and Coralline Crags may be of the same age as the Faluns of Touraine, as, though the fauna of the former is of a northern character, whilst that of the latter is southern, yet the two faunas depart almost equally from the nearest existing marine fauna. He regarded the Norwich Crag as older Pliocene, the Red and Coralline Crags as Miocene.

In 1840 the REV. W. B. CLARKE,‡ said that the word Crag is applied in Suffolk only to shelly beds; but he objected to the separation of the beds with shells from those without [though it is a question to what beds he refers]. He believed that the Crag was formed as sand banks, inhabited by *testacea*, in a tidal course, exposed to violent fluctuations of the sea and to drifts from land-waters.

In 1841 SIR C. LYELL§ returned to one of the subjects discussed in his paper of 1839, comparing the fossil contents of the Faluns of the Loire, etc., with those of the Crag, and, though there is a great difference therein, referring both deposits to the Miocene epoch.

In 1844 PROF. HENSLOW‖ described the concretions (phosphatic nodules) from the Red Crag, and concluded that they are coprolitic. He also noticed, for the first time, the occurrence of petro-tympanic bones of cetaceans.

In 1846 the same author¶ again noticed the occurrence of phosphatic nodules in the Crag, and that they are of the same character as some from the London Clay.

In this year PROF. OWEN** described the Mammalian fossils of the Red Crag, and concluded that the Cetacean ear-bones and teeth had been derived from Eocene beds, from the [mistaken] idea that a Cetotolite had been found in the London Clay, being recorded as "from Harwich Cliff."

PROF. HENSLOW recurred to the subject of his paper of 1846, two years later,†† stating that nodules which he once thought to be coprolitic are really derived from the London Clay, and thinking that various bones have been so as well, true Crag fossils differing from these older fossils in not being mineralized.

In this year (1848) was published the first instalment of S. V. WOOD's great work,‡‡ the greater part of which of course refers only to the fossils;

---

* *Mag. Nat. Hist.*, ser. 2, vol. ii., pp. 162, 163, 224, 225, 285, 286.
† *Mag. Nat. Hist.*, ser. 2, vol. iii., pp. 318–330. Abstract in *Proc. Geol. Soc.*, vol. iii., no. 63, pp. 126–130, and short note in *Bull. Soc. Géol. France*, t. x., p. 321.
‡ *Trans. Geol. Soc.*, ser. 2, vol. v., pp. 362–364.
§ *Proc. Geol. Soc.*, vol. iii., No. 79, p. 443.
‖ *Proc. Geol. Soc.*, vol. iv., pp. 281–283. Reprinted in *Quart. Journ. Geol. Soc.*, vol. i., pp. 35–37 (1845).
¶ *Rep. Brit. Assoc.* for 1845, *Sections*, pp. 51, 52.
** A History of British Fossil Mammals and Birds. 8vo. London. p. 542.
†† *Rep. Brit. Assoc.* for 1847, *Sections*, p. 64 (1848).
‡‡ A Monograph of the Crag Mollusca. Vol. i., Univalves.

but in the Introduction he classes the Coralline Crag as Miocene, the Red Crag as Pliocene, and the Mammaliferous (Norwich) Crag as Pleistocene; the first classification being given up in a later part, Bivalves, No. 3, pp. 301, 302 (1856).

In 1849 Prof. Prestwich* established the fact that the fossiliferous clay and sand of Chillesford overlies the Red Crag, and sometimes overlaps on to the Coralline Crag. These Chillesford Beds were the result of tranquil accumulation, whilst the Red Crag shows every sign of a disturbed condition of the waters. He gives a list of pits in Coralline Crag, in Red Crag and in Chillesford Clay, between the Alde and the Butley River.

Dr. Buckland† said that none of the Crag phosphatic nodules are coprolites, and believed that the phosphatic matter came from putrefying fish, and was absorbed by the London Clay, from which formation the nodules have been derived.

T. G. Ringler-Thomson‡ described the position of the bivalve shells as being with the concavity downwards and the umbo generally in an easterly direction. By experiment it was found that water deposits separate bivalve shells with the concavity upwards, and univalves with the mouths upwards. These positions not being common in the Crag, it was suspected that wind might have affected the position of the shells, as it was found to do experimentally. He concluded that the water must have left the Crag shells dry, and that they were then subjected to an easterly wind.

In 1851 the Rev. W. B. Clarke§ classed the Coralline Crag as Miocene, the Red Crag as Pliocene, and the Mammaliferous [Norwich] Crag as Pleistocene, and described the nodule-bed at the base of the Red Crag and its contents.

T. J. Herapath‖ noted the economic value of the nodule-bed, and gave analyses showing that the nodules and bones are rich in phosphoric acid.

In describing the Tertiary beds of Belgium, in 1852, Sir C. Lyell¶ referred to the Suffolk Crag, which he believed to be of the same age as the Upper Crag of Antwerp.

In another paper** he noted the occurrence, near the top of the shelly Crag at Wherstead, of a bed of unrolled flints, with some flint-pebbles, the upper parts of the stones being encrusted with barnacle-shells, whilst the lower surfaces are free, and inferred that the action of the currents which brought the Crag here was suspended for a time, so that the smallest pebbles were not overturned, as otherwise the barnacles would be found on the lower side or on both sides.

In the same year Prof. J. Phillips†† gave a general description of the Crag, and controverted Mr. Thomson's theory of the shells having been left in their position by wind (1849), the position of the shells (concave side downwards) being that which shells take in settling to rest from agitation in water. He believed that the Red Crag was deposited in a shallow bay, receiving matters from wasting cliffs and shifting sands, by a current of varying intensity.

In 1854 we have a suggestion from Prof. Johnston‡‡ that the phosphorus of the phosphatic nodules was derived from animal remains in higher beds, dissolved out by acids, and re-deposited at a lower level.

Prof. J. Phillips in 1855§§ seems almost to have foreshadowed the opinion of S. V. Wood, Junr. (1864), for he speaks of the Crag as a deposit in character much like a modern shelly beach, and regards it, with little doubt, as an old beach of the German Ocean.

---

* *Quart. Journ. Geol. Soc.*, vol. v., pp. 345-353.
† *Journ. R. Agric. Soc.*, vol. x., pp. 520-525.
‡ *Quart. Journ. Geol. Soc.*, vol. v., pp. 353, 354.
§ *Ann. Nat. Hist.*, ser. 2, vol. viii., pp. 205-211.
‖ *Journ. R. Agric. Soc.*, vol. xii., pp. 91-105.
¶ *Quart. Journ. Geol. Soc.*, vol. viii., pp. 282, 286.
** *Rep. Brit. Assoc.* for 1851, *Sections*, pp. 65, 66.
†† *Rep. Brit. Assoc.* for 1851, *Sections*, pp. 67, 68.
‡‡ *Rep. Brit. Assoc.* for 1853, *Sections*, p. 52.
§§ Manual of Geology. 8vo. London and Glasgow. p. 402.

S. V. WOOD in 1859 drew attention to the extraneous fossils of the Red Crag,* and remarked that this deposit shows the action of strong tidal currents, is more littoral in character, and, for its small area, contains a larger percentage of derived fossils than any other formation. He suggested that Christchurch Bay (Hampshire) shows like conditions to those of the Red Crag sea. The number of its derived shells, many of which may have come from the Coralline Crag, are a hindrance to applying the percentage test of age to the Red Crag. The terrestrial vertebrates are intruders, though opinions differ as to where from. He defended Charlesworth's divisions from being abolished because they contain the same mammals. These three divisions (Coralline, Red, and Mammaliferous) show great changes of condition, so that the Red Crag is a deposit of a distinct period. He differed from OWEN as to the Cetotolites having been derived from the London Clay, thinking that they have come rather from the Coralline Crag, or some other bed of newer Tertiary age. Most of the fish-teeth may have come from the London Clay, as well as some shells and many crustacea; there are few fossils from Secondary beds; it seems, therefore, that the Red Crag sea was chiefly bounded by London Clay land, the fossils from which were introduced into the Crag by coast-action. The sandstone nodules, mixed with the phosphatic nodules, some of which contain casts of shells, he regarded as of older Crag age, though there is no such bed in our existing Coralline Crag. We may have in the Red Crag the contents of destroyed parts of various Tertiary beds. This paper concludes with a list of the derived fossils.

The first paper on the Crag by S. V. WOOD, JUNR. appeared in 1864.†
He says that in the Red Crag we have, in England, the initiatory stage of the events that began by the encroachment on the land of a bay of the Northern Ocean, progressed by the extension of that bay into the Eastern Counties, and at last involved a larger area in submergence.

The Red Crag is divided into two parts, one with none of the characters of a deposit formed under water, the other with those characters. Of the former there are four stages (beach stages), whilst the latter is more or less horizontal.

The lowest three stages of the beach Crag are not quite constant in their direction (that is, the direction of the so-called false-bedding), and cannot be well identified in different sections; but the uppermost stage, from its thickness and from its having been less denuded by a succeeding stage than the others have been, can be accurately identified. The direction of the oblique laminæ of this fourth stage is from N.N.E. to S.S.W. at angles varying from 25° to 35°, south of Hollesley.

The constancy of direction and the parallelism of the planes precludes any idea of false bedding, under water, and in one place only in Suffolk (Butley) is there any indication of a water-deposit. At Walton Naze, however, there is, below other Crag, a greyish-brown bed, without stratification, but yielding shells in the condition in which they died, bivalves with the valves united (which happens in no other Red Crag bed) and not containing those derived Coralline Crag shells that make up so much of the mass elsewhere.

The fifth or water-deposited stage does not always occur over the lower stages. It is under this stage alone that the workings of phosphatic nodules occur, and where beach stages rest on the London Clay the nodule-bed does not occur. This bed thins off as the fifth stage Crag leaves the clay and rises over the beach stages. Though this stage is water-deposited

---

* *Quart. Journ. Geol. Soc.*, vol. xv., pp. 32–45.
† *Ann. Nat. Hist.*, ser. 3, vol. xiii., pp. 185–203, pl. xvii. Just as I was returning the first proof of this memoir, came the news of Mr. Wood's death, and I take this opportunity of bearing witness to the great effect his constant work has had in directing attention to the Drift and Crag of East Anglia: indeed he may be said to have rescued the Drift of that district from being almost a byeword of reproach amongst geologists, and to have shown what long and careful work is needed to understand it. Although always ready to defend his theoretical views his only object was to get at the truth, and he was not ashamed to own himself in the wrong. In common with many others, I have to thank him for much kindness. W. W.

yet the shells are not like those of the above-noted bed at Walton, but are as worn as those of the beach stages, from which they seem mainly to have been derived.

The beach stages seem to have resulted from a sea forced back by the growth of beach it had heaped up, until, by a slight subsidence, the sea planed down the old beach and again began the process of beaching up.

At Chillesford the fifth stage passes up into the sands and clays described by PRESTWICH (1849). Our author concluded that the Fluvio-marine (Norwich) Crag is as old as the Red Crag, and probably older than the fifth stage.

Six pages are devoted to the Drift, and an appendix gives the places of sections of Red Crag, noting the stages shown.

DR. P. CARPENTER in 1865* noticed that Crag species now live along the American coast, and concluded that in the early days of existing species there was a closer connection between the North Pacific and European than between the East and West American seas. Certain forms once thought peculiar to the Crag are found to have descendants or representatives in the districts of Vancouver and California, and 24 Crag species have been identified on the West Pacific coast.

In the same year PROF. E. R. LANKESTER† treated of the sources of the mammalian fossils, which seem to have been derived from various beds, and almost all of which are heavy and much mineralized. The sea in which the molluscan fauna of the Crag lived, broke up Pliocene, Miocene and Eocene beds, the fish-teeth and phosphatic nodules coming from London Clay, whilst the mammalian remains probably come from the Middle Antwerp Crag and an early Pliocene or a late Miocene bed.

The same author‡ regards the Norwich Crag as a much later deposit (though giving no reasons), and, judging by the percentages of extinct species, the Middle and Lower Antwerp Crag as older than both the Red and the Coralline Crag; and thinks, from the number of mammalian remains from the Middle Antwerp in our Red Crag, that these are the débris of a formation which existed in England, but was broken up by the Red Crag sea.

S. V. WOOD, JUNR.,§ referred to the subjects of his paper of 1864, inclining to the belief that the horizontal Crag is the re-deposit of the material of the beach Crag, and doubting that the former is part of the Red Crag [an opinion founded on reasons which the author would probably not hold as altogether valid now]. He corrects the statement in his last paper that phosphatic nodules occur only under the horizontal Crag, being satisfied that some thin traces referred to this stage from the presence of nodules, really belong to the beach series.

In 1866 the REV. O. FISHER‖ came to the conclusion that the Chillesford Clay underlies the Fluvio-marine or Norwich Crag (an error abandoned afterwards), having found brown clay at the bottom of the Thorpe pit. Beneath the Chillesford Clay (in the Aldborough and Orford District) comes sand, with shells of Mya in their burrows, then other sand, and then the Red Crag.

R. A. C. GODWIN-AUSTEN¶ criticized the percentage test of age as liable to fluctuation; paralleled the Scaldesian beds of Antwerp with the Red Crag, both consisting largely of derived shells; limited the Crag sea in Suffolk at Bentley, Ipswich, and Woodbridge, but included as of Crag age, beds which are now known to be later, such as those of Grays and Kelsey, giving a map of the Crag-sea area. He thought that there is a great break between the Crag and the Boulder Drift.

In the same year S. V. WOOD,** controverted FISHER's conclusion, noted above, agreeing with that of his son, as to the passage upwards of Red and

---

* Geol. Mag., vol. ii., pp. 152-154.
† Quart. Journ. Geol. Soc., vol. xxi., pp. 221-226.
‡ Geol. Mag., vol. ii., pp. 103, 104, 149-152.
§ Remarks in Explanation of the Map of the Upper Tertiaries of Norfolk, Suffolk, etc. (with Map and Sections as separate sheets). Privately printed.
‖ Quart. Journ. Geol. Soc., vol. xxii., pp. 19-28.
¶ Quart. Journ. Geol. Soc., vol. xxii., pp. 229-232, 237-239, 245, 246.
** Quart. Journ. Geol. Soc., vol. xxii., pp. 538-552.

Norwich Crag into Chillesford Beds, giving the name *Scrobicularia* Crag to the top, or horizontal, stage of the Red Crag. He referred chiefly to palæontological evidence, which shows one of the most rapid faunal changes, measured by the thickness of the beds in which it occurs. The oldest part of the Red Crag is palæontologically nearer the present time than to the Coralline Crag; and the former shows evidence of change by stages, the oldest having some affinities with the Coralline Crag, but more with the Mediterranean sea, whilst the newer stages have few shells, and those of northern type. The oldest stage is that of Walton Naze, the fauna of which shows a connection with more temperate seas, and an absence of northern forms. The next division is that from which were got the chief part of the shells described in the Monograph on the Crag Mollusca, and which occurs between the Stour and the Deben, and on the left bank of the estuary of the latter: it has mostly a highly oblique bedding, referred to beach action; shows an intermingling of the Walton fauna with the northern one of the succeeding horizons; and some shells seem to have been derived from the Coralline Crag. The next division occurs around Butley, Chillesford, and Sudbourne, and though in structure like the last, has a dissimilar fauna, but with many forms that occur at Sutton. Above this is the uppermost division of the Red Crag, marked by the incoming of *Scrobicularia piperata*, the fauna of which is small in number of species. Separated from this by a few feet of sand is the Chillesford sand (Mya-bed of FISHER). MR. S. V. WOOD, JUNR. added, some diagram-sections in illustration, with a list of the actual sections on which they are based.

PROF. E. R. LANKESTER in 1867[*] referring to the suggested correlation of the Coralline Crag with the Black Crag of Belgium, asked, if this be the case, how is the occurrence of the remanié teeth of species of sharks and Cetacea in *both* of our Crags to be accounted for? No unworn specimens occur in our Coralline Crag, as they do in the Black Crag. Whence, then, did the abundant remanié Cetacean and shark fauna of our Red Crag come? He again concluded that the Black Crag is an older deposit of the Crag sea, which had its representative in Suffolk, and from which first the Coralline and then the Red Crag has derived its sharks' teeth and Cetacean bones.

The REV. O. FISHER[†] defends his views of the year before; but, in a postscript, allows that they are partly wrong.

The REV. L. JENYNS[‡] noticed Henslow's discovery of the use of the fossil phosphates; but did not bring forward anything new.

In 1868 PROF. E. R. LANKESTER[§] referred to his published opinions, especially as to the derivation of the bones of the "coprolite-bed" from Diestian deposits. He noted the finding of 30 or more species of mulluscs in the sandstone-blocks (box-stones) which seem to be Diestian, and of the largest *Carcharodon* tooth he had seen (in the same). The "coprolite bed" is a littoral accumulation, formed, just before the Coralline Crag, from the detritus of London Clay and Diestian, with fragments of subaërial and fresh-water accumulations (whence its *Mastodon, Rhinoceros, Tapir, Hyæna, Sus,* and *Cervus* teeth). He objected to the name "coprolite-bed," because there is probably not one coprolite in it, the nodules being masses of London Clay which have received some 50 per cent. of phosphate of lime from the quantities of fossil bones with which they are associated on the sea-shore. He explained the rarity of bones of terrestrial Mammals, as compared with those of Cetaceans, from the fact that the former came on to the beach in a different state to the latter, which were derived from Diestian beds. The fresher bones would be more easily acted on by the sea than those already mineralised.

R. A. C. GODWIN-AUSTEN[||] gave a summary of our knowledge of the Crag, reviewing the conditions under which it was deposited, remarking

---

[*] *Geol. Mag.*, vol. iv., pp. 91, 92.
[†] *Quart. Journ. Geol. Soc.*, vol. xxiii., p. 175.
[‡] *Proc. Bath Nat. Hist. Field Club*, vol. i., No. i., pp. 9-24.
[§] *Geol. Mag.*, vol. v., pp. 254-258.
[||] *Geol. Mag.*, vol. v., pp. 469-478; *Geol. Nat. Hist. Repertory*, vol. ii., p. 229; and *Rep. Brit. Assoc.* for 1868, *Sections*, p. 70. (1869.)

that the Red Crag is a complex assemblage, in spite of its small vertical size, and that at Walton Naze alone do we find this old sea-bed in its original state, undisturbed, elsewhere the Red Crag being re-arranged and relatively of shallow water accumulation.

The REV. J. GUNN* placed the Chillesford sands and clays above the Forest Bed.

E. CHARLESWORTH said that† at no very distant day the Red Crag will have to be expunged from the list of British strata, its destruction being brought about partly by the encroachment of the sea, and partly by its being broken up to get at the layer of phosphatic nodules at its base. [Our author seems to forget that Red Crag occurs so many miles inland that the first cause will not be effective until a very distant day, and that it is only in parts that the nodule-bed occurs to a workable extent.] He noticed that the phosphatic matter often encloses the fangs of the sharks' teeth, the tooth proper being left free, and that it is only such teeth as have been derived from the London Clay that are thus included in phosphate, from which he concluded that all the phosphatic stone (as distinguished from bones) in the Crag have been derived from the London Clay.

In 1869 the REV. O. FISHER‡ regarded the Norwich Crag and the Red Crag as of the same age, as they seem to pass into one another; gave up his opinion that the clay under the Crag at Thorpe (near Aldborough) is Chillesford Clay; and remarked that the [lateral] passage from Red Crag to Norwich Crag seems to occur where the two provinces are separated by a ridge of Coralline Crag.

In 1870 PROF. E. R. LANKESTER§ treated of the composition of the nodule-bed at length. The bone-bed under the Suffolk Crag, and the stone-bed under the Norfolk Crag have a different fauna from that of the shelly beds above, the two sets of beds not being of the same age, nor formed under the same conditions. Though in England we have no Diestian beds (=the Lower or Black Crag of Antwerp), yet the cetaceans, sharks, etc. of the Suffolk bone-bed are the remains of an equivalent bed that has been destroyed.

From the occurrence of different shells in the higher and lower parts of the Red Crag, it is inferred that this deposit represents a considerable time. In its earlier period the Red Crag had a fauna not very different from that of the Coralline Crag, and with some survivors from the still earlier Diestian; in its later period none of these forms remained, but boreal forms were added, and at this period the Norwich Crag began to be formed, continuing to a later time than we have evidence of in Suffolk.

The contents of the Suffolk bone-bed differ from those of the Norfolk stone-bed, the former having derived its contents from sources not accessible to the latter, such as London Clay and Diestian beds [there is, though, nothing to show that London Clay was not open to the Norfolk bed, and indeed we know that it was]; and therefore our author could not see community of origin and date for the two beds.

He gave a detailed account of the sandstone nodules that occur in the bone-bed which he calls box-stones, the name boxes having been given by the phosphate-diggers to those that show shell-remains on being broken. The majority of these contain no fossils. After examining a vast number he concluded that all have been derived from one deposit, and that of Diestian age; and that it is probable that they are of the same age as the Lenham sandstone of Kent. They represent a period separated by a wide gap from the Red and Coralline Crags.

Lists of the fossils found in these stones, and of the Mammalia from the bone-bed are given.

C. JECKS‖ regards the sections of the Crag (Coralline, Red, &c.) as only different parts of one continuous deposit, generally in estuarine or shallow water, and subject to gradual changes of temperature.

---

* *Geol. Nat. Hist. Repertory*, vol. ii., p. 259. (*Brit. Assoc.*)
† *Geol. Mag.*, vol. v., pp. 577–580. Paper read to Norwich Geol. Soc. and printed in full in *Norwich Mercury*, Oct. 10. Separate copies in folio, pp. 3.
‡ *Geol. Mag.*, vol. vi., p. 142.
§ *Quart. Journ. Geol. Soc.*, vol. xxvi., pp. 493–502,? includes the paper in *Rep. Brit. Assoc.* for 1868, *Sections*, pp. 70, 71 (abstract).
‖ *Rep. Brit. Assoc.* for 1869, *Sections*, pp. 91, 92 (7 lines only).

In the following year Prof. Prestwich contributed a set of three papers on the Crag. The first of these is on the Coralline Crag, with which we are not now concerned, but the second* is devoted to the Red Crag, which is described as lying in an excavated area in the Coralline Crag, wrapping round the isolated reefs of the latter and filling the hollows between [it should be noted that the reefs are comparatively small and the hollows of wide extent]. He divided it into two only, instead of the five stages of Wood, the lower part marked by oblique lamination, and the upper by horizontal bedding. The phosphate-bed occurs at the base of the lower division, the direction of the lamination of which varies to almost all points of the compass, and this false-bedding is most general in the upper part of this division. Sometimes beds have been eroded before the deposition of those over-laying them, (see *post*, Fig. 18, p. 69). He had seen ripple-marks in only one place, Bawdsey Cliff, where each of the clayey laminæ of one bed had a ripple-marked surface. Another feature sometimes seen there seems to show that the shoals of the Red Crag sea were sometimes left dry, their surfaces fissured by drying, and the cracks filled with the matter of the bed next thrown down: elsewhere a layer has been pressed down into those below, causing a wavy structure, and the upper part then planed down.

The introduction of the oxide of iron, which colours the beds, seems to have been subsequent to their formation, and in one case it has segregated in flattened concentric rings [in section] many feet in length.

The lower division generally abounds in shells, mostly broken up: double shells are not common, and, excepting the old shore at Sutton (see *post*, p. 68), it is not easy to fix on a place where the shells are on the spot where they lived. Notwithstanding the great number of shells, the abundant ones are few. In places, especially away from the centre of the district, the beds are almost shell-less, or the shells are in patches. This may be owing to the original absence of shells; but also to their removal by percolation of rain-water, for where the beds are consolidated by iron-oxide casts are sometimes met with.

He alluded to the difficulty of marking the line between the two divisions (the upper of which he once called "the unproductive sands," from the absence of fossils, which, however, have since been found in places), and noticed sections showing a line of erosion between them. The upper division is the Chillesford Sands and it is succeeded by the Chillesford Clay, which is also classed with the Red Crag.

Details of many sections are given with lists of the fossils from some.

The fossils are of two kinds, those proper to the formation and those derived from other formations, these latter being important. Some of these may have been doubly derived, from the Coralline Crag, which got them from the older beds. With regard to the *Mollusca* there is a difference of opinion as to which are derived species; but he is inclined to think that the greater number of those found in the Suffolk Crag and not also in the Norfolk Crag have been derived from the Coralline Crag.

The lamination that Mr. Wood refers to beach-action he thinks has been produced by the shifting of shoals and sand-banks at the bottom of the sea, which was shallow and studded with reefs of Coralline Crag; whilst in winter the distant Chalk and Tertiary shores were fringed with ice, which floated off with large flints and deposited them in the Red Crag. The constant shifting of materials would result in the heavier parts, as bones, pebbles, and phosphatic nodules, being left behind and thus tending to accumulate in the basement-beds. The consequence of the reconstruction is that the shells are much broken up. The direction of the currents seems to have been from east to south-east, and the Red Crag sea seems to have been open to the north, but probably closed on the south. There is no distinction in the fossils from top to bottom of the lower division, after the deposit of which there was a slight subsidence. From the lower part of the upper sands having been formed from the lower Red Crag there is a similarity in mineral composition; but as the sea-bed became more depressed the sands became finer, and then pass up into the micaceous sands and clays of the Chillesford Beds.

---

* *Quart. Journ. Geol. Soc.*, vol. xxvii., pp. 325–356. (1871.)

In the third part of this set of papers* Prof. Prestwich referred chiefly to the Norwich Crag area, and concluded that this was divided from the more open sea of the Red Crag by a barrier of Coralline Crag, the northern area with streams flowing into it, and carrying in land and freshwater shells.

A list of the Mollusca of the Red and Norwich Crags, to a great extent on the authority of Mr. J. G. Jeffreys, is given.

In the same year (1871) A. and R. Bell† suggested the terms Lower, Middle, and Upper Crags, instead of Coralline, Red, and Norwich. They hold that there is no evidence for separating from the fauna of the Red Crag any species except such as are of Eocene or older date, regarding the signs of a supposed derivative origin as not really such. They proposed to class as Middle Crag the lower deposits from Walton Naze westward to Bentley and eastward to Butley and Hollesley, as Upper Crag the uppermost beds of the Red Crag, the Scrobicularia Crag, and the Norwich Crag. There is no order of succession physically, but only palæontologically. The fauna of the Red Crag has two aspects, a deep-water one and a shallow-water one, and this explains the difficulty in comparing different pits.

J. E. Taylor‡ concluded that the Norwich fluvio-marine Crag is an extension of the Red Crag, that, after depression, the Upper Norwich (marine) or Chillesford Crag was deposited, and that there is an unbroken sequence from Coralline Crag to the latest Drift deposit.

A. Bell§ controverted Taylor's view that Chillesford sand occurs at the Butley Crag Pits and gives a long list of the fossils found there. It should be noted that he classes Chillesford Beds as Pre-Glacial, as distinguished from Crag.

In 1872 the last-named author‖ reviewed Prestwich's papers. He thought that the presence of Diestian fossils in the Crag may be explained otherwise than has been supposed, and defended his views of the year before.

A. and R. Bell¶ give a fuller version of their paper of 1871, with a review of some of Prestwich's work, and a long list of fossils.

S. V. Wood, Junr., and F. W. Harmer** treated of the beds with which we are now concerned, giving a map and sections. They regarded the oblique lamination of the Red Crag as different from false bedding, and as the result of beach-action (as in Mr. Wood's paper of 1864), the deposit being the remains of a set of banks that were more or less dry at low tides and from time to time partly swept away and again accumulated. If the mass of the Crag had been deposited under water we should expect to find the large stones, often so abundant at its base, scattered throughout. The conclusions of Mr. Wood's paper of 1864 are adopted here, the stone-bed is regarded not as a land-surface, but as the result of cliff-waste, and the mammalian remains of the Red Crag are looked upon as wholly derivative, occurring only in the nodule-bed at the base, which is clearly a bed of erratics.

G. Scorr†† included in the Red Crag beds of rough red sand without shells, at the top, and described the bone-bed.

Sir C. Lyell in 1873‡‡ noticed the gradual lowering of temperature shown by the shells of the Crags, those of the Coralline Crag representing a climate like that of the Mediterranean; those of the Red Crag one like that of our own seas, and those of the Norwich Crag being almost Arctic. He thought that the large unrolled white-coated flints of the nodule-bed were probably carried by ice.

Next year,§§ in describing the Red Crag, he compared it to shifting sandbanks, like those of the Dogger Bank.

---

* *Quart. Journ. Geol. Soc.*, vol. xxvii., pp. 452–496.
† *Geol. Mag.*, vol. viii., pp. 255–265.
‡ *Geol. Mag.*, vol. viii., pp. 314–316.
§ *Geol. Mag.*, vol. viii., pp. 450–455.
‖ *Geol. Mag.*, vol. ix., pp. 209–215.
¶ *Proc. Geol. Assoc.*, vol. ii., no. 5, pp. 185–218.
** Part 1 of the Supplement to the Crag Mollusca, pp. v–xiii.
†† 19 *Ann. Rep. Brighton Nat. Hist. Soc.*, pp. 64–68.
‡‡ The Geological Evidences of the Antiquity of Man. Ed. 4. 8vo. London. pp. 248–254.
§§ The Student's Elements of Geology. Ed. 2. 8vo. London. p. 176. (1874.)

In the same year S. V. Wood* reviewed the palæontology of the Crag. Species formerly abundant had of late eluded search, though within a few yards of, and at the same horizon as, the place of former occurrence; but some once thought rare had become more plentiful.

He criticised the work of Mr. Jeffreys on Crag Mollusca, and thinks that if any period can be called "the cradle of the British Mollusca," it is the Red Crag rather than the Coralline.

The list of extraneous fossils (of his paper of 1859) needs additions. The only part of the Red Crag free from derivatives is that at Walton Naze. The Red and Fluvio-marine Crags and the Chillesford Beds he regarded as parts of one formation, during the accumulation of which only slight changes in the position of sea and land occurred. The list of the Marine Mollusca given shows almost the same per-centage of forms not now living in the case of the older Red Crag as in that of the Coralline.

J. E. Taylor, in his "Sketch of the Geology of Suffolk,"† said that the Box-stone Deposit, or bone-bed, may be part of the same old land-surface as the Norfolk stone-bed, and that the enclosed fossils of the box-stones seem to have roughly determined the shapes.

In this year I drew attention to a great extension of the Crag area, to the south-western part of Suffolk.‡

In 1877 Dr. J. E. Taylor, in an account of an excursion to the Crag District,§ suggested that the Baltic represents the condition of the later period of the Red Crag better than anything else, the water being partly brackish, with freshwater shells side by side with marine ones, as in the Fluvio-marine Crag.

S. V. Wood, Jun., and F. W. Harmer‖ refer to the unfossiliferous sand that often occurs above the shelly Crag. This seems in some places to pass down into the Crag by thin seams of comminuted shells; at others the bedding is independent of the shelly Crag beneath; sometimes it has the same oblique lamination as the Crag, apparently disconnected masses of which are imbedded in it here and there. Notwithstanding certain difficulties, they accept my view that this sand is Crag deprived of its shells by the infiltration of water, casts of the shells being left where there is ironstone; for in one case a layer of pebbles extends continuously from the shelly Crag into the sand. They do not agree with Prestwich in referring this sand to the upper or Chillesford division of the Red Crag, because the casts of shells in the ironstone are not of species characteristic of the newer (or Butley) part of the Red Crag or of the Chillesford Beds.

In the same year, in describing the patches of Red Crag at Walton Naze, Beaumont, and Harwich,¶ I suggested that the shell-less sand above was but the result of the alteration of the shelly Crag below, and in a note devoted to this subject** showed that what had been supposed to be a line of erosion was only one of irregular alteration, the lines of false-bedding of the shelly Crag being sometimes continued into the sand above. This irregular dissolving away of the shells explains the apparently isolated masses of Crag in the sand, and this unfossiliferous sand extends beyond where the shelly Crag had been observed.

E. Charlesworth, in reprinting a notice, by Prof. Lankester, of the Crag fossils in the Ipswich Museum (from the *Suffolk Chronicle* of August 4), recurred to the subject of the prospective exhaustion of the nodule-bed, and in the following year†† he gave us a note on English Crag History, referring especially to his earlier work, and remarking that the Red Crag is the record of a past state, like that where our Crag cliffs are now being washed by the sea, in the bed of which new formations are in progress, partly made up from remains of the present fauna, and partly from the fossils carried away from the land.

---

* Supplement to the Crag Mollusca. Part ii., pp. 190-221.
† White's "History Gazeteer, etc."
‡ *Quart. Journ. Geol. Soc.*, vol. xxx., pp. 403-405.
§ *Proc. Geol. Assoc.*, vol. v., no. 3, pp. 108-113.
‖ *Quart. Journ. Geol. Soc.*, vol. xxxiii., pp. 74-78.
¶ The Geology of the Eastern End of Essex . . . *Geological Survey Memoir*, pp. 10-16 (1877).
** *Quart. Journ. Geol. Soc.*, vol. xxiii., pp. 122, 123.
†† Fossil Exploration of Suffolk Crag (Orford Castle) and Hampshire Eocene Cliffs, pp. 8. 8vo. London. Privately printed, 1878.

In the same year (1878) I described the sections of the westerly extension of the Crag (at Sudbury)* noted in my paper of 1874, and suggested the possibility of some sands that had been classed as Drift turning out to be Crag, a question also alluded to in a later Memoir.†

In 1879 Mr. S. V. Wood in his Second Supplement to the Crag Mollusca,‡ treated of the introduction into Crag lists of new species on unsatisfactory evidence, either from doubtful identification, or as being simply derivatives, and gave an addition to the Synoptical List of Mollusca in the First Supplement.

In 1880 S. V. Wood, Jun.,§ remarked that the formations from the Red Crag onwards can be studied as one group, all having accumulated during one movement of depression and re-elevation, recurring to the conclusion that the Red Crag was accumulated between high and low water, when the rise and fall of the tide was great. He noted that whilst at Chillesford, etc., the Red Crag passes up into the Chillesford Clay, at Walton Naze (where older Crag only occurs, there is no such passage), and concluded that during the accumulation of the Red Crag there was a gradual elevation in the southern part of its area, and of depression in the northern; so that the Walton Crag first became land, and then the parts just to the north; whilst the sea encroached around Butley, Chillesford, etc., depositing newer beds of a foreshore-character on that side of the remnant of Coralline Crag, on the northern side of which the Red Crag takes the fluvio-marine character. Further depression resulted in the deposition of the laminated Chillesford Clay over Red and Coralline Crag alike, separated, however, from the Red Crag by sands, horizontal in their upper part, where they contain shells with both valves united, in their central part full of shells of *Scrobicularia*, but passing down into the obliquely-bedded Crag.

In 1882 we had our last contribution from the pen of S. V. Wood,‖ who gave a list of the Mollusca from the Red Crag at Felixstow, distinguishing the species that have been derived, firstly, from beds older than the Red Crag, secondly, from earlier Red Crag beds; and a supplementary list for Walton Naze, by Mr. R. Bell. The contrast between the Crag of Walton and that of Felixstow is striking, and the fragmentary condition of many shells at Felixstow, that are abundant in a perfect state at Walton, must be owing to derivation. It seems that between the deposit of these two divisions of the Red Crag certain species had ceased to exist in the Crag sea, whilst others had been brought in. In the Butley Crag this change is further marked. He traced the sequence of events during the Pliocene period in England, and re-stated the conclusion that all but the top part of the Red Crag was formed as banks between high and low water mark, which were continuously undergoing destruction and re-accumulation.

Mr. S. V. Wood, Jun., added some remarks in correction of the map and section in the First Supplement (1872); and whilst classing much of the sand over the Red Crag as Lower Glacial, allows that some is merely Crag from which the calcareous matter has been dissolved.

In 1884 E. G. Bell¶ noticed that few traces of land and freshwater shells have been found in the Red Crag, which is the more notable as the deposit must have been formed at no great distance from shore. All the specimens are of living British species of very wide range, and they are first found in this bed. He notes the finding of three additional species in the lower part of the Crag at Walton Naze, and remarks that their present geographical range, compared with that of the land-shells from the Butley Crag, leads to the same conclusion as that deduced from the marine species, the shells of Walton being mainly southern, whilst at Butley there are more of northern kinds.
W. W.

---

* The Geology of the N.W. Part of Essex . . . „ etc. *Geological Survey Memoir*, pp. 30, 31.
† The Geology of the Neighbourhood of Stowmarket, p. 5. (1881.)
‡ *Palæontographical Soc.*, pp. i., ii., 54, 55.
§ *Quart. Journ. Geol. Soc.*, vol. xxxvi., pp. 457–459.
‖ In the posthumous Third Supplement to the Crag Mollusca, edited by his son, S. V. Wood, Jun., pp. 13–24.
¶ *Geol. Mag.*, dec. iii., vol. i., pp. 262–264.

CHAPTER V.—RED CRAG—*continued.*

DETAILS.

IN describing the Red Crag in detail it will be convenient to break up our area into districts, by means of the river-valleys, whilst at the same time keeping to the more or less continuous outcrop as far as possible. We may begin, therefore, with the southern side of the Stour, and work towards the east, where the Red Crag of Harwich and the neighbourhood has already been described.* Then, returning to our western boundary, and working down the valley of the Stour on its other side, following the windings caused by its tributaries. Then in like manner up and down the two sides of the Orwell, along the coast, up and down the valley of the Deben, and thence eastward.

South of the Stour (Essex).

In this part only few very narrow and mostly short disconnected outcrops, from beneath the Glacial gravel and sand, could be safely identified as Crag. W. W.

Ironstone like that of the Red Crag, but without impressions of shells, occurs in a cutting on the abandoned Mistley and Thorpe Railway, near its junction with the Harwich line. It is overlain by light-grey clay, traces of which occur above the London Clay (with a little ferruginous sand intervening) in the neighbouring cutting on the Harwich line.

The large gravel-pit in the gardens at the N.E. corner of Mistley Park showed the following section in 1875 :—

		Ft.
Drift	Coarse very obliquely-bedded gravel, with fragments of ironstone	6 to 8
	Greyish-blue mottled plastic clay	1 to 1½
	Gravel and sand	about 3
Red Crag.	Ferruginous sand and ironstone (one cast of a shell)	2 to 4
	Phosphatic nodules and bones 2 to 3 inches.	
London Clay.		

The coarse gravel cuts off the clay, &c., so that on the northern side of the pit it rests on the ironstone.

In the lane near the school a little N.W. of the gravel-pit, the gravel cuts off the Crag and rests on the London Clay.

On the southern side of Mistley Park, near Oak Grove, the Crag is represented by 2 or 3 feet of ferruginous loam, with laminar ironstone, resting on a thin seam of phosphatic nodules. The junctions with the underlying London Clay and with the overlying Drift gravel were seen in a road-section.

On the road west of Brickkiln Wood, south of the Park, on the northern side of Furze Hill in the Park, and in the lane near by, laminated ironstone occurs, but there is no good section.

In a gravel-pit ½ of a mile S.W. by S. of Langham Church the Crag occurs in the form of ferruginous sandstone crowded with impressions of shells. Traces of similar stone more or less fossiliferous occur on the high road at Blackbrook Hill, and in the intervening fields. In the two large gravel-pits on the top of Blackbrook Hill the Crag is occasionally touched in the deeper excavations, and shelly Crag was noted here by the REV. W. B. CLARKE.† From Stratford Bridge to Langham Church it is frequently indicated in casual exposures, phosphatic nodules occurring sparingly, and also impressions of shells.

---

* The Geology of the Eastern End of Essex. *Geological Survey Memoir*, pp. 15, 16. (1877.)

† *Trans. Geol. Soc.*, ser. 2, vol. v. (1840.)

Traces of Crag with phosphatic nodules, pieces of bone, and impressions of shells occur in the valley between Boxted Street and Boxted Church, mostly on the S.E. side, but no section was seen.

W. H. D.

Between the Stour and the Brett.

Here, too, we have only disconnected outcrops, the most westerly of which is near the edge of the map, south of Chilton, where, however, there is some doubt as to the age of the sand (see p. 9), but it is quite possible that there may be some length of outcrop there. W. W.

North of Nayland the unfossiliferous sand has been mapped in the main valley, and there is a road-section at Starling Hill, a little south of Harper's Barn, showing Drift gravel over rather coarse reddish-brown ferruginous sand, slightly clayey in parts, to a thickness of 5 feet.

The sand crops out, to a greater extent, on either side of the little valley westward of Stoke.

Crag sand has also been mapped on both sides of the lower part of the Boxford Valley, where a sharp feature has been produced by it, and though no fossils were found, its resemblance to Crag warrants its being so classed. There was a small section, at the head of a little hollow, three quarters of a mile S.E. of Polstead Church, in 5 feet of coarse red sand with ferruginous layers.

Valley of the Brett.

On the right bank two small outcrops have been mapped near Shelly At the back of the Hall a section showed the following beds :—

Red Crag. { False bedded ferruginous sand, with bands of ironstone.
Sand, with crushed shells, and with phosphatic nodules and flints.

London Clay (junction not shown) with a layer of septaria, at one part of the pit, where it is at a higher level than the Crag.

Up the rest of this valley no Crag has been made out on this side ; but there is more on the left side. F. J. B.

The Chalk Pit, marked on the Map, just south-westward of Monks' Eleigh Church, gave the section fig. 9. Just to the left the Boulder Clay laps over to the Chalk.

Fig. 9.

Section in Chalk Pit, Monks' Eleigh (about 25 yards long).

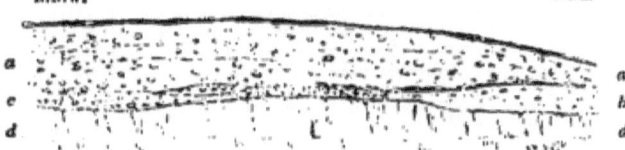

a. Boulder Clay ; 4 to 8 feet.
b. Coarse Gravel, at S.S.E., elsewhere only a trace, and finer ; up to 4 feet.
c. Red Crag. Light-coloured sand, with iron-sandstone, ironstone (? cast of shell) and at the bottom flints, flint pebbles and phosphatic nodules, a piece of bone and several sharks' teeth ; up to 2 feet.
d. Chalk with a few flints ; 12 feet.

W. W.

South of Hadleigh the sand is fairly shown, and at Layham brickyard it has yielded casts of shells (see p. 21).

About a third of a mile N.W. of Raydon, in a gravel-pit just south of the road, Crag sand, with many crushed shells, has been touched at the base. In the road by the houses at Sully's Hill, seven eighths of a mile south-westward from Raydon Church, I saw a small exposure of crushed shells.

Valley of the Stour, between the Brett and the Orwell.

A little north of Hill House, Stratford St. Mary, a pit showed 7 feet of brown ferruginous sand, with thin layers of ironstone, and a scattering of gravel, which last was in places cemented into a conglomerate by the iron-oxide. A road-cutting at the back of the house is also in like sand, false-bedded, and underlain by coarse yellow sand.

On Stratford Common, about half a mile eastward, was a pit, 10 feet deep in the sand, which here, too, had lines of gravel here and there, and ferruginous layers towards the bottom. There were also hollow balls of ironstone, with ochreous contents.

West of Brantham the sand again crops out, and also up the tributary valleys of Capel and Bentley. In the road-cutting south of Brantham Bridge some shells were seen.   F. J. B.

We have now reached the country where the Red Crag is in great part a highly fossiliferous deposit. In the railway-cutting at Bentley Station there is Drift gravel and sand, overlying the unfossiliferous sand, with shelly Crag beneath, and in a pit on the other (eastern) side of the valley, nearly half a mile above the station, there is a like section to that next to be noticed.

The large Crag pit at Danes Barn, just E. of Bentley Station, shows more than 30 feet of false-bedded sand, in great part a grit, mostly ferruginous but partly light coloured, partly compact and evenly bedded, with layers of iron-sandstone and of ironstone (also occurring in concretions) which sometimes contain impressions and casts of shells in the upper part of the section. There are gravelly layers, with phosphatic nodules, as well as flint pebbles, one of which layers (near the bottom) contains a good many angular flints. The bottom 4 to 7 feet is shelly Crag, the shells ending off at top regardless of bedding, the bottom gravelly layer (which shows a slight northerly dip), being above the shells on the S., and in them on the N. A few feet greater depth would reach the London Clay. I class the whole of the sand of this well-known section (the "Bentley Pit") with the Crag, there being no real division in it, the absence of shells being due clearly to nothing but dissolution after deposit. The top part is inaccessible.

Sand with casts of shells was seen north-eastward of Brantham Bridge, and again about a third of a mile north of the farm marked as "Stutton Vale," where it runs up nearly to the highest ground, whilst in the two little side-valleys eastward of this farm there is further evidence of the occurrence of the decalcified Crag.

A little pit on the eastern flank of the valley, about a quarter of a mile N.N.E. of Stutton Bridge, showed ferruginous sand, with a thin layer of shelly Crag near the top, and with iron-sandstone in the lower part, over shelly Crag.

Southward and eastward from this the Drift gravel and sand seems to overlap the Crag, which latter, however, was again seen at the head of the little valley, about half a mile westward of Stutton. It is quite possible, however, that here, and to the east, there may be more Crag than has been mapped, as it is very difficult to distinguish between Drift sand and decalcified Crag.

In the Tattingstone valley there is a considerable outcrop on both sides, except in the lowest part, near Holbrook, where from the cause just mentioned little has been mapped.

A small pit (on the right side of the valley) about halfway between Tattingstone Wonder and Alton Hall showed about 10 feet of Crag, false bedded and full of shells and pebbles; the upper part with many thin layers of iron-sandstone. There are many shells of *Mya* here. The old pit just northward of Tattingstone Wonder is in the ferruginous sand, capped by gravel.

The following section of the Hundred-house pit at Tattingstone (1828), is given by MR. CLARKE*; but I do not know the exact spot:—

	Earth [soil] 2 inches.
Red Crag 14 feet	Sand and clay, agglutinated by iron, in very thin layers.
	Large very white shells, here and there a flint or sandstone pebble crusted with *Balani*.
	Clayey shale, a line thick.
	Very perfect white *young* shells, teeth and palates.

---

* *Trans. Geol. Soc.*, ser. 2 vol. v., p. 381.

"The beds converge to the western corner [are false-bedded] at an angle of 25° to 30°. The shells on the east side are large, on the west small." His section of a pit at Tattingstone Park (on the same page) probably refers to that where the Coralline Crag was touched. See before, p. 26.

A Crag-pit nearly half a mile N.N.W. of Tattingstone Church, on the southern side of and close to the farm, showed more than 20 feet of Red Crag (with some small faults), consisting of false-bedded sand, passing down irregularly into false-bedded shelly Crag. There were marly phosphatic nodules in certain layers, and lenticular masses of ironstone and ferruginous loam, chiefly without shells. The shelly Crag was very rich in *Pectunculus*, and with a tendency to layers of *Fusus contrarius*. Some of the lower part was made up of broken-up shells.

A small pit on the eastern side of the little valley, eastward of the farm named Bentley Lodge, gave the most conclusive proof of the dissolution of the shells of the Crag by infiltration of carbonated water having been the cause of the irregular junction of the shell-less brown sand with the ordinary shelly Crag, the section being as follows:—Very coarse dark brown sand, almost all a grit indeed; with a gravelly layer, 1 to 2 feet thick, above the middle, containing phosphatic nodules and ferruginous casts of shells, the stones small and scattered. Just under the gravelly layer a little iron-sandstone, with casts of shells, below which the sand is false-bedded and passes down into the shelly Crag, the line between being clearly one of dissolution of the shells and not of erosion, as it cuts across the beds, to a lower level towards the stream. Near the bottom is a second bed, 1 to 1½ feet thick, of small scattered pebbles and phosphatic nodules, with iron-sandstone, and, moreover, with shells or casts of shells, according to the position of the bed with regard to the line of dissolution, the bed being at one part in the shell-less, and at another in the shelly sand.

As Prof. Prestwich saw the Red Crag resting against a cliff of Coralline Crag at Tattingstone, whereas when I was there this was not to be seen, I gladly reproduce his section,* with his consent, and by the kindness of the Council of the Geological Society. The section as seen by me has been described at p. 27.

Fig. 10.

Section in a Pit at Park Farm, Tattingstone. (Prestwich.)

Vertical scale about 12 feet to an inch.

1. Coarse gravel. Drift.
Red Crag { 2. Ochreous sand with seams of ironstone, &c.
3. Crag with a few coprolites.
4. Light-coloured Crag.
5. White sand.
6. Brown loam.
7. Not described.
8. Coralline Crag.
× Face of old cliff; depth not shown.

* *Quart. Journ. Geol. Soc.*, vol. xxvii., p. 342. (1871.)

PROF. PRESTWICH remarks that "flat pieces of the thin limestone seams of the Coralline Crag are common in the Red Crag around Tattingstone."

A pit on the western side of Crag Hall between Tattingstone and Holbrook, showed the Red Crag, in part hardened into stone, with some small phosphatic nodules, pebbles, and flints, chiefly in one bed. Another old pit on the southern side of the same place showed the like.

Down the hill south of Brook Farm (Holbrook) a deep forked ditch in the field, cut for drainage in 1872, showed sand, several feet thick, the lower part light-coloured, and at the bottom sometimes with broken-up shells, over London Clay. Below the fork there was sandy wash.

Below Holbrook the Drift seems to overlap the Crag until we get east of Harkstead, when the latter sets in again.

"Coprolites" have been worked three-quarters of a mile east of Harkstead Church, on the western side of the little valley; and, on the other side, about a quarter of a mile N.E. Further down this same valley, and west from Erwarton, was a section of brown and light-coloured false-bedded sand, with shells at bottom, and here also "coprolites" have been got. Again, there are old coprolite-workings just west of South Hall and about a third of a mile S.E. of Erwarton Hall.

Before reaching the point where the valleys of the Stour and of the Orwell unite, the Drift gravel and sand seems to overlap the Crag.

Valley of the Orwell, up the Right Side.

Around Shotley it is difficult to classify the sand, whether with Crag or Drift.

At Nether Hall, about a mile S.S.E. of the church, I saw 8 or 10 feet of fine sharp light-coloured and brown sand.

On the flank of the hill S. and S.E. of Shotley Low Farm (north of the village, there are traces of old Crag-pits, now ploughed over, and on parts of the hill top the soil is gravelly.

At Cowton Bottom, the following section was seen and I was told that 50 tons of phosphate had been got here:—

    A little gravel.
Red Crag { Sand, with phosphatic nodules in the lower part.
          { Shelly Crag at bottom.

Along the overgrown wooded river-cliff east of Pin Mill gravel, sand, and shelly Crag are often to be seen. The slope is very wet and swampy, as is the case very generally along the junction with the London Clay in this part, where that junction is often masked by sandy peaty soil.

At Chelmondiston are two pits (1872) with the following section:—

    A little gravel.
Red Crag { Sand, mostly coarse and ferruginous, partly false-bedded, with small quartz pebbles and a few gravelly layers. Sometimes cemented into an iron-sandstone. Passes down into the next.
          { Shelly Crag, shown irregularly at the bottom.

Through Woolverstone Park there are few signs of anything, but from what little can be seen there seems to be sand beneath the gravel; and as there is evidence of Crag on both sides, east and west, it seems the safer plan to mark an outcrop of that throughout. The cliff is overgrown, and to some extent cultivated (garden), but I could see sand in places along it.

By the road north-westward of Freston Tower a coprolite-working has been opened since I was there, and I am indebted to my friend DR. J. E. TAYLOR of Ipswich, for the following note of it (dated 1882):—

    Soil, about 9 inches.
Red Crag { Sand; about 4 feet.
         { Current-bedded Crag, full of ironstone; about 4 feet.
         { Nodule-bed; about 10 inches.
    London Clay.

Sand and Shelly Crag are to be seen along the road.

About half a mile W.S.W. of Freston Church are two sand pits close together. One, close to the hill-top (where there is gravelly sand), is in brown yellow and light-coloured sand, fine and without stones; 8 feet or more shown, the lower part being somewhat bedded and with a few very thin layers of grey loam. The lower and smaller pit is of about the same depth, in coarse brown sand with small flint-pebbles and pieces of flint; the lower part of a lighter colour and with few stones, and at the bottom there is light-coloured sand. Whether any of the sand here belongs to the Crag is hard to say.

A pit in Wherstead Park, just west of Gate Farm, showed (in 1872) nearly 10 feet of shelly Crag, for the most part a coarse ironshot grit with broken shells, containing a few pebbles and phosphatic nodules.

A small circular pit in the field close above the springs in the hollow S.W. of Wherstead Vicarage (S. of the church), gave the following section of over 15 feet of Red Crag, with strongly marked current-bedding:—

    A little flaggy iron-sandstone, almost wholly made up of casts and impressions of shells.
    Ferruginous grit with small pebbles and occasional casts of shells, passing down into the like with shells for the most part.
    A layer so full of pebbles as to be almost a gravel, with shells; sometimes a mere line, sometimes over 6 inches, running evenly across the pit.
    False-bedded ferruginous grit with shells and iron-sand-stone, passing down into—
    Lighter-coloured grit, crowded with shells.

These divisions are really of no account, and probably occur but for a short distance, the whole being one mass with hardened layers and a few phosphatic nodules; but the section well illustrates the dissolving away of shells, and their record by means of ferruginous casts.

The larger old pit at the spring is mostly overgrown. It reaches to a higher level, and its section is as follows:—

    Fine sand, orange buff and grey, with a few clayey layers (? Chillesford Sand of authors), about 10 feet thick, and apparently resting evenly on:—

Red Crag { Coarse ferruginous sand, with hard layers, a few pebbles, and (about 3 feet down) casts of shells in iron-sandstone. Shelly Crag shown below.

From the position assigned to the following section of a pit, "about 500 yards south of the vicarage-house of Wherstead,"* it would seem to be one not now to be seen:—

    Sandy and gravelly beds, without fossils, 8 feet.
    Shelly red Crag: near the top a layer of unrounded flints, with some flint-pebbles. The upper parts of these stones encrusted with barnacles. One flint 22×16×7 inches. 10 to 12 feet.

Just south-eastward of the Vicarage was a small pit in coarse ferruginous sand with pebbles, the stone-layer at top having casts of shells; and a little higher up the valley an overgrown pit shows sand above shelly Crag.

Westward from Wherstead the Crag occurs for some way up the Washbrook Valley, to Copdock on one side, and further on the other.

A small pit, up to 13 feet deep, just south of Therrington Hall, and close to the railway, partly overgrown or hidden by talus, showed, at the eastern corner, gravel, chiefly of chalk-pebbles and flints, with Boulder Clay wedged into it and a little on it. From below these ferruginous sand (? Crag) rises up nearly to the surface at one spot. Then shelly Crag rises up, and occurs all through the central part of the pit. The upper part of the Crag is much hardened into stone by iron, and has a bed of scattered small phosphatic nodules and pebbles: the lower part is the usual shelly sand, with a few small pebbles and nodules. The London Clay is touched below, and whilst at one spot there seems to be no nodule-bed, at another, but 4 feet off, there is a fair quantity of it, and elsewhere a bed of blackish, roundish stones (with the nodules) forms the bottom of the pit. At the western side the Boulder Clay scoops into the Crag and seems to be the only bed touched.

At Belstead Hall some sections on the west of the farm-buildings showed, in 1875, brown and grey bedded loam, and in places gravel, over

---

* Sir C. Lyell, *Rep. Brit. Assoc.* for 1851, *Sections*, p. 65.

grey Boulder Clay. Just north was a hole in brown sand, with a few broken Crag shells lying about: this sand must go under the Boulder Clay. In the ditch Boulder Clay and London Clay (the latter at one spot only) have been turned out, and a few phosphatic nodules.

Just above the Swan Inn, half a mile north of Copdock Church, I noticed traces of Crag, but too small to be mapped.

In a pit just north of Gusford Hall there was a little patch of gravelly sand at top at one part, over Red Crag, consisting of ferruginous sand above and shelly Crag below. The road-cutting just above shows more of the coarse sand, with a bed of scattered small pebbles and phosphatic nodules, and, at another place, with iron-sandstone.

The cutting along the pretty lane over a quarter of a mile west of the house at Stoke Park, gives a fair section of the Red Crag. Bright ferruginous sand, and some of a light colour, with a few small pebbles, dovetailing into shelly Crag, some of which also is light-coloured. Just before getting to the edge of the wood the junction with the London Clay is laid open, with a thin nodule-bed at the base of the Crag, and some septaria in the clay.

A small pit in a plantation about a quarter of a mile a little S. of W. of the house, showed at one part a little gravel over about 4 feet of brown and light-coloured sand, below which shelly Crag was touched. At another part, above the top of this, some 3 feet of gravel came directly over shelly Crag, so that the sand is probably Crag.

The bottom of the Crag was touched along the top of the railway-tunnel, and there seems to be a trace of the nodule-bed at Stoke brickyard, just to the east (see p. 11).

In the pit on the southern side of Gippeswick Hall (New Place on the Geological Survey map) the section was much hidden, but showed sand with gravel, over sand, and Crag, at the bottom of which apparently a few phosphatic nodules have been found. Between this and the house London Clay is touched.

Westward from this the Crag soon ends, the Drift gravel and sand coming down to the London Clay before we reach the high road. A trace of shelly Crag, however, occurs further westward, under the eastern end of the patch of Boulder Clay on the road N.N.E. of Poplar Farm, and perhaps again at the edge of the gravel and sand about a third of a mile to the north.

The Crag in the railway-cutting west of Handford Bridge is, to a great extent at least, not in place; but only masses in the Glacial Drift.

Valley of the Orwell, down the Left Side.

It is possible that some of the sand, with a gravelly layer at the base, at the large Bramford pits (see pp. 14, 15) may belong to the Crag rather than to the Drift, with which latter, however, it was thought safer to map it.

It is not until we reach the eastern part of Ipswich that Crag can be mapped; but then there are signs of its occurrence in the little valley above Brooks Hall, N.W. of the town, and the pits at a brickyard on the west of the Cemetery Road gave the following section:—

Drift.—Light-coloured false-bedded gravelly sand, lying irregularly on
Red Crag?—Brown sand, at a lower level than which is
London Clay.

On the opposite side of the same small valley, at the back of St. Margaret's Terrace, there is a little Crag over the London Clay.

On either side of St. Helen's Vale there is a narrow outcrop, and at the St. Helen's Pottery a little Crag was shown (see p. 13). We have thence a continuous outcrop to Orwell Park.

The ground being laid out for a new house (1875) a little W. of Rose Hill (Felixstow Road) touched the old brickyard, S. of Cavendish Road, at its eastern end, where London Clay is shown. A little higher there was shelly Crag, up to 7 feet thick, with phosphatic nodules at the bottom, immediately over the nodule-bed there being a layer of blocks of dark septariform stone. Above there was ferruginous false-bedded sand (? decalcified Crag), and at the top of the hill gravel.

A large old pit just eastward of the house in Holywells gives the following section:
   Drift Gravel.
   Red Crag { Sand and shelly Crag.
             { Phosphate-bed.
   ? London Clay.

A sand-pit at the southern edge of the park, and about an eighth of a mile east of the Cliff Brewery gave a like section, as below:—
   Drift sand and gravel, up to 6 feet.
   ? Red Crag { Loam and sand, bedded, partly ferruginous, (somewhat
            { like Chillesford beds), up to 4 feet.
            { Light-coloured and brown sand, about 18 feet.

The pits at the head of the valley, about two-thirds of a mile east of Greenwich Farm and south of Holywells, showed the following succession:—

Red Crag. { Ferruginous sand, with some layers of a lighter colour, some thin loamy layers, and some gravelly layers (with phosphatic nodules). There are hard bands, as usual, and in one pit a mass of hard ferruginous sandy loam, showing marked prismatic structure (vertical to the plane of bedding) as at the pit by Bentley Station.
        { A little shelly Crag.

London Clay apparently at the bottom, which is much hidden by springs, &c.

On the lane south of Greenwich Farm sand is seen resting on the London Clay, and further south, on the slope facing the river, the phosphatic nodules have been worked.

A Crag-pit close to the shore of the Orwell at Piper's Valley, gave the section below:—
   Irregular gravelly sand at top.
   Red Crag. { Dark ferruginous coarse sand, with small pebbles and phosphatic nodules.
         { Very shelly Crag, with a ferruginous bed at top (and with small pebbles and phosphatic nodules) about 8 feet shown.
   London Clay seems to occur irregularly underneath.

The junction of the two parts of the Crag slopes towards the river, and here as elsewhere, I believe, the difference between them is owing to the shells having been dissolved out in the upper part. On the north-eastern side the Crag is abruptly cut into by sand, partly fine and light-coloured.

Just S.W. at the beginning of the tumbled cliff (by the cottage) there is a little gravel over sand, with shelly Crag just below, and at the base London Clay, which throws out many springs along this sloping cliff.

About two-thirds of a mile N.N.W. of the remains of Alnesbourne Priory was another pit in sand and gravel over sand over shelly Crag.

Just before we reach Orwell Park the Drift sand and gravel seems to overlap the Crag; but the latter appears again in the side-valley of Nacton, and sand and Crag are then to be seen in places along the winding outcrop.

A pit about a quarter of a mile north of Levington Church gave the section below, for a few yards in extent, the rest of the pit being much overgrown (1874):—

   Small pipe of gravel.   FEET.

Red Crag. { Ferruginous sand, with a few casts of shells in iron-sandstone (at the clearest and highest part of the pit) - - - 6 or more.
       { Shelly Crag, with some small phosphatic nodules, flint-pebbles, &c. - - 0 to 1½
       { Sand, full of broken-up shells (sometimes dissolved out in the top part) - About 4
       { Sand with thin layers of ironstone - About 1
       { Shelly Crag, shown - - - to 3
       another 3 feet being hidden by fallen earth.

The section in another pit, just W. of the farm more than half a mile N. of Levington Church, was as follows (1874):

Red Crag.
- False-bedded sand, some very coarse and ferruginous, some fine; with nodules of ironstone, pieces of iron-sandstone (sometimes many very small pieces), some iron-sandstone with casts of fossils (only a foot from the surface of the ground), and a few small flints: about 12 feet.
- Shelly Crag, a few feet.

London Clay, touched at one place (in the ditch along the edge of the little wood, which is shown too near the stream on the Map). Sometimes there are a few phosphatic nodules at the junction with the Crag; but sometimes none.

The outcrop of the Crag here is close to the highest ground, leaving but little room for Drift to come on.

The Crag pit on the eastern side of the same little valley over a third of a mile N.E. of Levington Church showed, in 1874, from 20 to 25 feet of false-bedded sand, mostly brown and coarse, but a little grey and buff (finer). The top, 15 feet or more was apparently unfossiliferous, but casts of shells (*Cardium*) were found in some of the ironstone, of which there is a good deal, partly in concretions, partly in thin flaggy layers. There are also fine gravelly layers (of flint and quartz pebbles, with some phosphatic nodules). The bottom 5 or 6 feet is the usual shelly Red Crag, but there is no marked line of division between this and the rest.

At Stratton Hall, E.S.E. of Levington, a cutting at the back of the farm (near the road) gave an almost continuous section, except for overgrowth, about a quarter circle round the homestead. At one part there was a little gravel over brown sand, whilst eastwards there seemed to be shelly Crag beneath the latter, and S.E. (at the back of the farm-house) the brown sand contained a shelly mass close to the top, proving it to be Crag.

Around Moston Farm (between Levington and Trimley) the Drift seems to overlap the Crag; but at the spur southwards from the farm the latter crops out again for a short distance, and in the Crag-pit, marked on the Map, the following section was shown (1874), the greatest depth being over 20 feet:—

A little gravel, up to 5 feet.

Red Crag.
- Brown sand, with pebbles of flint and of quartz, and phosphatic nodules, especially in a layer at the bottom. This bed occurs at one part only (? a long lenticular mass): 0 to 3 or 4 feet.
- False-bedded shelly Crag, of a rather light colour, with pebbles and phosphatic nodules here and there, sometimes a thin layer at the bottom: 8 or 10 feet.
- A small wedge of pale purplish sand at one part: 6 or 8 inches.
- Brown rather clayey sand, with many short lenticular masses or nodules of whitish clay, flint-pebbles, and phosphatic nodules: 1 to 3 feet.
- Light-coloured (buff and grey), ironshot, fine, sharp, false-bedded sand, in places with small nodules of ironstone and very small pebbles of flint and of quartz.

The tolerably well-marked and even junction of the lowest bed (which it occurred to me might possibly belong to the Coralline Crag) with that above showed a slight S.W. dip, as far as could be seen. Near the entrance there was a little shelly Crag, which seemed to dip under the lowest sand, but perhaps it is not in place, and I was told that London Clay had been found beneath the sand; it certainly occurs along the edge of the wood just below (south) at a level but slightly lower than that of the pit-bottom, if at all at one part.

A new coprolite-working (1874) at the top end of the little wood about a mile N.W. of Trimley Churches, and close to the railway, gave a good section, as follows:—

Wash of loam, partly with stones, partly bluish-grey (peaty); probably formed by the springs: up to 6 feet.

Red Crag.
- Shelly Crag, mostly from 3 to 4 feet, but up to 6 feet. At the S.E. end of the pit there were some beds without shells, below others with shells.
- Phosphate-bed, with many shells of *Pectunculus*, at one part over 3 feet (the *Pectunculus* shells being then mostly at the bottom). The upper part not rich in phosphate. Above the rich part, at the bottom, there was often a mass of brown sandstone, which contained many specimens of *Mytilus edulis*.

At some small coprolite-workings at the back of a cottage about three-quarters of a mile W. of N.W. of Trimley Churches the following was the section :—

Fine sandy gravel and soil, 8 feet at most.

Red Crag.
- Brown false-bedded sand, 3 or 4 feet, passing down into the next.
- Shelly Crag, just shown, but has been found about 3 feet deep.
- Nodule-bed, about 6 inches.

London Clay below.

Coprolites have also been worked just S.E. and N.E.

At the western end of Lower Street, west of Trimley Churches, a very shallow pit, close by a small pond below (W. of) the farm, showed evenly false-bedded shelly Crag, the dip of the false-bedding eastwards, over a little light-coloured sand. A larger old pit just above (E.), in the outer part of the farm-enclosure showed sandy and gravelly soil over irregularly false-bedded, dark brown, ferruginous coarse sand, with some iron-sandstone (the top part flaggy and containing casts of fossils) over false-bedded shelly Crag.

Both these pits are on the northern side of the lane; on the southern a larger pit, more than 20 feet deep, gave this section :—

A little gravelly sand.

Red Crag.
- Dark brown ferruginous false-bedded sand, with a little fossiliferous iron-sandstone (or rather grit) at top in parts.
- False-bedded shelly Crag, with a long lenticular layer of light-coloured sand. Nodule-bed said to be found about 5 feet down.

Round Grimston Hall, half a mile west of Trimley, coprolites have been largely worked, and in 1874 there was the following set of sections :—

1. Pit just S.W. of the house. Brown sand, partly gravelly, on shelly Crag, 2 or 3 feet, on London Clay. There were no coprolites at one part, but some at another, about 7 feet down, whilst at another the London Clay, usually 8 or 9 feet down, came up irregularly nearly to the surface.

2. A little north of the farm, on the western side of the lane to Trimley. A little gravelly sand over Crag, false-bedded at top in parts, irregularly without shells; 8 feet or more, to water; said to be 16 feet to the nodule-bed.

3. Smaller pit at the eastern edge of the lane, opposite and a little lower. Sandy soil and brown sand, with a thin gravelly layer at the bottom, about 6 feet, over shelly Crag.

4. A coprolite-pit, in full work, just N.E. of the farm, was about 22 feet deep, and gave this section :—

Soil.
Loamy or clayey earth, lying irregularly on the bed below. 2 to 5 feet.
Sand, with a little gravel and loam, false-bedded (? lower part may be Crag), resting fairly evenly on the next bed; about 7 feet.
False-bedded shelly Crag, with a very long lenticular mass of mauve-grey sand which was unfossiliferous, but contained some stone with pieces of shells. Coprolites in shelly sand at the bottom. 6 to 8 feet.
London Clay, some dark grey.

The watercourse just south of the farm had been cleared, and showed a great thickness of sand, the result of wash from above. North of the house this watercourse is dry, or filled in, but a deep hole near the house showed 3 or 4 feet of washed sand over London Clay.

PROF. E. R. LANKESTER described the following section "in a pit at Trimley on the Orwell" as showing the Suffolk Bone-bed, "without any superimposed Crag;" but the red sand has been shown, since his description was written,* to be mere decalcified Crag.

	FEET.
Soil	1½
Clay, with flints	4½
Red sand, with a tooth of *Elephas meridionalis*	12
Bone-bed: phosphatic clay-nodules, sandstone nodules and slabs, bones, teeth, &c., with greyish-white sand	1½

Westward and southward of Walton the Crag again seems to be overlapped by the Drift in parts.

In an old pit, in a field, on the southern side of the footpath from Blofield Farm eastward, I saw 6 or 7 feet of sandy soil and sand with thin layers of clay, over shelly Crag (only just shown).

Along a hedge, less than a quarter of a mile to the south and high up, London Clay and a little Crag were to be seen: apparently an irregular junction.

The cliff-top a little eastward of Walton Ferry House Inn shows a little shelly Crag, irregularly over which there is in parts gravelly sand, that seems indeed to cut out the Crag altogether sometimes.

At the most southerly of the cuttings on the Felixstow Railway, except the little one already noticed (p. 25) and to which it almost joins, London Clay occurs at the southern end, but the Crag soon comes on, and it is not far before the former is lost (the line rising), the nodule-bed at the base of the Crag occurring, however, some little way beyond. There are some thin layers of gravel in scoops in the Crag, and also some sandstone (not transported blocks, but hardened in place and sometimes enclosing shells). The upper part of the Crag is without shells and disposed in great wavy masses. Farther on there is evenly bedded fine sand, with clay-partings (very different from the usual coarse false-bedded sand) nearly to the bottom, with shelly Crag below, and also above (nearly to the top); so that this finer bed is clearly *in* the shelly Crag and not above it (like the Chillesford Beds). Further on all is sand, with no shells, up to the bridge over the line, a little beyond which some shelly sand comes on above the other, and capped by 4 or 5 feet of brown sandy soil. Before getting to the footpath across the line nearly all the cutting is in a wash of loam, sand, and gravel.

Felixstow Cliffs and Pits.

One of the best known sections of the Red Crag is along this range of cliff from Martello Tower Q. to East End Farm, a distance of more than two miles, along great part of which shelly Crag is to be seen, so that the fossils can often be easily collected. The junction with the London Clay is shown in places and the Crag is cut back by the two small heads of valleys for a little way. For convenience the whole of the cliff-section will be described, without separating the parts where there is no Crag.

PROF. J. PHILLIPS has noted the occurrence of a band of Crag in these cliffs, for half a mile, in which the lamium range in one direction (S.W.) and are sometimes curved, with the concavity upwards.†

---

* *Geol. Mag.*, vol. v., p. 257. (1868.)
† *Rep. Brit. Assoc.* for 1851, *Sections*, p. 67.

Beginning at the western end, the London Clay occurs up to the top, by the Ordnance Hotel, and is shown, at the bottom, to be grey, bedded, and with a slight easterly dip.

Before reaching the enclosure of Martello Tower Q. the Red Crag comes on at the top, and the London Clay shows parallel joint-planes, and has layers of a yellow sulphur-mineral.

At the back of the Suffolk Convalescent Home, there is false-bedded Crag (the dip of the false-bedding being westward), capped by more even beds (much hidden), with a layer of *Mya* shells at the junction. The Crag here sinks to a lower level.

Then the section is much hidden; but the junction of the Crag and the London Clay is shown by springs, near the bottom and along the back of the houses. Gravelly patches occur here and there at the top.

Where the road goes up from the beach there was a good section in false-bedded sand, and above it another cutting, with some gravelly sand at the highest part, and false-bedded sand apparently lying irregularly on shelly Crag; the irregularity, however, is owing, in great measure at all events, to the dissolving away of shells.

From this spot the cliff is for awhile hidden by a house and grounds, beyond which comes the long section that best shows the Crag here. The cliff is much masked by landslips, and overgrown; but the Crag is seen to rise close to the surface and to go low down, the junction with the London Clay being marked by moisture and richer growth of vegetation.

At first some brown clayey loam, partly gravelly, was shown at top. There were occasional layers of laminated loam in the Crag, and some small phosphatic nodules; but no layer of nodules was seen at the bottom. At one part it was over 30 feet from the top to the London Clay. At a clear place, just before reaching the next enclosure, the section showed five or six recognizable beds in the Red Crag, as below:—

	FEET.
1. A bed consisting chiefly of shells of *Mya*, but with some of *Cyprina*	6 or more.
2. An apparently lenticular mass of fine light-yellow sand, with clayey layers at top and bottom	
3. False-bedded Crag, the false-bedding almost wholly westward	6 or 7
4. False-bedded Crag, with loamy layers, the false-bedding westward	5 or 6
5. An even bed, of *Mya*, &c., rather white, with phosphatic nodules about	2
6. False-bedded Crag, the false-bedding eastward, less shelly than the rest and with ferruginous layers.	

London Clay.

Then, in an enclosure, and at the back of the house, shelly Crag, without any divisions, was shown to a thickness of 20 feet or more, and just beyond the house a wash of stony sand at the top, beyond which the section was again hidden.

Shelly Crag is cut into at the back of the Bath Hotel, and at the house (Hermitage) beyond the enclosure of Martello Tower R. the junction of the Crag and the London Clay was seen.

The land bordering the shore is then low, and the beds are hidden for some way; but London Clay was shown at Felixstow Cottage, and east of that house it rises up, as a cliff, when it was seen to be well bedded, with a slight south-westerly dip, and showed some small faults with a north-easterly downthrow.

At the end of the Cottage grounds Crag comes on at top, and the dip of the clay changes to north-eastward, at an angle of about 5°. The Crag is patchy, thin, and covered by loam, &c.

A little further, by some steps up the cliff, there seemed to be a fault throwing down the London Clay 12 feet or more south-westward, and here there was no Crag for a few yards. Then the bedding of the clay was horizontal, except for a fault of about 2 feet downthrow to the N.E. At a zig-zag path up the cliff (to the last enclosure marked on the Map—? Martello Place), the clay occurs up to the top, except for wash; whilst just beyond there was some laminated loam at the bottom of the thin covering of Crag.

Then the London Clay rose close to the surface for some way, with a thin capping of Crag and loam; and then it came to the surface, except for soil, until the Crag came on again, and was being worked for phosphates close to the cliff.

The London Clay rose to the surface again, at about the highest part of the cliff (showing the irregular way in which the Crag comes on), with a little patch of Crag (a few nodules at bottom) opposite and just beyond where the lane runs near to the cliff; whilst a little further the nodule-bed again came on, and shelly Crag, for some 150 yards. This part of the cliff gave the best exposure of the London Clay, the bedding of which was often slightly waved. Some of the lower beds are rather sandy, and some thin layers with green grains were seen in the bottom part of the cliff, and, more clearly, on the shore (which I saw at one time much bared from shingle). At one place a broken *Cyprina* shell occurred in the clay, and at another, some two feet above the base of the cliff, a nest of the same about a foot long by four inches deep at most; the shells with both valves together, but so friable as to defy extraction. This is the only case in which I have seen any trace of shells in the London Clay of this coast, the only other fossils noticed being remains of plants, which are very frequent in the state of casts in iron-pyrites, so much so indeed that in places the scanty beach was chiefly composed of them.

As the ground falls, to the little valley running up to the Church, there is London Clay only. Down the side of the valley there is a fairly thick wash of stony loam, with rearranged, or slipped, masses of London Clay. In this loam I found pieces of bones, some of which seemed to have been cut.

In the bottom of the hollow there is, over the loam, a mass of peaty sand (in which I found the tooth of a pig), the product of the springs of the valley, and like that generally seen along the damp valleys of the neighbourhood.

On the other side of the valley the loam again occurs, and then the cliff consists of London Clay. At the highest part Crag comes on above, with some nodules at the bottom, and here and there some whitish marly earth. The Crag capping occurred for about 200 yards, as far as the hedge from East End Farm.

At the last the London Clay dips very slightly N.E., and, a few yards beyond the ending off of the Crag, blown sand was seen to be strangely banked up against the cliff, which then slopes down to the sand and shingle tract of Bawdsey Haven.

The natural sections of the cliffs are not however the only ones in which Crag has been seen at Felixstow. Since the time when I surveyed that part the phosphatic nodule-bed at the base has been worked close to the western part of the cliff.

In December 1882, some years after the Geological Survey of the district was finished, Mr. S. V. Wood noted the section shown in Fig. 11, along the cutting of a new road up the cliff just north of the Convalescent Home, and passing over Col. Tomline's water-tank, and he has kindly allowed me to copy and use his drawing and notes.

Mr. Wood regards the brickearth 2 as belonging to his Lower Glacial, the sand 3 as belonging to his Bure Valley Beds, and the loamy sand 4 as probably so also, though he expresses a doubt as to whether it may not belong to the Crag. Not having seen the section myself I am loth to give a decided opinion; but I may suggest the possibility of all the beds belonging to the Crag, with a representative of the Chillesford Clay, though we have no trace of the latter elsewhere in this part. The apparent transgression of 4 over 5 does not go much against this, as no true bedding is shown in 5 or 6.

Fig. 11.

Section in a New Road-Cutting just N. of the Convalescent Home, Felixstow. (S. V. Wood, 1882.)

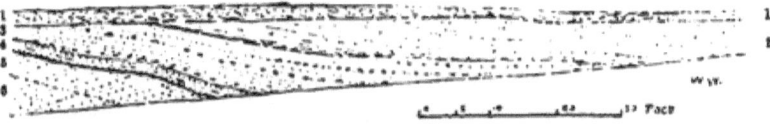

1. Soil.
2. Reddish-brown brickearth, like that of the brickyard at Derby Road, Ipswich, passing down into—
3. Yellow sand with orange-coloured bands and patches, and some very fine shingle.
4. Dark brown bedded loamy sand.
5. Obliquely bedded Red Crag, without shells (decalcified).
6. Obliquely bedded shelly Red Crag.

There is no line between 5 and 6 really, the line here merely represents the ending off of the shells.

In a pit about a third of a mile south-westward from the church the shelly Crag was well seen, and here my friend Mr. W. E. Hardy found a shell of *Cardium echinatum*, which the late Mr. S. V. Wood describes (in a letter) as "a perfect specimen, very rare to my researches, a variety with angular ribs."

In an old pit, close to the northern side of the road, about a third of a mile S.E. of the remains of the Old Hall, there is a little gravelly sand (Drift) at top; but the Crag comes up close to the surface.

I saw workings in the nodule-bed, close to the cliff-edge, in the field east of Martello Place, and, just to the north, the coprolite-work in the meadow east of Felixstow Church, gave the following section (1874):—

A little soil.

Red Crag. { Crag, in parts shelly to the top, somewhat evenly bedded (though with small current-bedding), with layers of laminated loam and clay, chiefly in two beds; about 12 feet.
Nodule-bed, with flints, a foot to 2 feet.
Shelly Crag; up to about a foot, in parts.

London Clay.

The beds seem to rise southwards, where it is only about 8 feet down to the nodule-bed.

W. W.

CHAPTER VI.—RED CRAG—*continued*.

DETAILS.

Valley of the Deben, up the Right Side, to the Brightwell Valley.

In its range up the valley of the Deben and its tributaries, the outcrop of the Red Crag is continuous, except for two short interruptions at Kirton, where the Drift overlaps, and it is of a most winding character, being much cut back up the side-valleys, so much indeed as to be in many places within a mile of the outcrop on the left side of the valley of the Orwell. Here, too, the nodule-bed has been much worked, and many good pit-sections occur; these indeed are so many that it has been convenient to break up this side of the Deben Valley into four sections.

An old pit about half a mile N.W. of Felixstow Church is, I believe, the site of a nodule-working.

The nodule-bed was worked, in 1874, in the field in the angle of the roads half a mile northwards from Walton Church; but the shallow pit was filled in before I could note the section.

In the Crag-pit just above the cottage, marked Mill House on the Map, in the little valley N.E. of Trimley, the false-bedded shelly Crag does not end off sharply at top; but in its upper part is interbedded with unfossiliferous sand, which latter alone occurs at the top part of the pit. It is all probably Crag, as close by (higher up, towards the village) another pit is in coarse ferruginous sand, partly hardened into iron-sandstone, especially towards the top, where the stone contains casts of shells. Above this is finer unfossiliferous sand of a lighter colour (? Drift). The iron-oxide has nought to do with the bedding, but has infiltrated.

At the Sand-pit, marked on the Map, more than half a mile W.S.W. of Falkenham Church, the section was :—

Sand and gravel, with pieces of iron-sandstone (containing impressions of shells) at the bottom: up to 6 feet or more.
False-bedded coarse ferruginous sand, with impressions of shells in places: up to 8 feet?
Shelly Crag touched at the bottom.

A small section was to be seen (1874) in an old pit, marked on the Map, on the eastern side of the lane nearly a mile S. of S.E. from Falkenham Church, as follows :—

Irregular hollow of brown and buff sand (? Drift) at one part.

Red Crag.
{ Brown coarse sand, with some small pebbles and a few phosphate nodules; some layers of broken-up iron-sandstone, or grit, with casts of shells; about 4 feet thick; and then the bottom part lighter-coloured and false-bedded.

Signs of shelly Crag in some parts of the bottom.

Shelly Crag also occurs in the pond at the back of the farmhouse, and in the lane there is a very small patch of gravel over the upper sand.

In a pit about a fifth of a mile eastward of Falkenham Church the upper part of the Crag is without shells.

About half a mile northward of Falkenham Church there was a nodule-working, in 1874, on the eastern side of the track, one pit, then being filled up, showed a mass of sand. Just before getting to this pit London Clay seems to occur at the surface (unless brought there) at the same or a higher level.

Close by, to the E.N.E., a smaller pit showed some feet of sand, with a few phosphate nodules and some box-stones at or near the bottom, though sometimes the sand rested on London Clay without any nodules occurring.

Some 200 yards south, and nearly at the same level, was a well in London Clay.

Another pit just S.E. of the end of the lane from the church, pointing northward towards Corporation Farm, was in brown sand, with sometimes a little shelly Crag (at W. end only) and a few coprolites at the bottom, resting irregularly on London Clay, which seemed to rise up nearly vertically for about 3 feet at one place.

A neighbouring coprolite-work, about 16 feet deep, nearly half a mile N.N.W. of Falkenham Church, gave the following section (1874):—

		FEET.
Soil and sand, sometimes gravelly at top, false-bedded		12 or 14
Red Crag. { Shelly Crag,	- about	1 or 1½
{ Coprolite-bed,	- about	1 or 2
London Clay.		

At the farm by the edge of the marsh, about 1¼ miles east of Kirton, a small quantity of coprolites has been got below gravelly sand, with clay beneath, no shelly Crag having been found. The road to the farm is made to a great extent of box-stones. This must be a small outlier.

At Kirton a coprolite-working, some 20 feet deep, about a quarter of a mile N.E. of the church, gave the following section (1877):—

Glacial Drift. Sand and gravel, 12 to 15 feet; a little loamy in places, and then forming what the foreman called a "loam-horse," which dammed back water at one end.

Red Crag. { Brown false-bedded sand, with a little shelly Crag at the E. end.
{ Nodule-bed.

Another working, a little eastward, and just south of Corporation Farm, gave this section:—

Glacial Drift. Nearly all light-coloured sand, with gravelly layers. There were two "loam-horses," one a mass of brown and grey clay, with stones, going nearly to the bottom of the pit; the other almost meeting a small hump of London Clay, that stuck up to some height, right through the nodule-bed. The sand was browner at bottom, where there was for the most part a line of gravel, but the division from the Crag was not well marked: about 15 feet thick generally.

Red Crag. { Brown sand; 6 to 8 feet.
{ Mostly 2 or 3 feet of shelly Crag.
{ Nodule-bed, resting unevenly on the London Clay, and thick on each side of the hump of the latter.
London Clay.

The loam-horses for the most part ran downwards obliquely and not vertically.

The nodule-bed has been also worked, I believe, a little north of Corporation Farm.

Brightwell Valley.

The outcrop of the Red Crag reaches up this tributary valley for six miles from the boundary-line in the main valley, close up to Ipswich Racecourse, and in the midst of this the nodule-bed has been worked more than anywhere else.

A coprolite-working on the western side of the farm, nearer a mile N.N.E. of Kirton church, gave the section below (1877):—

Glacial Drift. False-bedded, fine, sandy gravel, resting irregularly on the bed below; up to nearly 20 feet thick (including soil) in a scoop on the E. side.

Red Crag. { Brown sand (no shelly Crag seen).
{ Nodule-bed.

London Clay, brown at top, dark grey below.

About a fifth of a mile farther west is the site of another coprolite-working, which had been given up before I was there.

The line of pit on the western side of the little valley, about three quarters of a mile west of Kirton church, gave the following section (1874) :—

Drift. Brown sandy false-bedded gravel, chiefly of subangular flints and flint-pebbles, at one part resting rather irregularly on the bed below; up to 8 feet.

Red Crag. { Sand: the upper part brown, yellow, and partly white, and fine: the lower part a brown grit, passing down into the next; 6 to 10 feet.
{ Brown shelly Crag.

A pit on the southern side of the little valley a little west of the farm half a mile southward of Kembroke showed the following :—

Glacial Drift. Buff and brown false-bedded sand, with gravel, up to 7 feet thick, resting irregularly on

False-bedded brown Crag sand, the top part buff at one place. The junction hard to make out in parts.

A pit just northwards of Kembroke, gave the section below :—
Glacial Drift. A little gravel and sand.
Red Crag, about 25 to 30 feet, false-bedded. Brown sand at top, shelly sand below. No nodule-bed.
London Clay.

About half a mile from this, in an old pit a mile E.S.E. of Bucklesham Church, and on the southern side of the head of the little valley, I saw gravel, up to 4 feet thick, over Crag sand ; the top part fine, yellowish-brown, and somewhat bedded; the rest ferruginous, coarse, with scattered layers of small pebbles, &c., somewhat bedded at first (with slightly loamy layers), then false-bedded, and to a great extent hardened to a soft iron-sandstone.

Just east of the house marked "Hall" on the Map, about three quarters of a mile east of Bucklesham Church, I saw the layer of phosphatic nodules overlying London Clay, and there are springs here above the junction of the Crag and the clay.

A Crag pit nearly a quarter of a mile north of Bucklesham Church, on the eastern side of the little valley, about 30 feet deep, showed (1877) ferruginous sand, with shelly Crag below. A great wavy mass of poor ironstone, with the small rude columnar structure also seen at Ipswich and Bentley, scooped into the shelly Crag, and a little of the latter was also interbedded in the sand above.

Just west of the church a section showed a trace of Drift gravel over Crag sand, with shelly Crag beneath.

A pit about half a mile N.W. of Bucklesham Church (on the S. side of the little valley) gave the following section :—

Small patches of gravel at the highest part.

Red Crag ; 20 feet ? { Coarse false-bedded ferruginous sand, with ironstone (sometimes containing casts of shells) and a layer of pebbles and phosphatic nodules.
{ False-bedded shelly Crag.

London Clay has been turned out of the stream a little lower to the east.

The section in another pit, in a field about three quarters of a mile W.N.W. of Bucklesham Church, was as follows :—

Loamy soil, up to 3 feet.
Gravelly patches.

Red Crag { Coarse brown sand, false-bedded (especially in the lower part), with stones.
{ Shelly Crag has been touched below.

Just opposite this the coprolite-work on the western side of the lane about a quarter of a mile S.E. of Foxhall Lodge, gave the following section, in 1876.

Drift. Gravel and sand; up to 8 feet.

Red Crag. { Sand.
Shelly Crag.
Coprolite bed; about 25 feet or more from surface.

Mr. S. V. Wood has kindly communicated a drawing, made five or six years later, in which the gravel is shown to reach up to 15 feet in thickness, and to rest irregularly on sand, which he classes as Lower Glacial, with loamy bedded sand beneath.

The coprolite-working on the eastern side of the lane close to the last gave a section about 27 feet deep (1875):—

Glacial Drift.—Light-coloured sand and gravel, resting irregularly on the next; up to 8 feet thick.

Red Crag. {
Ferruginous, coarse, false-bedded sand, with the usual gravelly layers (containing small phosphatic nodules). Some casts of shells in ironstone.
Shelly Crag, a few feet. The lines of false-bedding pass from this into the shell-less sand above, showing both to be really one bed. Towards the east a mass of shell-less sand came in under the shelly Crag, which was then thin; but further east more of the latter came in below.
Nodule-bed, full of shells, over a foot thick, and has been found up to 4 feet. No water in this pit.

The coprolite-working about a third of a mile to the east, also on the northern side of the little valley, showed completely (1877) that the shell-less ferruginous sand is simply decalcified Crag. In parts the shelly Crag went up to the top of the pit, except for soil, whilst in others the shell-less sand occurred to some depth, ended off suddenly against the shelly sand, and had the structural lines of the latter continued through it. At one part the two dove-tailed together, a long strip of the shelly Crag running into the midst of the sand, and a long strip of the latter running also into the former.

Another coprolite-working, just east of the last, gave the following section :—

Red Crag; about 35 feet or more. {
Ferruginous and yellowish false-bedded sand, with ironstone; the lower part shelly, and the shells ending off most abruptly, across bedding, etc. Beds waved, and showing a small fault (about a foot downthrow). There are some pipe-like hollows, or funnels, of sand, which have been water-channels, and in which the shells have been dissolved away.
Nodule-bed, over a foot, and has been found up to 4 feet thick.
Shelly sand, 2 or 3 feet, and then a few more nodules.

Grey London Clay touched.

The pit at the back of the barn about half a mile N. of Bucklesham Church showed, in 1877, 8 or 10 feet of brown bedded loam and sand with some thin grey layers, and at the bottom part thin ferruginous layers; resting in waves on sand and shelly Crag, of which only 2 or 3 feet was to be seen. Can this loam represent the Chillesford Clay?

The nodule-bed has been worked about a quarter of a mile east of Foxhall Lodge, and at the old coprolite-working at the southern edge of the plantation on the eastern side of the Lodge, the following beds were to be seen, in 1875:—

Drift. {
At top some grey stony loam, not unlike weathered Boulder Clay, in pockets; up to 3 or 4 feet.
Gravel and sand, apparently thick.

Ferruginous sand, of the Red Crag, as in the workings just south and above described.

A small Crag pit, nearly a third of a mile east of the large pond, Bixley Decoy, showed ferruginous sand and shelly Crag, with a gravelly layer (pebbles and phosphatic nodules) for the most part above the shells, but also with shells above it partly; so that the line of shell-ending has nothing to with the bedding.

A like section was seen in the small sharp-sided island in the marsh, just east, in a large pit, nearly 30 feet deep. The whole of the sand is false-bedded, and there are impressions of shells in some of the ironstone and iron-sandstone, of which there is a good deal. The gravelly bed here is probably a continuation of that just noticed.

The sand-pit in the little hollow by the hedge (marked on the Map) about half a mile nearly N.W. of Warren House (Felixstow Road), showed a little gravel, in parts, over ferruginous sand (Crag), at the lower part with iron-sandstone containing, at one place, a few casts of shells (*Mytilus*).

In the other terminal branch of the valley, too, the outcrop reaches nearly as far, to Rushmere Common. In this branch, at the western edge of Foxhall Heath, the road down to the valley, more than a mile S.S.W. of Kesgrave Church, shows the following succession :—

At top brown sand, with traces of fine gravel, and just below is sand, with a thin line of gravel at the base (Drift).
Grey and brown bedded loam, with little sand (? = Chillesford Clay); nearly 18 inches, passing down into—
Ferruginous sand (Crag).

A fifth of a mile lower down the valley sand and shelly Crag are to be seen, and again, about half a mile westward of Foxhall Hall, where there is gravel above the Crag sand, as in two other pits close by.

Just S.W. of the Hall was another like section of gravel over sand and Crag, and, close by, in 1875, the new coprolite-working on the southern side of the Hall was 27 feet deep, and gave the following section, remarkable for the occurrence of shelly sand beneath the mass of the nodule-bed (see also section, p. 61) :—

Glacial Drift.—Sand and gravel.

Red Crag.
{
Ferruginous and light-coloured false-bedded sand.
Shelly Crag, with a nodule (or gravel) bed some 16 feet down (from surface).
Main nodule-bed, a foot or more thick, where open to view underlain by—
Sand, with broken-up shells and a few nodules; about a foot.
}

Dark grey London Clay touched.

Here, as elsewhere, the ending off of the shells in the Crag has nought to do with the bedding. At the northern end this plane of decalcification rises to the east, where the ground falls, which is exceptional.

The large working directly opposite, and E. of, the farm was abandoned towards the end of 1874. There is here a greater thickness of the sand and gravel at top, and the total depth was 30 feet. A long wedge of shelly Crag was to be seen in the shell-less sand, capped by a ferruginous bedded loam, with an irregular prismatic structure, which loam was probably the cause of the preservation from dissolution of the shells beneath.

The large adjoining coprolite-working, further east of Foxhall Hall, gave a fine section in 1876, when the beds shown were as follows :—

Drift.—False-bedded gravel and sand, resting irregularly on the sand below; up to 15 feet (or more).

Red Crag.
{
Ferruginous sand, with ironstone (impressions of shells), and scattered phosphatic nodules; of irregular thickness, being merely decalcified Crag.
Shelly Crag, with a loamy ferrugincus bed about the junction with the shell-less sand. The bottom 6 feet or so with phosphatic nodules and flints (some large), either in layers or scattered freely throughout. At the most easterly part (not then worked) there was at the bottom a loamy, firm, ferruginous bed, up to 3 feet thick, probably not far above the nodule-bed.
Nodule-bed, at a depth of 33–36 feet; about a foot thick; with water, showing the presence of London Clay.
}

It is this last section, I believe, that Mr. WOOD refers to,* and, by his kindness and that of the Council of the Geological Society, his woodcut is reproduced:—

FIG. 12.

Section in a Coprolite Pit by Foxhall Hall. (WOOD.)

The actual section was in terraces, here omitted; height 15 feet.

c. Glacial Drift.—Bedded gravelly sand, passing at the base into false-bedded gravel.

Red Crag. { b. Red sands and partly hardened loamy sand, horizontally bedded.
{ a. Unaltered shelly Crag.

At the back of the farm, about half a mile west of Brightwell Church, a section showed a trace of gravel over sand with ironstone and a layer of phosphatic nodules.

Another pit at the Hall, and just east of the church, gave a like, but better, section as follows:—

Glacial Drift.—Trace of gravel.

Red Crag. { Light-coloured sand, with fine gravelly patches. I could not well get at this, which seemed to belong to the Crag; up to 6 feet?
{ Firm brown iron-sand, partly very coarse and with pebbles, etc. ? 20 to 25 feet.
{ Shelly Crag at the bottom, at W. part.

Below this farm the Crag is shown in springs to the marsh-level.

At Newbourn Hall and church there is hard shelly Crag.

At the Crag pit, marked on the Map, in the little valley about three-quarters of a mile E.N.E. of Brightwell Church, there was a wash of sand and gravel down the slope, over false-bedded ferruginous Crag sand, in parts full of casts and impressions of shells in ironstone. At the base was seen dark red shelly Crag, false-bedded (southwards), with phosphatic nodules at top in places, hardened and consequently standing out as a sort of crag. Immediately south, indeed joining this, another opening showed gravelly soil over a good thickness of the brown sand, with a floor of shelly Crag.

Just eastward of Walk Barn there is Drift sand and gravel over sand and shelly Crag; and in an old pit, about a quarter of a mile E S.E. sand and shelly Crag occur beneath Drift (see p. 80).

Through the strip of wood in the valley-bottom about a quarter of a mile N.W. of Newbourn a set of springs was cut back, on the eastern side, in 1877, into very shelly Crag.

The large Crag pit, marked on the Map, at Newbourn, nearly a quarter of a mile N.E. of the church, was about 40 feet deep, wholly in Red Crag, the eastern end being overgrown. The decalcified sand is in part rather light-coloured at top, partly fine, and is of course irregularly divided from the shelly Crag beneath. This latter contains a great

---

* *Quart. Journ. Geol. Soc.*, vol. xxxiii., p. 81. (1877.)

variety of shells, many well preserved (and I believe this pit would prove a good collecting-place): it is mostly firm, so as to stand vertical in section, dark, false-bedded, and often with many phosphatic nodules and flints: at one part a nearly horizontal yellowish line occurs cutting across the false-bedding, and showing how little dependence is to be placed on colour. At the western part of the pit the process of dissolution of shells was shown, the shelly Crag in places passing into a sort of marl, and there being many more or less vertical marly veins, the marl being the result of the dissolving away of shells from the sand. At the bottom of the pit there are springs, and the London Clay occurs at the lowest part.

I first saw this section on a very windy day, when I noticed a peculiar appearance at the top part. This was owing to what may be called miniature reversed earth-pillars. The formation of earth-pillars through the protecting action of stones (whereby the clay, &c. immediately beneath is preserved from weathering, whilst the unprotected parts around are carried away, leaving irregular pillar-like masses) is well known; but in this case the current of wind blowing obliquely up the face of the pit, carried away the loose sand except where resisted by small stones, leaving small pillars (two or three inches long) *above* the protecting stones.

A long cutting in the stackyard at the farm, about a quarter of a mile eastward of Newbourn Church, near by the Crag Pit, again showed very shelly Crag, with many phosphatic nodules, flints, etc. There were here more or less vertical funnel-like places where the red matter had been washed out and the Crag bleached, the shells also being dissolved out to some extent.

Valley of the Deben, up the Right Side, between the Brightwell and Finn Valleys.

At Hemley there is sand, and at Hemley Hall a sand-pit, on the southern side of the farmyard, gave the following section:—

Drift ?—Light-coloured, somewhat bedded sand; up to 7 feet. Hardly to be distinguished from the underlying.

Red Crag. { Brown false-bedded sand; up to 12 feet or more. Shelly Crag and phosphatic nodules, in part of the floor of the pit.

An old pit, 12 feet or more deep, in a field about half a mile S.S.E. of Waldringfield Church, showed these beds:—

Drift.—Gravel and sand; up to 5 feet (with soil). At the N. end with lumpy patches of pale sandy Boulder Clay at the bottom. Rests irregularly on the Crag sand.

Red Crag. { Ferruginous sand; 6 inches to a few feet. Shelly Crag.

The old pit at the cross-roads south of the church shows a little shelly Crag with sand above, and in a field nearly a quarter of a mile S.E. of the church, the traces of an old ploughed-over pit showed pale grey sandy Boulder Clay, gravel, and Crag. The Drift would seem to be a small (unmappable) tongue ploughing into the Crag.

Just N. of this there was, in 1877, a long deep trench (? the beginning of a coprolite-pit) running northward down to the little side-valley. At the top part there was Red Crag, the London Clay being touched at a depth of about 10 feet. Further on, before getting to the hedge, the latter came up irregularly above the bottom of the narrow trench, going down again by the hedge, beyond which the ground slopes more sharply northward and the Crag ends off, black peaty earth coming on at top and thickening down the slope.

Close by, S.S.E. of the church, a new coprolite-working showed, at its eastern end, an irregular hollow of Drift over the Crag, to a depth of 17 feet at one spot. The Drift consisted of fine whitish gravel (forming the chief mass) underlain by whitish clay (partly a fine Boulder Clay), and then, in places, more gravel. In other parts of the pit there were some smooth-sided broad pipes or hollows of sand in the Crag. The nodule-bed, up to 3 feet thick, rested irregularly on London Clay.

Directly eastward of the church there is yellow sand, over brown sand, over red sand, all apparently belonging to the Crag.

The large coprolite-working N.E. of Waldringfield Church, which was nearly given up in 1876, except close to the road, gave the following section :—

    Glacial Drift.—Gravel and sand, at the highest part ; up to 8 feet thick, with soil.

    Red Crag. { Loamy ferruginous bedded layer, partly mottled.
                Sand, some fine.
                Shelly Crag.
                Nodule-bed ; said to be up to 4 feet thick in places.

    London Clay touched (not seen by me).

Mr. Stollery, the foreman, who had a large collection of shells from the Crag, told me that the working had been carried to a depth of about 40 feet; that, in places, some six inches of Coralline Crag had been got beneath the nodule-bed; and that he had found *Pholas* shells bored into the London Clay to a depth of some inches.

At the sand-pit, marked on the Map, less than half a mile north-westward of Waldringfield Church there is shelly Crag at the bottom; and in a pond on the north this and London Clay both occur.

A pit on the western side of the road, a mile and a quarter N.W. of the church, showed a little Drift gravel over sand and shelly Crag.

Just east of the road, nearly a mile southward from Martlesham Church, there was a like section, with more of the gravel at top, and also with London Clay at the bottom.

About a quarter of a mile westward of this last, and about a mile southward from Martlesham Church, is the site of an old coprolite-work, also showing gravel over sand and shelly Crag; and it is probably here that Mr. Wood noted the section reproduced in Figs. 13, 14.

Figs. 13, 14.

Sections in a Pit, South of Martlesham.*

 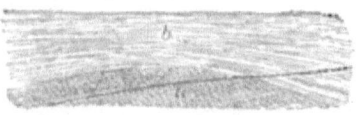

    c. Pipe of sand crossing both altered and unaltered Crag.
    b. Bedded sands, = *a*, altered.
    a. Shelly Crag.
    x Layer of flint-pebbles, running through both shelly Crag and sand.

Near the head of this little valley, by "Shepherds Lodge," was a pit showing a little gravel over brown sand, the latter probably Crag.

On the west of the road, about three quarters of a mile south of Martlesham Church, is the site of another old coprolite-working, which, like the former, shows a little gravel over sand and shelly Crag.

Valley of the Finn.

Up the southern side of this valley the Red Crag crops out for nearly five miles, when the Drift seems to overlap and to rest on the London Clay, which happens again about a mile lower down on the northern side. There are also outcrops up the side-valleys.

Shelly Crag may be seen near Kesgrave Hall, and a pit a little higher up the same side-valley just north of "Sunk Houses," about a third of a mile west of the Hall, gave (in 1874-78) a very marked junction of Drift and Crag, the section (which is the one alluded to by Mr. Wood)† being :—

---

* Reproduced from *Quart. Journ. Geol. Soc.*, vol. xxxiii., p. 75, through the kindness of the Council of the Geological Society.
† *Quart. Journ. Geol. Soc.*, vol. xxxiii., p. 75. (1877.)

Glacial Drift.—Brown and light-coloured sand and gravel, false-bedded, resting irregularly on the bed below; up to 8 feet or more.

Red Crag.—False-bedded, coarse, deep rich brown, ferruginous sand, with layers of iron-sandstone (some full of impressions of shells), and a good many small pebbles and flints; up to about 13 feet seen. Wet at bottom of pit (about 2 feet lower).

The railway-cutting east of Bealings Station was mostly overgrown when I saw it (1878), the extreme eastern end quite so. A little way in, however, I saw a streak of shelly Crag in the shell-less brown sand on the southern side. Then the northern side showed ferruginous false-bedded sand over, and passing into, shelly sand, the London Clay beneath being sometimes touched in the ditch; as was also the case in the ditch on the south as the ground rises. Further on shelly Crag was again seen in the sand, at one part (on the southern side) a mass of the former being underlain by the latter. Where the cutting is deep only the lower part was open to view, and showed the sand both above and beneath shelly Crag. At the slight hollow, upper beds (brown sand with a gravelly base) sweep down to about the level of the line. At the next deep part the top was overgrown, and only ferruginous sand was seen. Further on, as the ground falls, sand and gravel sweep down over this sand, at one place to the level of the rails; and this section (Drift over Crag) seems to extend to the western end.

The short cutting touching Bealings Station is in the brown sand of the Crag.

The cutting west of this (and near Kesgrave House) shows at the highest part light-coloured sand, with a gravelly tendency at top. The bottom part is in brown sand with shelly Crag, the latter mostly below the level of the rails.

The next, a shallow, turfed cutting, is in sand.

Then comes a long cutting, southward of Playford Hall. At its eastern end a patch of Drift (Boulder Clay and sand, see p. 89) comes down over the brown sand of the Crag; but how far it extends eastward is uncertain. Between the two bridges over the line the brown sand is shown along the lower part, about 160 to 170 yards from the second bridge there seems to be a little Boulder Clay at top on the southern side, and the hollow beyond seems to be partly filled with washed-in material. Westward of the second bridge the lower part was tolerably clear, showing brown and light-coloured false-bedded sand (Crag).

The next cutting, which almost touches the above, about two thirds of a mile south-westward of Playford Church, is short. The lower part was re-opened in 1876, and showed the following section, the beds rising slightly eastward, so that the upper only occurred on the west:—

? *Drift or Crag.*—Brown sand, with layers of loam, passing down into like sand with layers of gravel.

Red Crag.—Bright ferruginous sand, with lighter-coloured sand below. I found one piece of shell in this.

An old pit, south of Playford Hall, and just north of the railway, gave the following succession:—

Dark ferruginous sand; up to 6 feet, or more.

Light-coloured finer sand, with a few small thin patches of grey and brownish clay at the top, and slightly micaceous; up to 3 feet.

Dark ferruginous sand; 12 feet shown, but the bottom part hidden.

I take all these beds to belong to the Red Crag; the middle bed is a sort of hint at the conditions of the Chillesford Beds, of which we have no certain knowledge in this district. At the northern part of the pit (ploughed over) there seems to have been a patch of Boulder Clay.

A little to the west, in the wood just north of the railway-cutting last noticed, there is a sharp cliff, with springs at the foot, pointing to the outcrop of the London Clay from beneath the Crag.

The short railway-cutting north of Rushmere Street was turfed throughout, but seemed to be in sand, with a loamy bed in it, judging from the line of dampness and the growth of willows.

The other side of the valley, as also the left side of the Deben to near Alderton, was mapped by Mr. DALTON, whose notes follow.   W. W.

From Tuddenham St. Martin to near Playford the Red Crag is either absent or too thin to be seen in the absence of sections. It appears a little above Playford, but offers nothing worthy of notice above Martlesham. In Whin Hill railway-cutting it has its usual character, of a ferruginous current-bedded mass of shells and sand. The section of this railway-cutting, now much overgrown, has been described by Prof. PRESTWICH* as showing the following beds:—

[Glacial Drift.]—White sand and gravel; 3 feet.

Red Crag. { Yellow sand, with a few patches of shells at the base; 15 feet.
Shelly Crag; 12 feet [no nodule-bed].

London Clay.

The base of the Crag is exposed in a pit on Kingston Farm; but here also there is no phosphato-bed.

Valley of the Deben, down the Left Side.

From the edge of the map near Woodbridge the Red Crag has a continuous outcrop round to the Butley River, not only fringing the plateau of Glacial gravel, but rising high in the intermediate valleys, and near Shottisham, constituting the watershed. Its thickness varies considerably, owing to the inequality of the surface on which it was deposited, and which at Sutton rises higher than most of the Red Crag, and, in fact, formed an island in the sea of that period. But little of the Red Crag east of the Deben is decalcified, its shells being retained even on the watershed (see p. 70).

The junction with the London Clay was shown just N.W. of Ferry Farm (south of Woodbridge), and the low cliff, a quarter of a mile south of the farm, consists of red sand without shells.

Much of the ground between Nettle Hill cliff, and Sutton Hall has been found productive of phosphate, and some of the abandoned pits are still partly open.

The "Bullock-yard pit" exhibits the cliff of Coralline Crag against which the Red Crag has been deposited.

Prof. PRESTWICH's figures (15–17, p. 68), show the structure of this point better than any merely verbal description. He remarks that the sections here show "that there are two submerged cliffs, that they pass round the hill, and that the mass of Coralline Crag, forming the higher part of the hill, has been an old reef in the Red Crag sea."†

South of Shottisham Creek the Crag descends to high-water level for about half a mile, rises to Church Farm, and again descends at Ramsholt, whence it ranges but little above High Water Mark to Ramsholt Dock. It rises again to Peyton Hall, passing above that and Poplar Hall. W. H. D.

The sand-pit, marked on the Map, two thirds of a mile westward of Alderton Church showed the following beds (1874):—

A little gravelly sand.

Red Crag. { Brown false-bedded sand, mostly coarse; in the upper part some small pieces of ironstone, with casts and impressions of shells, also some small, vertical, stalactite-like incrustations of ironstone (as in the Crag of Bawdsey cliff); = decalcified Crag; about 12 feet.
Shelly Crag (in the lower part of the pit), the shells ending off irregularly at top; 15 feet.

Between Alderton and Bawdsey the valley of the Deben is barely separated from what remains of that of the Ore or Alde, and the Red Crag is just cut through, leaving the Bawdsey Mass as an outlier, so that at one part there is little more than a third of a mile of low-lying London Clay between the two sets of marshes.

---

* *Quart. Journ. Geol. Soc.*, vol. xxvii., p. 334. (1871.)
† Ibid., p. 339.

Sections at Sutton. (PRESTWICH.)
Vertical scale about 12 feet to an inch.
Reproduced, from *Quart. Journ. Geol. Soc.*, vol. xxvii., p. 340, by the kindness of PROF. PRESTWICH and of the Council of the Geological Society.

FIG. 15.
Section in the Bullock-yard Pit, 54 feet above Low-Water Mark.

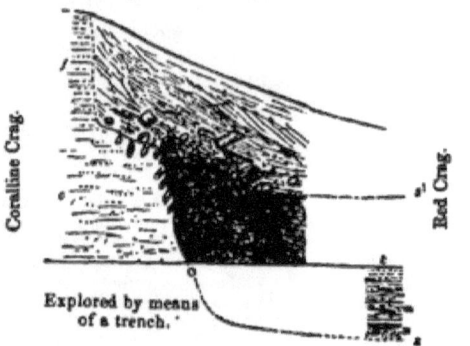

t. Floor of pit 31 feet above Low Water Mark.
*s*¹ Upper shore-line, with blocks of Coralline Crag, flints, coprolites and shells above it.
m. Seam or shells of *Mytilus edulis*, almost all with both valves.
n. Bed of coprolites and large flints.
s. Lower shore-line.

FIG. 16.
Section in the same Pit, but at right angles to the above.

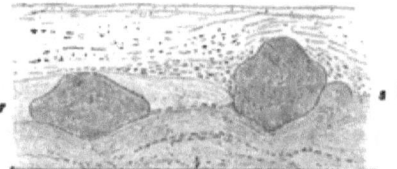

Red Crag with two large blocks of Coralline Crag, the larger may weigh more than a ton. 1 must have fallen before, and 2 after the deposition of the bed *r.* There were also many smaller blocks, some bored by Annelids, others covered with *Balani*; as well as flint-pebbles, coprolites, and unworn flints.

FIG. 17.
Section in the Pit near the Barn, at the Western Part of the Ridge.

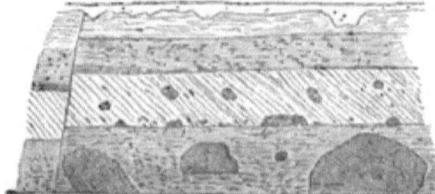

Red Crag with many blocks of Coralline Crag, and here and there flints and phosphatic nodules. Shows the section of the lower shore on the eastern side of the reef. "The occurrence of these transported blocks of Coralline Crag is peculiar to these pits " (p. 341).

I believe that the nodule-bed has been worked just S.E. of Manor House, Bawdsey, and, in 1874, there was a small working in a field about a third of a mile S.W. of the church. At the spot where the bed was shown it was about 3 feet down, and capped by shelly Crag. Along the lane close by, the ditch (in the same field), shows London Clay for some way.

Prof. Prestwich has figured a section at Ramsholt, showing erosion of the lower beds of the Red Crag before the deposition of those above, which is here reproduced, through the kindness of the Council of the Geological Society (Fig. 18.)

Fig. 18.

Section in Red Crag at Ramsholt.[*]

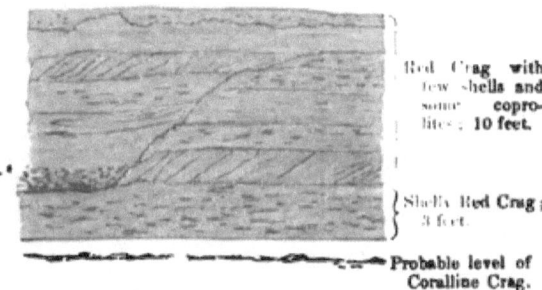

*Seam of coprolites.

Red Crag with few shells and some coprolites. 10 feet.

Shelly Red Crag; 3 feet.

Probable level of Coralline Crag.

Bawdsey Cliff.

The south-western part of this range of cliff gives us one of the best sections of the Red Crag. As there is (or was) often a shelf near the base of the Crag, this out of-the-way spot is very favourable for the collection of fossils, which occur here in great number and variety, as well as in a good state of preservation. The list given by Prof. Prestwich[†] has been much added to.

In this case, as with Felixstow, the whole cliff-section will be described here, and not the Crag alone.

At the S.W. end, marked by the site of the Martello Tower, in an earthwork at the top, there is gravel, resting irregularly on Red Crag, on London Clay, the last not rising more than 8 feet above the base of the cliff.

Going N.E. the clay rose slightly, and in part the thick gravel rested on it, cutting through the Crag.

Then the gravel thins off, and a good thickness of false-bedded Crag was shown. At top were fragments of a very shelly bed (*Mya*, etc., as at Felixstow), succeeded by a mass of sand mostly without shells, whilst the lower part was shelly. Here also, as at Felixstow, were layers of loam.

The Crag is very massive, being much bound together, and there are hollows without shells, resulting from the dissolving away of the shells.

Opposite Cottage Barn a very even junction of the Crag with the London Clay was shown, the latter being sometimes 12 feet or more up the cliff.

---

[*] *Quart. Journ. Geol. Soc.*, vol. xxvii., p. 327.
[†] *Quart. Journ. Geol. Soc.*, vol. xxvii., p. 337.

Then, from the cliff being a little lower, less Crag occurred, and the top part was without shells.

As the ground rises the shelly Crag reached to the top, the prevalence of *Cyprina*, *Mya*, and *Tellina* in certain beds being remarkable, and flint pebbles and phosphatic nodules occurring throughout.

The ground still rising there comes on, at top, fine buff sand, with a layer of gravel at its foot, and then, above this apparently (on still higher ground), coarser brown sand with layers of gravel. These beds are probably of Glacial age. Along this highest part the cliff has become a steep, rough, grassy slope, masking the London Clay at the foot, probably because of the sand at the top, which, being much looser than the Crag, washes over the face of the cliff.

As the level of the ground falls slowly shelly Crag came near to the surface by the hedge running down to near Middle Barn. A little further the Drift ends off, the upper part of the Crag being unfossiliferous sand, and the cliff resuming its rougher form.

The London Clay was masked by fallen earth, and, as the surface of the ground sinks, the Crag seemed to go to a rather lower level. When the cliff gets low the clay was shown 7 or 8 feet up, capped by a little sand and shelly Crag, which capping ended off about 150 yards before reaching the Sea Mark, beyond which the London Clay alone, except for soil, forms the low slope to the track to Bawdsey Hall. Then the diminutive cliff is overgrown, but consists of London Clay with a loamy soil, the latter perhaps thickening further on, until at Martello Tower W. there is only about 3 feet of brown loam. Then the surface of the ground sinks until there is almost nothing above the beach-level, and then rises slightly to a height of about 6 feet, clay being shown just before getting to the road at East End (? from shingle having been taken away from the front). Then the surface falls again, and the slight bank is overgrown, to Martello Tower X., where the sea-wall begins. Along all this part there was a narrow belt of shingle above high-water mark.

In front of the sea-wall, by Tower X., Crag occurs at the edge of, and below, the shingle, as well as just N. It has also been found along the ditch, inside the sea-wall, northwards from the tower nearly down to the marsh.

Valley of the Ore.

On the London Clay, west and south-west of Martello Tower X., there are some spots of Red Crag, too small to be shown on the map.

At Shingle Street I saw the junction of the Crag with the London Clay in a ditch north of Martello Tower A. A.   W. W.

East of Alderton the Red Crag descends to the sea-level and skirts the marsh northward to Hollesley, when the outcrop up the small valley joins that of the Deben on the N.W.

This inland stretch of Red Crag, from Hollesley to Shottisham, calls for but few remarks. The Crag is mostly shelly, probably partly from the protection of the Boulder Clay not long since removed (speaking geologically), but mainly from its porosity and depth. Where no retention of carbonated waters takes place, the rapidity of percolation prevents any notable solution of calcareous matter, whilst the amount of carbonic acid gathered by rain water on the barren wastes must be very slight, and will be further reduced during percolation through thick beds of fine sand of the Glacial Series.

Coprolite has been raised in the fields E. and S.E. of Caldwell Hall, S.E. of Boyton, and pockets of it have been found under the alluvium thereabouts. N.E. of the Hall the Red Crag extends beneath the alluvium, overlapping the Coralline Crag, here worked for phosphates, as mentioned above, p. 28.

The valley separating Boyton and Capel St. Andrews shows London Clay rising to an unusual height, for this part, on both sides as far as Boyton Ford. Coprolite is raised at Capel Farm.

There is now no trace of the large workings for the nodules that were once opened on the north of Stonebridge Marshes.

The Gedgrave ridge is an exception to the general absence of decalcification east of the Deben, consisting entirely of red sand, though capped Pre-Glacially by Chillesford Clay (since removed) the Glacial covering being only coarse gravel.

W. H. D.

CHAPTER VII.—GLACIAL DRIFT.

General Remarks.

It should be understood that the term Glacial Drift does not imply that all the beds so-classed were deposited under strictly glacial conditions: it is used in a chronological sense, like the terms Carboniferous, Cretaceous, &c.; and therefore includes all beds formed during what is known as the Glacial Period, a time when, though ice asserted its supremacy, there were seasons, or places, with a somewhat milder state of things. Not only do we find Boulder Clay, the clear result of ice-action; but also, though to a less extent, sandy beds that seem to have been deposited by the sea, and loamy or clayey beds which, from their laminated structure, must have been formed in still water.

There is no need to enter here on the subject of the classification of the various divisions of this Drift, one of the most controversial of questions, and it will be enough to point out the succession found in our own limited district, without seeking to impose the same on other tracts, near or far off. This is a comparatively simple matter, though not without difficulty, there being some difference of opinion with regard to the exact position of the local brickearth (see p. 83).

Disregarding some doubtful high level gravel, above the Boulder Clay, but of the classification of which one can say nothing with certainty, the Glacial Drift of our district may be divided into two, for classificatory purposes (for descriptive purposes it will be treated under three heads, founded on lithological characters). The upper member is the deposit sometimes distinguished as the Great Chalky Boulder Clay, but which it is perhaps better to term simply the Boulder Clay; other like beds, at lower horizons in the series, being sometimes equally chalky. Below this there occurs a thinner and more varying set of deposits, consisting chiefly of sand and gravel, but containing in some places (though rarely in our district) a comparatively thin mass of Boulder Clay, and in others beds of loam or clay, that form a valuable brickearth.

The Boulder Clay is the Upper Glacial of Wood and Harmer, the sand and gravel their Middle Glacial, and the brickearth, to some extent at least, their Lower Glacial. However, the strong division insisted on by Mr. Wood as occurring between the Middle and Lower Glacial beds, is not clear to me.

Gravel and Sand.

In describing the details of the Glacial gravel and sand it will be convenient to follow the same order as with the Red Crag, the latter being almost everywhere capped by the former, the only exceptions being where small patches of Boulder Clay occur on the Crag.

South of the Stour (*Essex*).

This part was mapped by Mr. DALTON, who reports that "the Glacial gravel and sand, with irregular bands and lenticular masses of loam, ranges almost continuously along the southern side of the Stour Valley, being absent only at Little Horkesley, and to the south, where the Boulder Clay overlaps and rests on the London Clay. Gravel is dug in many places, but there are no sections requiring special notice, except those already mentioned as showing Crag " (p. 44).

Valley of the Stour, Left Side, above the Boxford Valley.

The outcrop is continuous in this tract, and runs up the tributary valley to Assington.

About five eighths of a mile a little west of south from Chilton Church, and above the large old chalk-pit, is a sand-pit about 20 feet deep, with the following succession:—

Glacial Drift.
- Boulder Clay, at the entrance (N.W.), below which the other beds probably dip.
- Gravel, of flints, flint-pebbles, quartz-pebbles (very small ones abundant), and others; with beds of coarse brown sand.
- Brown sand.
- Brown and grey fine sand, with layers of pipe-clay, causing a moist surface; 10 feet or more.
- Coarser, sharp, grey sand; shown to 6 feet at the western end.

At the highest part there is only a little gravel, but at the north-eastern end the beds sink sharply northwards, and gravel comes on.

Another pit close by, and just half a mile south of Chilton Church, shows the same beds, with more of the lowest sand (? 10 feet), here false-bedded. The northerly (or north-westerly) dip is also shown, and more strikingly than in the former section, as here it reaches as high an angle as 75°, and brings in Boulder Clay above the gravel.

More than a quarter of a mile N.W. of the Pottery (south of Chilton), and about 100 yards in rear of the targets at the rifle-range, a pit laid open 10 feet or more of this sand, which here is gravelly, mostly coarse, bright-coloured, with a few large concretions and very many smaller fragments of ironstone, and with some small patches of shining black sand.

At the targets the way down to the marker's place (in front) is in coarse, brown, ferruginous sand, with fine gravel, some pieces of brown hematite and some phosphatic nodules, about 4 feet thick, and strongly suggestive of Crag, over brown London Clay.

At the Pottery, a pit above the kiln, and touching the lane on the north, showed in parts a thick wash of brown loam over the sharp bright yellow and ferruginous Drift sand, with small flints and pebbles. The junction of this sand with the London Clay was shown in a pit a little north-east (see p. 9).

On the railway about a mile S.W. of Little Cornard, and barely separated from the larger cutting (on the north), is another, short, small, and over-grown, in gravel on the south, but in sharp sand over brown loam (like basement-bed of London Clay) at the other end.

From here eastward to the Bentley Valley, the ground was surveyed by MR. BENNETT, whose notes will be used in the following description.

Boxford Valley.

The outcrop up this valley is at first continuous, and then interrupted, consisting at last of mere isolated patches, some not in the bottom.

W. W.

Just N.E. of Mascals Farm, and about a mile west of Boxford Church, there is sandy gravel, with seams and lenticular patches of sand and loam, and much waved, about 9 feet deep.

At Brook House, nearly a mile south-eastward from Great Waldingfield Church, there is a small protrusion, surrounded on all sides by Boulder Clay. A pit shows gravel both on the clay and also rising up through it, and in the road up the hill S.W. Boulder Clay was seen banked against the gravel boss, a patch of loam in which dipped at a high angle.

In the small patch, nearly a mile N.E. of Little Waldingfield Church, the gravel-pit, marked on the Map, showed in one place Boulder Clay over coarse gravel with a little iron-sand, whilst in another place there was a lenticular patch of loam in the gravel, there about 12 feet thick, and bent up in an arch.

At the village there is a larger outcrop. Here a pit, on the western side of the road, north-west of the church, gave the section below, the bedding of the gravel following the hollow of the Boulder Clay:—

Boulder Clay; 0 to 4½ feet, in a slight hollow, the bottom, 6 inches, brown.

{ Pinkish gravel; 9 inches.
{ Sandy gravel; 14 inches.
{ Rather coarse gravel, with large flint pebbles; 3 feet.

A little eastward of the church another pit showed 10 feet of chalky gravel and sand, covered by a thin layer of Boulder Clay.

Southward of Streets End Farm, Boxford, a pit showed the following beds:—

Rather coarse sand, with lines of gravel, 3 feet.
Clean stiff brown clay, 6 or 7 inches.
Rather coarse gravel, with a little brown sand, 1½ feet down.

At Hole Farm, N.E. of Groton, there is fine, buff, sand and pebbles, capped by 6 feet of buff sandy loam, and at Spout Farm, about a quarter of a mile lower down this branch of the valley, a gravel-pit showed pebbles of black flint and of quartz in a sandy matrix, with some subangular flints.

In a pit at Creak Hill, by the lane nearly a mile east of Polstead Church, the beds seen were as follows:—

Rather coarse, sandy, subangular gravel; 6 feet.
Gravel and sand interbedded, the sand buff, coarse, and much false-bedded; 5 feet.

About 30 chains to the east, on the other side of the slight valley here, and on the northern side of the road, close to the cottages, there was a section of coarse subangular red gravel, with a little coarse red sand.

Valley of the Brett.

There is a good exposure up this valley, and where the sand is in force, as near Hadleigh, some steep slopes have resulted from its denudation.

In a farmyard a quarter of a mile north of Shelly Church, there is very coarse gravel, containing much chalk, and in one part so clayey as to resemble a very stony Boulder Clay, with fine buff sand beneath.

At the back of Semer Union, marked on the Map as Cosford Union House, a pit gave the section shown in Fig. 19; and another pit, a fifth of a mile south of Semer Church, that shown in Fig. 20.

Fig. 19.

Section in Drift at Cosford Union House.

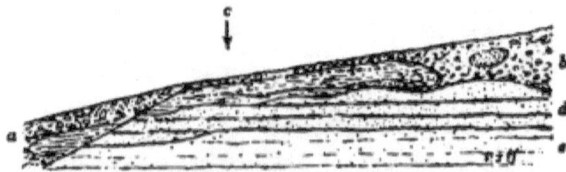

Scale 16 feet to an inch.

a. Coarse gravel, with a lenticular patch of stiff brown clay.
b. Rather coarse brown sand, with a little gravel; up to 7 feet.
c. Lenticular patch of brown and grey sandy clay, with thin bands of sand (? reconstructed Thanet Sand); about 3 feet. Does not come to the surface.
d. Fine, bedded, buff sand, with partings of pipe-clay and thin bands of grey sand.
e. Fine, white, rather sharp, bedded sand; 3 feet, shown, said not to be bottomed at 15.

GLACIAL DRIFT.

FIG. 20.

Section South of Semer Church.

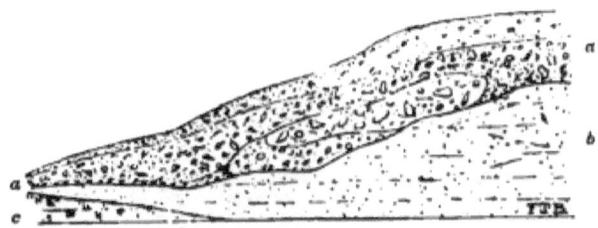

Scale 16 feet to an inch.

a. Rather coarse brown sand, with a little gravel, containing a lenticular mass of Boulder Clay and coarse gravel, and at the lower part a few phosphatic nodules.
b. Fine bedded light-brown sand. [It struck me that this might be Crag.—W. W.]
c. Brown sandy clay. [Base-bed of Thanet Sand.—W. W.] In the cut this, by mistake, has been shaded like chalk.

The junction of the Boulder Clay and the gravel near Monks' Eleigh Church has been already described (p. 45), and a pit by the cross-roads east of the church showed 5 feet of sandy loam over 6 feet of coarse gravel. Cinerary urns and the foundations of a wall are said to have been found in this pit.

In a pit on the eastern side of the road at Red Hill Green, Aldham, there is Boulder Clay, with sand and gravel rising up in a boss nearly to the surface, and hardened into rocky masses at the junction.

A pit just east of Hadleigh Railway Station gave the section, Fig. 21.

FIG. 21.

Section East of Hadleigh Railway Station.

Scale 8 feet to an inch.

a. Coarse slightly false-bedded sand, with lines of gravel, passing down into *b.*
b. Very pebbly gravel (mostly black flints), cutting across the bedding of *c.*
c. A confused mixture of sand and gravel, with lenticular patches of grey clay (*d.*)
e. Rather fine evenly bedded brown sand, about 3 feet.
 Fine white sand touched at bottom.

At the back of Benton End Farm, nearly a mile south-eastward of Hadleigh Church, a pit, much hidden by talus, showed over 6 feet of false-bedded sand, with lines of gravel, mostly of pebbles of quartz and flint and much-rolled flints, with sharp buff sand beneath.

The following section was seen in the second cutting on the railway S.E. from Hadleigh:—

Boulder Clay.
{ Evenly bedded buff sand, with lines of gravel near the top, and a line of pebbles at the bottom; 2½ feet.
Confused mass of pebbly gravel, with lenticular patches of loam and sand; 3½ feet, resting in hollows on—
Rather fine buff bedded and false-bedded sand; not bottomed at 2 feet. F. J. B.

The junction of the Boulder Clay with the sand and gravel is also shown at the western part of the next cutting, south of Cates Hill Farm, the rest of which is in Boulder Clay only. W. W.

About a quarter of a mile west of Raydon Church a pit showed 8 feet of bedded and false-bedded sand, the upper part buff, the lower reddish, with a few lines of gravel here and there. F. J. B.

Valley of the Stour, and Tributaries, between the Brett and the Orwell.

Most of the sections in this part of the left side of the Stour Valley have been already noticed, in describing the Red Crag (pp. 46–48), and there is little to add, although the sand and gravel now form the plateau, in the absence of the overlying Boulder Clay.

In the railway-cutting just north of Bentley Bridge, N.E. of the church, there is false-bedded gravel and sand with loam, whilst in the same cutting, beyond the next bridge, by Bentley Lodge, there is loam at the bottom.

In the road-cutting north of Brantham Bridge (southward of Bentley Station) there is at top, close to the cross-lane, a little ferruginous sand; then (below) a little greyish loam; then ferruginous gravel; then ferruginous sand, with some small pebbles, etc., which last is probably Crag.

Near Holbrook and Harkstead the Glacial sand seems to rest on the London Clay, no trace of the Red Crag being seen for the most part.

In a small pit just outside Holbrook Gardens, and south eastward from the Summer House, there was a very small hollow of gravel, over 7 feet of yellow whitish and brown sand, mostly fine.

It is doubtful whether some of the outliers of gravel south of Harkstead, which have been coloured as Glacial, may not belong rather to a later series.

Valley of the Orwell, and Tributaries.

The thin capping that hides the Crag from Shotley Gate for some miles N.W. is without interest, and the few sections where gravel has been seen above the Crag on the right side of the Orwell have already been described (p. 48-50). The soil over the plateau here is mostly loamy and sandy.

A small sand-pit about a quarter of a mile N.W. of Wherstead Church gave the following section:—

Gravelly soil.
Brown loamy sand, with layers of grey clay and of gravel; 4 or 5 feet.
Buff and brown fine sand; about 4 feet.

Up the Washbrook tributary, above Copdock, the Glacial Drift overlaps the Crag and rests on the London Clay, with but a slight exception on the left side.

Gravel has been worked on the west of Wherstead Heath.

The long railway-cutting south-eastward of Belstead is much overgrown, but the order of the beds at the central and north-eastern parts could be fairly made out as follows:—

Drift.
- Sand with gravelly layers; 12 feet or more (between the two bridges).
- Gravel, with many large flints and other stones; of irregular thickness (up to 4 feet), and sometimes seeming to pass down into gravelly sand.

Sand, probably Red Crag, at N.E. end.

The south-western part is shallower, and shows sandy gravel and gravelly sand.

In the road-cutting about half way between Belstead and Gosford Hall there is at top a little gravelly sand (Drift) on coarse ferruginous sand (Crag), and then, a little down the slope, Boulder Clay, which must bank up against the Crag, though no junction could be seen, the cutting being overgrown (1874). Then fine sandy chalky gravel, Boulder Clay, and buff loam (but the section is so overgrown that one cannot make out their order) down to the cottage.

The section of a brickyard at Copdock (? now abandoned) has been thus given by the REV. W. B. CLARKE,* who has also recorded 40 feet of gravel in a pit near by:—

[Drift.]
- Red diluvial clay 3 feet.
- Gravel - 3 ,,
- White sand - 24 ,,

London Clay. W.W.

At Hintlesham Priory, 1¼ miles N.W. of the village, a pit a quarter of a mile N.E. of the house, gave the section shown by Fig. 22.

FIG. 22.

Section in a Gravel Pit near Hintlesham Priory.

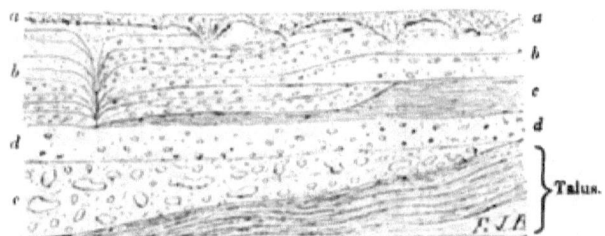

Scale 8 feet to an inch.

a. Red Clay (? weathered Boulder Clay); 6 inches to a foot (or more), resting irregularly on b.
b. Rather fine sand and gravel, with a singular piped structure, which goes down into the bed below, the part in the hollow is very fine chalky gravel; 4 to 5½ feet.
c. Wedge of fine buff loam; up to about 1½ feet.
d. Chalky gravel finer than that in b; about 1½ feet.
e. Very coarse gravel with lumps of chalk; 4 feet.

Blocks of the hard conglomerate at the junction of the sand with the Boulder Clay may be seen in the field south of Elmsett Church.

A gravel-pit a little N.W. of the church showed the junction with the Boulder Clay, giving the following section on its eastern side:—

Chalky Boulder Clay; about 3 feet.
- Rather coarse, sandy gravel, with pebbles of quartz and of quartzite; about 2 to 10 feet, cutting down over the bed below.
- Fine, buff, rather clayey sand; up to about 8 feet.

---

* *Trans. Geol. Soc.*, ser. 2, vol. v., p. 380. (1840.)

Whilst on the western side the succession was:—
Very stony Boulder Clay; up to about 4 feet.
Fine gravel, thickening towards the valley; about a foot to 4 feet.
Pebbly gravel, with a sharp dip towards the valley; about 5 to 8 feet.

F. J. B.

Returning to the main valley; at Stoke Brickyard, Ipswich, (see p. 11) the Glacial Drift seems to overlap the Crag and to rest on the London Clay, and a little more than a mile westward this condition sets in altogether, except for mere traces of Crag.

The railway-cutting westward of Handford Bridge (Ipswich) is now mostly overgrown, and little is to be seen of what must once have been a fine section. At the south-eastern end there is Boulder Clay, above which gravel seems to come on near the bridge for the high road. On the north-eastern side, before getting opposite the signal-box, I saw a crushed mass of shelly Crag (? with Boulder Clay wedged under). Near the signal-box, on the other side of the cutting (and about 6 chains from the bridge ?), the upper part of the cutting was turfed, but the lower part showed the following beds:—

A little fine sand.
Red Crag ⎰ Ferruginous sand; about 10 feet.
(? in place). ⎱ Shelly Crag, with some nodules.
Bedded London Clay at the box; up to 12 feet above the line.

A little further, on the same side, the London Clay rises to near the top of the cutting, and is capped by sand. London Clay also occurs at the bottom at the second telegraph-post from the signal-box, whilst at the third there is gravel. On the north-eastern side of the cutting, some way southwards of the second bridge over the line, I saw a mass of the plastic clay of the Reading Beds, of the London Clay, and of Crag, so disposed as to show that it was transported.

Just south of the bridge there is Boulder Clay over sand, and between the fork of the lines there seems to be gravel over the Boulder Clay.

Near Bramford the Glacial sand and gravel comes nearly to the bottom of the valley, where it is joined by the later river-gravel. Naturally the dividing-line between the two is not the most satisfactory one to draw.

The large old pit, marked on the Map, nearly a mile N.N.W. of Bramford Church is overgrown, but gravel and sand may be seen, with many pebbles of chalk. Near the S.W. corner there is a trace of Boulder Clay, either above or in the gravel, which proves the beds to be of Glacial age.

In an old pit, almost filled up, at the farm nearly a mile N.N.E. of Flowton, in Boulder Clay, there are blocks of sandstone and conglomerate, the hardened top of the sand and gravel beneath the clay.

The Drift of the higher part of the Gipping Valley has been described in the Memoir on Sheet 50, S.W., and we will now cross over and go down the right side.

The sections near Bramford have been described above (pp. 14, 15).

At a slightly higher level than the Whitton Leys brickyard (see p. 23), and on the other (N.W.) side of the lane, a shallow old pit showed sand and gravel, which, therefore, come on directly above the London Clay of the brickyard.

Along the high road north of Westerfield (at the head of a tributary valley) the section was nowhere clear (1876). At first, just out of the village, I saw, on the western side, sand, gravel, and Boulder Clay, the last seeming to be the lowest. Further on, on the eastern side, pale sandy Boulder Clay was seen over sand. Perhaps, therefore, the former clay is a bed in the sand and gravel. Of the sand-pits marked on the Ordnance Map here nothing is to be seen: they must have been given up years ago.

Northward of Ipswich there are several masses of gravel and sand, that come to the surface through the Boulder Clay, between the valleys of the Orwell and the Finn.

GLACIAL DRIFT.

In the most westerly of these an old pit in the corner of a field, about half a mile S.S.W. of Whitton Church, showed 3 feet or more of Boulder Clay (on the E. side of the N. end only), resting on light-coloured, rather fine gravel, largely composed of chalk-pebbles, with sand: the junction mostly hidden by talus. In this spot the line on the map between the Boulder Clay and the gravel is for the most part doubtful, the beds lying irregularly.

In another of these inliers a small pit, about a quarter of a mile S.E. of Whitton Church, showed a trace of Boulder Clay over gravel.

In another is the large old gravel pit, marked on the Map, on the eastern side of the Henley Road, about a mile north from Christchurch Park, which was overgrown in 1875, except at the northern end, where the following section was seen:—

Glacial Drift. { A little Boulder Clay, chiefly on the western side.
Gravel, both fine and coarse, with some loamy layers; 16 or 18 feet.

Shelly Crag, touched at the bottom, and at one place (N. end of W. side) rising up half way to the surface.

The next inlier is out by the railway, the long cutting of which, north of Ipswich, is overgrown, and mostly shows Boulder Clay only; but, about half way between the two main roads over the line, gravel occurs for a little way.

In the most easterly of these inliers, south of Westerfield, a pit about a quarter of a mile N.N.E. of Red House, showed small patches of Boulder Clay over gravel, up to about 10 feet deep, the upper part mostly fine, the lower coarse. At one place, under a piece of Boulder Clay, the gravel, with layers of sand, is hardened, especially the sand (which forms a stone) to a depth of 4 feet or so.

The neighbouring cuttings of the Felixstow Railway are described below (p. 89).

The long railway-cutting N. of Ipswich is overgrown. At the western end (where the cutting is on the S. side only) a little gravel may be seen at first; but Boulder Clay seems to come on suddenly, at about 40 yards (from the gate at the beginning). Beyond this I could see nothing but Boulder Clay, except that about half way between the two bridges over the line (for the lane and the Henley Road), the topsoil is gravelly, and before getting to the second of the bridges (the high road), where the cutting is deep, light-coloured sand is shown at the bottom.

Ipswich Cemetery is on the sand and gravel, except at the north, where there is a thin patch of Boulder Clay, the gravel beneath which is touched by some of the graves. The junction with the Boulder Clay is shown also in the cutting on the Felixstow Railway just east (see p. 89), and in the old gravel-pit, marked on the Map, about a quarter of a mile eastward.

The next cutting of the Felixstow Railway at Woodbridge Road showed gravel, sometimes coarse, over gravel and sand; and the next, southward of Spring Road, at its northern end passes through gravel, capped at first by a loamy soil, over sand with gravel, and it continues throughout in gravel and sand.

There are also pits in the gravel at Ipswich, both north and east of the town, as too over the plateau to the south-east, but none calling for notice.

The sections showing the junction of the gravel with the underlying Crag sand have mostly been described already (pp. 51–54); but besides these, there is a pit between the Felixstow Railway and road about two-thirds of a mile beyond Nacton Station, which passed through gravel, up to 10 feet thick, to sand that perhaps belongs to the Crag.

In the remains of an old shallow pit touching the southern side of the high road, over half a mile south-eastward of Trimley Churches, a little coarse brown sand or grit with some pebbles was seen (1874), and, from rabbit-holes, shelly Crag has been turned out, so that it can be but a few feet below the surface.

Valley of the Deben, and Tributaries.

The boundary-line of the Glacial gravel and sand follows that of the Red Crag, and is of an even more winding character, the cutting-back of the side-valleys having naturally affected the higher line more than the lower one.

There is hardly a noteworthy section, other than those sections already noticed in describing the Crag (pp. 58-65), until we reach the tributary valley of the Finn and the capping of Boulder Clay, though both gravel and sand are often to be seen.

An old circular pit, marked on the Map, in a field about a third of a mile northward of Newbourn, showed, on its eastern side, brown Drift sand, with a layer of gravel at bottom, up to 10 feet thick, over ferruginous Crag sand, up to 15 feet exposed. At the southern part the section was:—

Glacial Drift.	Sand, as before; 6 or 7 feet, mostly with gravel at bottom. Pale grey sandy Boulder Clay (stones small); from 0 to over 2 feet, with a little gravel at bottom.
Red Crag.	Ferruginous sand; a few inches. Shelly Crag, the clay above protecting the shells from dissolution.

The Boulder Clay was traceable for about 8 yards, and came in again close by, up to 3 feet thick, and resting on shelly Crag. The rest of the pit was more overgrown; but at the northern part there were also patches of Boulder Clay plunging down sharply into Crag sand, which latter comes up nearly to the top of the hill on the road (to new barn) close by.

Following the Finn Valley the pit on the hill-top, by the cross-roads south of Bealings Railway Station, is in chalky gravel.

Along the grassed lane north of Lucks Farm, and about a mile north of Kesgrave Church there is Boulder Clay over light-buff, white-speckled sand, sometimes with a little chalky gravel at top. I saw a very few small pieces of shell (*Cardium*, etc.) in some of the fallen sand. Higher up (S.) the Boulder Clay has weathered into stony loam or clay.

Close to the northern part of Lucks Wood (where there is Boulder Clay) is an old pit in sand, mostly ferruginous, with gravelly layers, partly hardened, and at first sight much like Red Crag, but probably Drift. There is no room on the map to draw the boundary-lines properly here, the railway having been engraved too near the wood.

A junction of Boulder Clay and sand, like that in the lane just noted, but not so clear, occurs also in the lane west of the wood, a little above the railway.

The long railway-cutting at Westerfield, which begins about half a mile east of the station, and reaches for more than a mile eastward, must have given a fine section when clear; but the following notes show all that could be seen in 1876, the measurements of distances (made by pacing) being only approximately right.

At about 70 yards from the cart-road over the line, at the western end, there is gravel (N.), and at 10 yards further a very little Boulder Clay comes on at top, on both sides for a short way, beyond which gravel and sand continue. At 145 yards a little shelly Crag was turned out at a telegraph-post (N.), and then a little Boulder Clay comes on at top (S.) At 165 yards, below gravel (S.) Crag occurs for about 10 yards, (brown sand, partly shelly, with phosphatic nodules at east). Then the cutting was overgrown for some way, but seemed to be all sand and gravel to the highest part. At about 260 yards the N. side was tolerably clear, showing gravelly sand, and at about 300 yards thin discontinuous Boulder Clay comes on over the gravel (the latter hidden by talus) with a stony loamy soil above. At about 340 yards the Boulder Clay is thicker (? in a little hollow) and seems to take up about 50 yards of the cutting. Then the sides were clearer and showed gravel, with bits of Boulder Clay at top, especially on the south, and at about 400 yards there seemed to be a good deal of the clay. At the half-mile post (540 yards, or 55 beyond the footpath across the line) there is loamy soil over Boulder Clay (N.), the gravel below being hidden by talus, and at 10 yards further the following succession was seen :—

    Loamy soil.
    A little Boulder Clay } 3 or 4 feet.
    A little chalky gravel
    Soft ferruginous sandstone; a foot or more.
    Gravel (bottom hidden by talus).

The Boulder Clay goes about 10 yards further, or probably more on this side (overgrown), as when it got clearer, at 620 yards, the clay was again seen for about 15 yards, and at 660 yards it was also seen, over gravel, on the N. side, whence it is continuous, and with a thickness of 5 or 6 feet, to just beyond 700 yards, or within 40 yards of the bridge of the Tuddenham road.

The following details of the southern side, at a spot about 150 yards west of this bridge, are from the note-book of Mr. S. V. Wood.

    Soil; about 2 feet.
    Boulder Clay, with small pockets of reddish-brown sand; 3½ feet.
    { Yellowish-white marl; 2 inches.
      Dark-brown loamy sand; 2 inches.
      Yellowish-white marl; 3 inches.
    Reddish sand, with angular flints and a few pieces of rolled chalk; 5 feet; then hidden by talus.

Mr. Wood remarks that on the opposite side of the cutting gravel, composed of rolled pieces of chalk, partly takes the place of the marl bands of the above.

Beyond the bridge the lower part (N.) is clear, and at 770 yards (from the beginning) shows gravel and sand, which, 30 yards further, is hardened into a conglomerate, huge blocks of which have been left along the bottom of the cutting. Boulder Clay occurs above, and, further on, between the two there is stony sand with thin irregular layers of fine Boulder Clay and continuous lines of race. This section, therefore, shows a passage from the Boulder Clay into the sandy beds beneath. At 870 to 910 yards, moreover, the bottom part of the Boulder Clay (all seen) is bedded and shows this passage.

At 930 yards, or 70 west of the centre of the next bridge, the Boulder Clay becomes patchy, and then ends off. Just before 930 yards, the S. side had been re-opened for ballast, and showed gravel and sand for about 100 yards. Then the sides were overgrown, but showed sand and gravel, capped with patches of Boulder Clay (S.); at about 1,030 yards the last is nearly continuous, and soon after on the N. side also. At 1,170 yards there is (N.) Boulder Clay over gravel and sand, with thin layers of Boulder Clay (as before), the lower part hidden, and on the other side the part of the gravel just beneath the Boulder Clay is hardened in places. At over 1,240 yards (or less than 60 before reaching the centre of the next bridge) the gravel and sand (N.) is hardened into a conglomerate, chiefly by iron. The sides were overgrown to just beyond the bridge, but at 1,330 yards, where the cutting had been re-opened (though at the time of my visit much hidden), the following section was seen :—

    A little Boulder Clay (? soon ends off).
    Gravel, beneath which there was soon shown—
    Pale sandy Boulder Clay, rising nearly to the top; bottom not shown, but there seems to be—
    Gravel and sand below (dry)

The lower bed of Boulder Clay seems to reach to the top at 1,450 yards (or 85 before reaching the footpath across the railway), except for patches of coarse gravel. At the footpath, where the cutting is shallower, gravel and sand occur. The shallow sides were then overgrown for some way, but seemed to be all gravel and sand, until, at 1,715 yards, Boulder Clay occurs at the bottom. Just beyond, the S. side was clear, except at top, and showed pale grey Boulder Clay (? gravel beneath). At 1,745 yards there is gravel and sand on the N., and still Boulder Clay on the S., but 50 yards further gravel and sand were shown beneath the clay, which last again occurs on the N. side at 1,825 yards, or about 100 yards before the cutting ends.

These notes of this long cutting may serve to show the irregularity of the Drift beds. W.W.

Gravel has been dug at several places between Tuddenham and Playford; but the pits rarely have any noteworthy feature.

About a quarter of a mile west of Culpho Hall, Playford (and at the very edge of the map), a sand-pit gave the following section, with a length of 30 yards or more (1877, 1878):—

Soil and sand, mostly with gravel at the base; ? up to 6 feet.
Alternations of grey loam with brown and buff sand. At the western end the lowest part all sand, the bottom loam having thinned out; a layer of gravel at the base; up to nearly 8 feet; thinning E.
Light-coloured false-bedded sand; 11 feet seen, but more found.

Possibly the last two beds belong to the Crag series, or they may represent Glacial beds somewhat older than the others of our district, as Mr. Wood, who saw the section in 1881, thinks. It would not be safe however to map them separately from the sand that usually underlies the Boulder Clay.

A pit about a mile N.E. of Bealings Station shows the Red Crag (mostly sand without shells). On the northern side a mass of Drift (gravel and sand) cuts down into the Crag almost vertically, and then, in and near the bottom of the pit, which is partly hidden by talus, there are masses of hard grit, apparently in place, some with broken-up shells. One of these masses of stone (hardened Drift) was traced continuously for 25 feet along the bottom of the pit, with a breadth of nearly 5 feet, and a thickness of over 2 as far as seen (not bottomed). W. W. and W. H. D.

Shell-fragments occur in the gravelly sands near Seckford Hall, in two road-cuttings, one half a mile W., the other 300 yards E., of the Hall, and in a well at a house, just out of the map, N. of the Hall, the section of which is given by Mr. S. V. Wood.*

A quarter of a mile west of Kingston Farm, the gravel, containing balls of stiff Boulder Clay, is seen resting upon Crag.

Returning to the main valley, the Deben, and including the tract beyond it, to the east, most of the Glacial Drift between Woodbridge and Boyton is sand, with gravelly parts near its base, especially about Ramsholt and Hollesley.

The gravel pits are few, for in this region of loose sand, roads are repaired with clay, often brought from a considerable distance.

A pit barely half a mile S.W. of Shottisham Hall shows 10 feet of sandy gravel capping 30 feet or more of Red Crag.

There is a small patch of gravel near the crest of the ridge of Gedgrave, resting on decalcified Crag.

W. H. D.

---

* *Quart. Journ. Geol. Soc.*, vol. xxxiii., pp. 106, 107. (1877.)

CHAPTER VIII.—GLACIAL DRIFT, *continued.*

BRICKEARTH OR LOAM.

ALTHOUGH here described under one head, it is quite likely that these loams do not all occur at one horizon in the Glacial Drift, some being above, whilst some is either in or below the sand and gravel. Of loam occupying the latter position there is, however, but little area of outcrop in our district; though Messrs. WOOD and HARMER believe that it underlies the gravel and sand to a large extent, and is indeed the base on which the later Glacial deposits rest in the north-western part of the district.* W. W.

Possibly some of the pebbly loam over the gravel and sand may be merely the result of the disintegration of the Boulder Clay, in which process the calcareous matter would be dissolved out, as in other districts.

South of the Stour (Essex).

East of Great Horkesley the gravel is much covered by a pebbly loam, forming a porous fertile soil.

In a brickyard at the back of the Crown Inn, Ardleigh, the section in 1875, showed finely-bedded brown and grey loam free from pebbles, with pockets of gravelly sand, slightly contorted, 8 to 10 feet thick, over whitish sand. W. H. D.

Between the Stour and the Orwell.

At the brickyard nearly a mile south-westward of Little Cornard Church there was a section at the eastern side, showing some 12 feet of brickearth, a sandy buff laminated clay at top, passing down into greyish-blue clean clay, with a marly fracture when dry; whilst to the west the clay was browner, more laminated, and with sandy partings. Still further west, the section was not clear, but fine, buff, here and there rather clayey, sand was seen, alternating with loam.

In the Boxford Valley a patch of loam has been mapped south-westward of Edwardston Church, and a road-cutting about 50 yards west of the church gave the following section:—

Sandy loam, with small chalk-stones, and lenticular patches of gravel and sand and of fine buff loam; about 3 to 8 feet.
Chalky Boulder Clay; from nearly 0 to nearly 3 feet.
Buff sandy loam; less than a foot.
Coarse gravel; up to 3 feet.

At the kiln, marked on the Map, a quarter of a mile east of Boxford Church, the pit was in buff sandy laminated loam, with lines of chalky gravel in the topmost part, the lower two thirds rather more clayey; seen to 18 feet, said to be more sandy again lower down, and to rest on Boulder Clay.

A pit northward of Aveley Hall, three quarters of a mile N.E. of Assington Church, gave the section below:—

Brown clay with a few stones [? weathered Boulder Clay] seeming to pass into
Chalky Boulder Clay.
Buff laminated sandy loam; 4 feet.

A pit, in a field three-quarters of a mile west of Polstead Church, showed 8 feet of grey clay, weathering white, sandy at top and stiff at bottom.

---

* *Quart. Journ. Geol. Soc.*, vol. xxxiii., pp. 102-109. (1877.)

At Coyts Tye, in the Boulder Clay plateau, more than two miles west of Hadleigh, there is a brickyard, in a mass of loam that seems to rise up from beneath the Boulder Clay, as described by Mr. S. V. Wood,* and the following section was noted:—

Brown, sandy, laminated loam; 30 feet.
Whitish sandy loam; 14 feet.
Whitish clay; not bottomed at 7 feet.

There is a fair deposit of brickearth on the western side of the valley of the Brett below Hadleigh, and more than half a mile southward from Layham Church, is a brickyard, with buff sandy laminated loam, very evenly bedded, dipping north, and not bottomed at 8 feet. F. J. B.

The small patch of loam on the plateau half a mile east of Beutley Church is probably above the surrounding gravel, as also is the mass in a like position south of Copdock; indeed this may be merely the result of the disintegration of Boulder Clay.

East of the Orwell.

South-east of Bramford a mass of loam is cut through by the railway, and seems to reach southwards close to the top of the pit shown in Fig. 1 (p. 7) as if it overlaid the Boulder Clay there, which clay is very probably not part of the wide-spreading mass above, but may be a lower bed, in or under the sand and gravel.

On the plateau east of Ipswich there are three exposures in which the brickearth is, or has been, worked.

At the abandoned brickyard, now (1875) a garden, between Woodbridge Road and Spring Road, near their junction, on the east of Ipswich, the section was for the most part hidden. At the western end I saw gravel and loam, below which brickearth was probably found; whilst at the northern side, along the Woodbridge Road, there was loamy and gravelly soil over brickearth, the bottom part grey. It seems that the brickearth dips westward.

The brickyard close by, on the southern side of Spring Road, gave no good section. The northern part of the pit showed—

Brown loam, gravelly at top (gravel in places).
Gravel; a foot or 2 feet, rising up from beneath at N.W. corner.
Boulder Clay; 3 feet shown.

At another part, a little S.E., the beds rose up the reverse way (eastward) and showed two small faults. The succession was:—

Brown loam, gravelly at top.
Gravel.
Thin peaty bed (clayey).
Loam, with gravelly sand at top.

At the southern end there was brown laminated brickearth, and grey earth has also been dug. Here, too, Boulder Clay has been got at bottom.

Brickearth has been worked just south, by the Boys' Home.

It is possible that this outcrop may only be divided by a wash of sand from the small outcrop that has been mapped a little S.S.W., just north of the road from Ipswich to Foxhall, which again in like manner may be connected with the third patch a little to the south, now to be described.

At the brickyard on the north of the Felixstow Road, about half a mile eastward of Bishop's Hill, marked on the Map, a small pit by the cottage, S. of the kiln, gave the section below:—

a. A little gravel, irregular; up 5 feet.
b. Grey brickearth, partly laminated; 0 to 3 feet.
c. Grey and brown sand; 6 feet shown, to water.

In the larger pit, reaching up to the kiln, at one place, east of the kiln, there was dirty gravel (a) over laminated and contorted brickearth (b?), and at another place gravel (a) over yellowish and brownish sand (c); whilst close by, towards the kiln, a little brickearth (b?) came in between,

---

* *Quart. Journ. Geol. Soc.*, vol. xxxiii., p. 109.

and seemed to thicken westward, as towards the kiln there was again a little gravel (a) over brickearth (b?), all but the top part of the latter being laminated and sometimes contorted. The section was not clear throughout, and I could not make out whether the sand is really at the bottom of all, or whether it may come in between two beds of brickearth.

At the overgrown loam-pit, marked on the Map, on the Ipswich Racecourse, at the southern end of this exposure, there seems to be sand and gravel at the top in places. There is also loam and some Boulder Clay.

In an old pit on the southern side of the high road, about half a mile south of Rushmere Church, there is Boulder Clay next the road, and this seems to underlie brickearth and gravel.

Rushmere Brickyard, on the northern side of the high road, over half a mile W. of Kesgrave Church, and therefore often called (though wrongly) Kesgrave Brickyard gives the best section in these parts.

At the cottage, by the road, I saw (in 1875) more than 20 feet of laminated brickearth, mostly grey, dipping south-eastward, and underlain by gravel and sand. Further north, and deeper, Boulder Clay has been found beneath the brickearth. At the northern part of the yard the following section was noted (western face):—

Gravel and sand; 6 feet or more, thinning to S.

Buff laminated brickearth, sandy, with layers of sand, and some thin lenticular gravelly layers (small chalk pebbles); over 12 feet (not bottomed).

Gravel and sand said to occur below.

On a later visit (1877) a cut in buff finely laminated brickearth in the S.W. corner of the yard showed six small faults (of a few inches downthrow) in a distance of about 6 feet. A few yards north of the cottage the brickearth was more or less a clay, with some buff sandy layers and stony at top. At the northern end there was brown gravel, up to 8 feet thick, passing down into bedded sand (with clayey layers and a few lenticular gravelly layers) which is the equivalent of the brickearth.

Mr. Wood regards all these exposures of brickearth east of Ipswich as parts of a large mass, reaching underground from the Valley of the Orwell to that of the Deben, and as belonging to the lowermost of his threefold divisions of the Glacial Drift.*
Whilst, however, I cannot disprove his theory, I am disposed rather to think that the brickearth may occur in the form of large lenticular masses in the sand and gravel, and in favour of this view would draw attention to the fact that sand and gravel does occur beneath.

At the western end of Foxhall Heath, and a mile S.S.W. of Kesgrave Church, there is a mere patch of clay and chalky earth.

At the brickyard within the triangle of roads, Trimley Heath, the pit was about 16 feet deep in 1874. The top 6 or 7 feet showed pockets of gravel, with stony loam above. The brickearth is light-coloured (buff and grey) sandy, but at the bottom sometimes clayey. Beneath it at the eastern face was brown sand, with a few flints and much water (? Crag); whilst at the mill, close by, a well, 18 feet deep, touched Crag and coprolites. At the western end of the yard, near the road, the brickearth was ironshot, the top part the more clayey, with pockets of gravelly sand and a little sand and gravel at top, the lower part being very sandy. At the southern part of the yard there is again fine sandy gravel at top, whilst at the bottom a foot of "rock" (? sandstone) has been found. There is no good evidence of the exact age of this brickearth, and, though it has been classed as Glacial Drift, it occurred to me that there was a distant possibility of its being Chillesford Clay.

At Kirton Kiln, just S.E. of Church Farm, at the time of my visit (1874), the eastern part of the not too clear section was a shallow cut in sand.

---

* *Quart. Journ. Geol. Soc.*, vol. xxxiii., pp. 103-106, with transverse sections.

The central part was deeper, and showed, on the east, a little Boulder Clay, above which came a trace of a gravelly bed, then light-grey brickearth, with some race, perhaps 10 feet thick, and then darker and stiffer brickearth with some nodules of ironstone. The junction of the two brickearths dipped sharply westward (about 45°), and the beds seem to be in a hollow, as further W. the lighter-coloured brickearth was again shown. At the shallow western part there was fine sand, below which a little gravel has been found. The arrangement of the beds seemed to be as in Fig. 23, but I could not see whether the Boulder Clay continued to the western side. Mr. S. V. Wood disagrees with this view, and regards the brickearth as a boss of his Lower Glacial (Contorted Drift) coming up through the sand (Middle Glacial).

FIG. 23.
Diagram-Section at Kirton Kiln.
E. Pit.   Central Pit.   W. Pit.

a. Dark stiff brickearth.
b. Light-grey brickearth.
c. Trace of gravelly bed.
d. Boulder Clay.
e. Sand.
The shaded parts show the pits, the rest is inferred.

At Felixstow there are signs of loam over a fair area about half a mile south-east from the church; but whether this is from the occurrence of loamy beds in the Crag, or of a bed above the Crag, I could not make out, there being no section, and therefore, though I mapped the loamy area, as well as possible, yet it is not shown on the published map. Some much later observations by Mr. S. V. Wood (made only in December 1882), and with which he has favoured me, show, however, the occurrence, north of the Convalescent Home, of reddish-brown brickearth like that at Derby Road, Ipswich, at the surface in the road-cutting, on the south, (see Fig. 11 p. 57), and further north, only about 2 feet down, beneath coarse gravel. Though this would seem to be a different mass of loam from that first noted, yet it points to the occurrence of Glacial brickearth in this neighbourhood.

The brickearth coloured in Ipswich is of doubtful age. It has Boulder Clay on one side and Valley Gravel on the other, and to which it is allied there is nothing to show. At the chapel at the S.E. corner of the crossing of Wilberforce Road and Clarkson Street, I saw buff, bedded loam, and a little to the S.W., close to the Boulder Clay and to the London Road, buff sandy and calcareous loam. The ground is again loamy on the western side of the patch of Boulder Clay, on the north of which it is hard to know where the London Clay and the brickearth join.

BOULDER CLAY.

This, the most wide-spread division of the Glacial Drift in the east of England, is here a bluish-grey clay, weathering brown by exposure to long-continued atmospheric actions, mostly crowded (in places so much as to cause a whitish colour) with rounded pieces of hard Chalk, of various sizes, and often showing the well-known glacial scratches. So full of chalk is this clay generally, that it has been named by Mr. S. V. Wood the Great Chalky

Boulder Clay, a name which, however, is open to the objection that other beds of Boulder Clay are sometimes as chalky. Besides pieces of chalk, flint, and flint-pebbles are of common occurrence, as also masses of septaria or cement-stones from various Jurassic clays, including the Lias. Fragments of trap-rocks, granites, as well as Carboniferous limestones and sandstones, and other sedimentary rocks also occur.

It is clearly a deposit of glacial origin, but various authors have propounded various views as to its formation, within the above limit. Without entering into this highly controversial question, and its overflowing literature, I may refer the reader to "The Great Ice Age" by PROF. J. GEIKIE for arguments in favour of the land-ice theory, and to the work of Messrs. W. H. PENNING and A. J. JUKES-BROWNE* for the shore-ice theory; whilst these and the floating-ice theory have been respectively upheld in papers in sundry geological journals.

In our district there is little evidence of the occurrence of beds of Boulder Clay in the sand and gravel or with the brickearth that underlie the great sheet of clay; but such layers do occur here and there. There are, too, patches of Boulder Clay, far off from the great mass, which may either belong to the latter or in some cases may be a lower bed; but all these are now described under one heading.

The Boulder Clay reaches to a thickness of about 100 feet, according to the evidence of well-sections; but this thickness is probably rare here, and for the most part there is much less of the bed.

Whilst generally resting on the Glacial sand and gravel, yet the Boulder Clay in places overlaps this lower member of the series, and lies on the London Clay, or on the Chalk. Again, whilst the mass is confined to the plateau on the west and north-west, there are places where tongues, or more often isolated masses, occur at lower levels.

The rather sudden ending-off of the Boulder Clay (roughly speaking along a line through Bentley, Ipswich, and Woodbridge), looks as if it might not have spread continuously over the whole of the plateau of gravel and sand to the east and south, on which comparatively few and small outlying patches occur, many of which may belong to a lower bed and not to the great mass that elsewhere overlies the sand and gravel. Had the Boulder Clay ever extended far over this plateau, as a continuous sheet, we should hardly have expected it to have been so clearly removed by denudation as to have left, as a rule, no trace whatever of its former existence. W. W.

South of the Stour (Essex).

The Boulder Clay ranges continuously from the west to near Breewood Hall and Pytchbury Wood south of Little and Great Horksley, beyond which the loamy soil to which it decomposes blends imperceptibly with the underlying pebbly loam, making the boundary uncertain.

The base is seen in several places about Mount Bures and Wormingford. On the railway near Mount Green the lower beds are rudely stratified.

W. H. D.

---

* Geological Survey Memoir on the Neighbourhood of Cambridge.

Between the Stour and the Orwell.

At and west of Leadenheath, and between Boxford and Hadleigh, the top of the Boulder Clay consists, for several feet, of a stiff brown and yellowish clay, with no chalk, and this is seen, in some sections, to pass down into the ordinary Boulder Clay, as if the chalk had been dissolved out by percolation, as elsewhere.

East and west of Burnt House Farm, on the tongue of clay between Polstead and Shelly the boundary-line is doubtful, as there is no feature, the clay being at the same level as the gravel that rises up from beneath.

Near Dairy Farm, about half a mile eastward from Semer Church, the following section was noted, showing a confused sort of junction of the Valley Drift and the Boulder Clay :—

> Sandy wash; 2 to 3 feet.
> Sandy loam, with nests of gravel, passing into Boulder Clay, with an interrupted layer of clean clay at the bottom; from a few inches to about 2 feet.
> Very chalky Boulder Clay, with small stones; 2 to 3 feet seen.
>
> F. J. B.

The section drawn in Fig. 24 is in a small old pit under a hedge, about a quarter of a mile westward of Layham Church, and is remarkable for showing what seems to be a very large boulder of chalk.

FIG. 24.

Section in an old Pit westward of Layham Church.

a. Soil with a little Boulder Clay, sand, etc.
b. Mass of chalk, with unrolled flints (? a huge boulder) passing sideways into—
b¹. Chalk rubble and chalky gravel.
c. Boulder Clay.

The cuttings of the Hadleigh Branch Railway mostly show Boulder Clay (see p. 76), and those between Raydon and Capel are wholly in it.

West and south-west of Ipswich there are a number of small patches, at various levels, some low-down on the London Clay; thus at Chantry the kitchen garden is mostly on Boulder Clay.

Between the Orwell and the Deben.

At the entrance of the northern of the two large chalk-pits, northward of Bramford, near the Chemical Works (where "Paper Mill" is engraved on the Map), there seems to be a very thin sheet of Boulder Clay draping the chalk, and sometimes a little gravel also. This may be a reconstructed bed, but I could make nothing of it.

A shallow old chalk-pit, about a quarter of a mile N.E. of Bramford Church, showed Boulder Clay, with a little sand and gravel, over the Chalk. Another old pit (overgrown) a few yards higher up the lane, and on its other (S.) side, is in Boulder Clay, with a little gravel and sand below, and the like occurs along the lane above, before it opens on to Whitton Leys.

The boundary between the Boulder Clay and the gravel at Westerfield House is doubtful, and the line engraved on the map is indeed arbitrary, gravel occurring here and there where Boulder Clay has been coloured. It is also impossible to draw that line rightly just E., as the map is wrong and the railway is represented thereon too near the lane (from being made too large).

The most northerly cutting on the Felixstow Railway (E.S.E. of Westerfield Station) beginning from the northern end, is in gravel on the western side. Then Boulder Clay occurs on the other side, with gravel below, and then Boulder Clay alone on both sides. Further on is a hump of chalk gravel, which seemed to have a little Boulder Clay above in parts as well as below. After this the cutting is in Boulder Clay with hollows of sandy soil, until close to the southern end, where gravel and loam rise up in places.

The next cutting is in Boulder Clay at its northern end, with gravel beneath in parts. At the bridge over (Tuddenham Road) the gravel rises high up, being covered only by about 4 feet of clayey soil and made ground. South of the bridge the gravel has been worked to a depth of 7 feet, partly below the level of the line. The slightly irregular junction of the Boulder Clay and the gravel runs a little further, and then, the line rising, the cutting is in the former only. At and beyond the next bridge over (lane) there are in the Boulder Clay some small masses of sand, and gravelly layers; whilst half-way (and more) to the next bridge there are some chalky masses (lumps of chalk and re-arranged chalk), at one part the cutting, some 7 feet deep, being more in chalk than anything else. Then gravel, with a hardened layer at top, rises up, but not to the surface, for a few yards, and then, some 30 yards further, gravel and sand, which rise to the surface in about 20 yards (cutting 5 feet deep), and the gravel continues to the bridge over, some 90 yards further. About 70 yards beyond the bridge a little Boulder Clay occurs above the gravel and sand, on the higher (eastern) side, and some 12 yards further an irregular layer of brown clay (0 to 4 feet thick) occurs in the gravel for 20 yards or more, the section, on the eastern side, being as shown in Fig 25. As the cutting falls southwards, the Boulder Clay ends off.

Fig. 25.

Section in the Cutting on the Felixstow Railway northward of Albion Mills, Woodbridge Road, Ipswich.

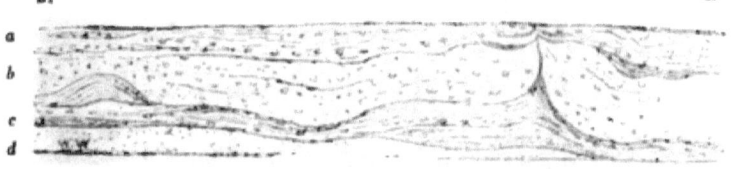

About 12 feet deep at most and 20 feet long.

Glacial Drift.
- a. Boulder Clay.
- b. Gravel and sand.
- c. Clay (in parts a Boulder Clay).
- d. Sand and gravel.

These railway-sections show how thin the Boulder Clay here is for the most part, and also how hard it may sometimes be to separate it accurately from the gravel and sand on which it rests irregularly.

Close to the top of the hill west of Tuddenham, on the northern side of the road to Westerfield, a pit was open, in 1878, to supply the brickyard just below (see p. 25). At first nothing else but the grey chalky Boulder clay was found; but in working westward a bed of light-coloured sand, mostly fine, and chalky gravel was shown in the midst of the clay, and there are signs of this bed also in the fields northward. Just above it there were gravelly masses in the clay.

At the lodge in the railway-cutting S.E. of Playford Hall, a small excavation, northwards from the face of the cutting, gave the section shown in Fig. 26.

FIG. 26.
Section on the Railway S.E. of Playford Hall.

a. Soil.
Glacial Drift. { b. Boulder Clay.
{ c. Light-coloured sand, gravelly, with a layer of gravel at bottom.
d. Red Crag. Buff and brown sand, with a little grey clay.

Just touching, on the north, in a pit from which Boulder Clay has been got for brick-making, I saw 10 feet of it, pale, sandy and standing with a vertical face. The northern part of this pit must have been in sand, and the Boulder Clay seems to be a small detached mass.

In a field at the north-eastern edge of Levington Heath an old pit shows Boulder Clay, under the hedge of the heath; but I could not see how it lay with regard to the sand.

At the back of the cottages, marked on the Map, nearly a quarter of a mile N.E. is another and larger old pit, which shows sand on the southern side, and Boulder Clay (overgrown and hidden) on the northern. Here, too, I could not make out how the two joined; but it looked as if the clay might go under the sand, which latter seems to come on again at the cottages.

Another and clearer pit, touching the lane just N.E., showed, at the western part, Boulder Clay, perhaps 10 feet thick, over light-coloured gravelly sand; whilst at the eastern part there is brown sand, with light-coloured sand lower down at one place. The relation of the Boulder Clay and the sand is again not shown; but the two must join somewhat abruptly, as there is only an interval of 10 yards between places where all is sand and all Boulder Clay.

The clay was again seen further N.E., in an old ploughed-over pit on the other (N.) side of the road, across the corner of the next field to a cottage, and through the garden. I was told that bricks had been made here.   W. W.

The Boulder Clay of the N. side of the Finn Valley consists of peninsulas and promontories of the widespread sheet which covers High Suffolk. Many of the pits in it are sunk through to the sand beneath, but there is no need to chronicle all such exposures. A small outlier occurs three-quarters of a mile E.N.E. of Playford, and a larger one half a mile W.S.W. of Woodbridge.

East of the Deben.

The patches of Boulder Clay eastward of the Deben are of uncertain age, seeming in places to lie beneath the surrounding Glacial beds, in others to be interbedded with them, and in others to overlie them. Such patches or masses as lie upon, or in hollows in, the Red Crag may of course be assigned with equal probability to any of the three of MR. S. V. WOOD's divisions of the Glacial epoch.

At Black House, nearly a mile S.E. of the Woodbridge Ferry, the Boulder Clay, seen in a small pond, appears to be beneath gravel.

The clay pit (marked on the edge of the map) north of Sutton Common gives no evidence of the relation of the clay to the surrounding sands.

The large patch of Boulder Clay E. of Shottisham, and the three small neighbouring patches on Bussock Road, are probably outliers of the great sheet of Upper Boulder Clay many miles away to the north; but it is possible that they are bosses of clay older than the surrounding sand and gravel.

The "Loam pit" at Walk Barn (marked on the Map), more than a mile south-eastward of Shottisham Church, shows sand over Boulder Clay over Crag, in an indistinct run-down section. In a district where sand is so much shifted by wind, this section is not decisive as to the age of the clay, which, with that next to be noted, may be older than the Glacial sands.

In a crag-pit at a farm about a third of a mile W.N.W of Hollesley Bridge there is a steep-sided hollow filled with Boulder Clay, the trend of the hollow being approximately parallel with the brook, to a former mouth of which, at Martello Tower AA, it points.

Four small but mappable patches of Boulder Clay occur near Hollesley. One of these, a quarter of a mile N.N.W. of the Rectory, is surrounded by gravel, the other two, south and south-east of the Rectory, lie upon Crag. Half a mile west of Hollesley Grove a pit on the line of junction of the Crag and the Glacial Drift shows at intervals in its run-down and bush-covered sides, finely laminated lavender-grey marl, abutting against and partly sharing in the irregularities of the surface of an underlying mass of Boulder Clay. At the western end a peak of clay rises through the marl. On the southern side the clay forms an uneven floor to the marl and rises up on the west like an overhanging wave, in the concave side of which the laminæ of the marl are crushed and contorted. This section has several features in common with some fine exposures in the adjoining district (50, S.E.), where a continuous belt of Boulder Clay, overlaid by brick-earth, extends for some miles between the Crag and the Glacial sands.

On the plateau eastward there are many small patches of clay, some too small to be mapped. W. H. D.

CHAPTER IX.—POST GLACIAL BEDS.

BEFORE describing the various beds massed under the above heading, it will be well to notice the difficulty there is in definitely assigning a Glacial or Post Glacial age to various deposits of gravel and brickearth. This difficulty arises, not altogether from doubt as to whether certain masses belong to the Glacial Drift, or are of later date; but also from the fact that the terms Glacial and Post Glacial are themselves indefinite, the Drift of the latter age in one district being perhaps as old as that of the former age in another part of the kingdom, glacial conditions having lasted longer in the one tract than in the other. These terms, therefore, should only be used locally, and in that sense they are now used, Post Glacial meaning only later than the Glacial Drift of the district.

The above remarks apply only to the first two sets of beds to be described, the later beds of the marshes and of the coast being far newer without doubt. W. W.

HIGH LEVEL GRAVEL.

The mass of gravel which has been mapped from Great Waldingfield to Assington is of doubtful character, both as regards age and origin. It is composed of angular and subangular flints, and is of slight thickness, being worked only to a depth of about three feet, in mere casual openings, fresh spots being dug into as more gravel is wanted. It may be that this is merely a sandy and gravelly bed connected with the Boulder Clay, on which it rests, and it may have resulted to a certain extent from weathering.

F. J. B.

RIVER OR VALLEY DRIFT.

These deposits are of freshwater origin, for wherever fossils are found in them these are of land or freshwater kinds. They are confined to the neighbourhood of the rivers and streams, and in our district indeed occur only along the lower levels of the valleys; and they have been formed by the rivers, at a time when these had greater power and were of greater volume than now; at a time when our island stood at a higher level than now, and probably joined the Continent.

1. *GRAVEL.*

This is naturally to a great extent made up from the older gravel of the hills; but flints are the chief constituent, in a sandy matrix, and the gravel is sometimes coarse. W. W.

Valley of the Stour and Tributaries.

Terraces of river-gravel occur along great part of the southern bank of the Stour; but in many places the London Clay outcrop reaches to the marshes. W. H. D.

There is also a fair spread of this gravel on the left bank, down to Stratford St. Mary, as well as up the tributary Boxford and Brett Valleys.

In a pit a little east of Chelsworth Church, in the Brett Valley, there was coarse subangular gravel, with a layer of grey loam containing a few land shells. Many bones have been found also, amongst them some of *Bos longifrons*. Bones have also been found at Stone Street, north-westward of Hadleigh. F. J. B.

Valley of the Orwell.

There is hardly any gravel in the lower part of this valley; but a fringe sets in on the western side some 3 miles before passing above the tidal stream, and then is almost continuous.

Near the southern mouth of the railway-tunnel, S.E. of Ipswich Station, the Valley Drift rises up above the level of the terrace skirting the river. The section is much overgrown and hidden; but on the eastern side of the cutting I saw loam and clay, with shells, over the gravel. There are many mammalian remains in the Ipswich Museum got from this cutting, I believe, and amongst them a number of elephants' teeth.

Prof. Prestwich, writing of this or of some neighbouring section, says that " several baskets were filled with the teeth and bones of Elephants of all ages, found in a few square yards of brickearth near the station at Ipswich."*

Above Ipswich there is often some difficulty in dividing this gravel from the like deposit of Glacial age, against which it ends off; but the feature of the slightly rising terrace bordering the river is mostly well-marked. At Ipswich, and more than a mile north of Bramford, there are two islands of gravel, surrounded on all sides by marsh, from above which they rise but little.

Through Ipswich town the difficulty of classifying the gravel was increased by the fact of Boulder Clay having been found at the surface from the London Road northwards, on the west of Wilberforce Street, from its occurring (though under sand) in the excavation for a house just west of St. Matthew's Church, and in the cutting for the sewer in Lady Lane, south-eastward of the same church, and probably in other places. I infer, however, that this Boulder Clay is merely part of a low-lying mass under the gravel.

Since the above was written Mr. H. Miller, assistant to Mr. P. Bruff, C.E., has kindly given me an account of the excavations of the Ipswich main sewer, from which the following is compiled:—

The sewer starts in the Bramford Road, a little beyond the tan-yard, and runs along that road to Victoria Street; then down that street, across the London Road and through private ground to Handford Road, by Mr. Bruff's Office at Handford Lodge; then eastward along Handford Road to near the Oil Mill, where it takes to the filled-up bed of the Little Gipping. The depth in this section of the work was only 13 feet at the most, averaging 9 or 10 feet. The beds were chiefly sand and gravel; but clay was touched in three places: about the middle of Victoria Street, the clay being chalky (=Boulder Clay); at the southern end of that street; and near the Oil Mill. The first of these was only 100 feet through; but the other two were humps about 100 yards through, and the levels were respectively 5, 4, and 5½ feet below the surface. A supplementary note from Mr. Miller, says that for a short distance along the Bramford Road the bottom of the trench was below the valley-gravel, and showed a fine silty clay with a few minute freshwater shells, recognized by Mr. G. Sharman as *Pisidium*, sp.

The sewer leaves the Little Gipping River before that reaches Commercial Road, and then runs along the southern part of Friar Street, College Street, Quay Street, the southern part of Fore Street St. Clement's, Duke Street, John Street, to S.E. of the gasworks, beyond which point its course is shown by the borings (see p. 129). Throughout the above section of the work the excavation was all in sand and gravel, varying from clean yellow sand in John Street to coarse gravel in Friars Road.

The most interesting part of this set of sections is the further evidence it gives of the existence of Boulder Clay under the gravel. A still more

---

* The Ground beneath Us . . ., p. 23. 8vo. London, 1857.

interesting piece of evidence, however, has since been given by the well at the New Mill, on St. Peter's Quay (see p. 118), which proves the occurrence of a deep channel, or hollow, of Glacial Drift at that spot, Boulder Clay having been found at a depth of nearly 120 feet below high-water mark, whereas near by in various directions the Chalk has been touched at depths of from less than 30 to 70 feet.

Mr. T. Miller, Engineer to the Dock Commission, tells me, too, that in dredging in the dock very variable soils are found, for instance, hard and soft chalk, sandstone boulders, (greywethers), soft and hard clay, brickearth, sand, and gravel.

At the back of the Cliff Brewery there is sand and loam, with gravel at the bottom, and with bits of shelly Crag; and at the low cliff at the southern end of this litttle patch the sand and loam rests on the bottom part of the London Clay.

At the foot of the sloping river-cliff, a little south of the cottage at Piper's Valley, south of Ipswich, there is a very narrow flat of gravel and sand; a low terrace that may have been formed merely of reconstructed material brought down by slips from the gravel and sand just above.

In the patch to the south, which seems to be about half a mile long, the gravel and sand may be seen against a sharp slope of London Clay in the cliff west of Pond Hall.

At the very small short piece of cliff south-westward of Broke Hall (and south of Nacton) there is irregular gravel and sand, with London Clay coming up irregularly to the surface at the highest part (not 8 feet).

Valley of the Deben.

On the western side of this valley there is a set of isolated patches, which, though small, often make a well-marked feature. These skirt the marsh, and in some cases reach up to the Red Crag, whilst in others ending off on the London Clay. The other side of the valley is free from gravel, except just below Woodbridge.

The gravel-pit, about 12 feet deep, a little W.S.W. of the cottage at top of Holm Hills, north of Felixstow, showed (1874) an apparent easterly dip; but this may be current-bedding; the direction, however, is the same throughout, and the dividing planes are even and finely bedded. The gravel is fine and sandy, and its upper part (following the apparent dip) brown and without shells; whilst the middle part is white and crowded with fragments of Crag shells, the lower part again being brown and without shells, and rather coarser.

In the gravel-pit at the farm, near the edge of the marsh, more than half a mile a little N. of E. of Falkenham Church, fine brown sandy gravel was shown (1874), to a depth of 10 feet, close to (and north of) the house. At one part, close to the garden-hedge, a small cut showed a little gravel over a little grey chalky clay, with small rounded pieces of chalk and pieces of flint. This Boulder Clay, which is far from any yet noticed, may have gravel underneath, not being at the bottom of the pit; but this could not be seen.

About the wood marked "Delf," more than half a mile S.E. of Waldringfield Church, the topography of the Map is hopelessly wrong, making the boundary-line of the patch of sand here doubtful. The sand, with here and there a little gravel, lies irregularly on the London Clay, as the last comes up in places, notably by the pond in the S.E. corner of the wood.

The small overgrown cliff E.N.E. of Waldringfield Church is in gravel and sand. At one part a pit showed about 20 feet of light-coloured sandy gravel, both fine and coarse, confused as regards bedding, and in places with broken-up shells from the Crag. By its position one would judge this to be river-gravel; but some doubt may be thrown on this conclusion by the occurrence of Glacial gravel near by at a comparatively low level, in hollows in the Crag (see p. 64). I was told that bones had been found here.

On the southern side of the valley of the Finn there is a narrow strip of gravel above Martlesham, skirting the marsh for more than a mile, whilst small patches occur S.E. of Little Bealings Church and about half a mile below Tuddenham.   W. W.

On the other side of the valley of the Finn, a strip of gravel accompanies the Bealings brook near its junction with the Finn.

The upper part of Martlesham Creek is bordered on the north by a gravel-terrace, extending up the Finn beyond the bridge.

Woodbridge stands partly on river-gravel, the terrace of which extends downwards nearly to Kingston Quay; a like terrace ranges down from the Ferry on the opposite side. W. H. D.

2. LOAM OR BRICKEARTH.

Besides occasional masses of loam in the gravel, there is sometimes a layer of this over the gravel (where the two occur together); the only notable occurrences, however, being in the lower part of the valley of the Stour, the most interesting mass being on the left side at and above Stutton Ness.

On the southern side of that river, just below Wrabness sluice, there is a low cliff, in bedded sand (mostly fine), and loam, with a little gravel in parts, and with broken shells at one spot.

On the shore south of Stutton Hall there is gravel, with London Clay at the base of the cliff mostly. A little lower (at the little bay S.S.E. of the Hall) there is the following section:—

    Brown bedded loam; about 6 feet.
    Pale grey and buff bedded loam, with a layer of brown clay, and with rare scattered flints and pebbles, and (in the grey loam) a few broken shells; about 6 feet.
    Bottom 2 or 3 feet hidden.

From this spot towards Stutton Ness there is a low cliff of brown and buff sand and loam with gravel, in which last I found pieces of bones and of an elephant's tusk; there are also shells, and the London Clay is shown at the base in places. About half way nearly all is loam, more or less bedded, with sandy and stony layers; then the cliff is very low, and at the bottom there is a greyish loam, which contains a number of land and freshwater shells (for a list, see p. 96), and also contains rare pieces of flint and pebbles; still further this is about 3 feet thick, and underlain by a little brown loam.

At the Ness there is gravel, with London Clay shown below in part, and at the eastern of the two points the latter rises nearly to the top of the cliff. A little north (after turning the point) there is loam with a little gravel at the bottom, over sandy London Clay.

The patch mapped below Stutton is somewhat doubtful, and may be the result of the wash of the London Clay slope.

Close to, and east of, the farm about half a mile N.N.W. of Tattingstone Church, an old pit showed about 8 feet of buff loam, with calcareous concretions, chiefly in one layer, and with a line of small pebbles, &c. in part, above the concretions.

I was at a loss what to make of this loam, which almost seemed to go under the neighbouring Red Crag. It is hardly like London Clay, and we know of no loamy equivalent of the Coralline Crag: on the whole, therefore, it seemed safest to regard it as a Post Glacial (Valley) Drift.

There is a shallower overgrown pit in the loam just north, the site of a former brickyard, and at the cottage further north, on the high road, there is loam on the east, below the cottage, and Crag on the west, above.

Like loam seems also to occur lower down the valley.

In another tributary valley above Holbrook Garden there is some grey and brown loam (not mapped) which may underlie the gravel that comes on at a higher level, or may be merely a wash from the hill-sides.

The long patch of loam mapped near Erwarton is doubtful, as also are the patches in the bottom part of the valley of the Stour, near Shotley, and below Chelmondiston, on the right side, and near Levington, west of Trimley, and south of Trimley, on the left side. These may be to a great extent the result of the wash of the London Clay slopes. W. W.

List of Fossils.

MAMMALIA (all from Ipswich, except the first, which is from Stutton.)

Arvicola amphibia, *Linn.*
Bison priscus, *Bojan.*
Bos primigenius, *Bojan.*
*Canis lupus, *Linn.*
—— vulpes, *Linn.*
Cervus capreolus, *Linn.*
—— megaceros, *Hart.*

Elephas antiquus, *Falc.*
—— primigenius, *Blum.*
*Equus.
Felis spelæa, *Goldf.*
Lutra vulgaris, *Erxl.*
Rhinoceros tichorinus, *Cuv.*
Ursus ferox, *Linn.*

On the authority of PROF. W. B. DAWKINS, *Quart. Journ. Geol. Soc.*, vol. xxv., p. 194, except the two marked * which were determined by MR. E. T. NEWTON, from the Collection of MR. R. FITCH, of Norwich.

MOLLUSCA (all from Stutton).

Gasteropoda.

Ancylus fluviatilis, *Müll.*
—— lacustris, *Linn.*
Azeca (Bulimus) tridens, *Pulteney.*
Bithinia tentaculata, *Linn.*
Carychium minimum, *Müll.*
Helix arbustorum, *Linn.*
—— fruticum, *Müll.*
—— fulva, *Müll.*
—— hispida, *Linn.*
—— ,, var. concinna, *Jeffr.*
—— ,, ,, plebeia, *Jeffr.*
—— nemoralis, *Linn.*
—— ,, var. hortensis, *Müll.*
—— nitidula, *Drap.*
—— pulchella, *Müll.*
Hydrobia marginata, *Michaud.*
Limax agrestis, *Müll.*
Limnea auricularia, *Linn.*
—— palustris, *Müll.*
—— peregra, *Müll.*

Limnea truncatula, *Müll.*
Planorbis albus, *Müll.*
—— complanatus, *Linn.* (=marginatus, *Drap.*)
—— contortus, *Linn.*
—— corneus, *Linn.*
—— glaber, *Jeffr.*
—— nautileus, *Linn.*
—— nitidus, *Müll.*
—— spirorbis, *Müll.*
—— vortex, *Linn.*
Pupa antivertigo, *Drap.*
—— muscorum, *Linn.*
—— pygmæa, *Drap.*
Succinea elegans, *Risso* (=Pfeifferi, *Rosm.*)
—— putris, *Linn.*
Valvata cristata, *Müll.*
—— piscinalis, *Müll.*
Zua (Cochlicopa) lubrica, *Müll.*

On the authority of MR. S. V. WOOD's Monograph of the Crag Mollusca, vol. ii., No. 3, pp. 306–308, the names corrected in a few cases by MR. G. SHARMAN. Mr. Wood's earlier list (see below) differs from this, both in containing names not herein, and in not containing names herein.

Lamellibranchiata.

Anodonta cygnea, *Linn.*
Corbicula fluminalis, *Müll.*
Pisidium amnicum, *Müll.*
—— henslowianum, *Sheppard.*

Pisidium pulchellum, *Jenyns.*
Sphærium (Cyclas) corneum, *Linn.*
Unio tumidus, *Retz.*

CRUSTACEA (*Entomostraca*). From Stutton.

? Cypris gibba, *Ramdohr.*

The Lamellibranchiata compiled by MR. G. SHARMAN from the body of MR. WOOD's Monograph. The Entomostracan on the authority of MR. WOOD's earlier list, *Mag. Nat. Hist.* vol. vii., p. 274.

Recent Beds.

Alluvium.

Along the courses of the larger streams there is generally a marshy flat, consisting of the mud that has been left by the streams in shifting their channels, associated sometimes with peat. It is this peat which, occurring generally beneath the marsh-clay, forms those submerged forests, of which so much has been written, and which are merely the seaward extensions of river-beds, the valleys of which have been cut back by the sea. I believe that these submerged forests occur at nearly all river-mouths (though rarely to be seen), and never elsewhere. It is probably the singularity of finding freshwater deposits of late date overflowed by the present sea, that has caused so much to be written on them, but it should be remembered that whilst the literature of the subject is chiefly confined to the beds as they appear at the junction of the river and the sea, the beds themselves reach inland far up the valleys.

Such an occurrence has been described by Dr. J. E. Taylor, as seen in our chief valley, the Orwell, a little below Ipswich, and was shown in excavating for a new channel through the mud-banks. According to Dr. Taylor* the section was as follows:—

Alluvium
- Black mud; 6 or 8 feet.
- Peat, full of recumbent trees, such as dwarf oak, pine, alder, &c.; also with impressions of leaves, fruits, &c. Several fine molar teeth of the Mammoth: layers of freshwater shells; 9 feet.
- Marl with freshwater shells.

Solid chalk.

"A series of thirteen excavations and dredgings . . . . . proved that the submerged forest extended for seven or eight miles [down the river]. The peat-bed on an average was about 9 feet (in some places 14 feet) below low-water neap-tides."

Dr. Taylor has since noticed a like occurrence at the northern side of the mouth of the Deben,† where, he says, the peat is only visible at low water spring tides, rests on the London Clay, and is about four or five feet thick at the most; but has evidently been much denuded. "Remains of trees are not plentiful . . . . . . and the peat contains an abundance of freshwater and marsh plants, but I found no freshwater shells." The only animal remains found were part of the skull and horn-cores of *Bos longifrons*: but bones had been washed out. "Among the plants a species of *Cyperus* was abundant, and *Sphagnum* was also plentiful."

I learn, from Mr. H. Miller, that the Ipswich main sewer was taken along the bed of the Little Gipping, from near the Oil Mill in the Handford Road to near the southern part of Friar's Road, and that this river-bed was shown by the excavations to consist of peat and silt, varying from 2 to 8 feet in depth, and resting on gravel and sand.

Mr. T. Miller told me that at the Drill Hall, Portmans Road, Ipswich, about 8 feet of mud were found, underlain by peat, on an average 3 feet thick, with branches, nuts, &c., and resting on gravel.

I heard from Mr. E. Buckham, the Town Surveyor, that at the new public-house The Gun, at the corner of Quay Street and Lower Orwell

---

* *Rep. Brit. Assoc.* for 1875, *Sections*, p. 82, and *Science Gossip*, No. 120, p. 279. (1874.)

† *Geol. Mag.*, dec. ii., vol. ix., p. 573. (1882.)

Street, the following beds were found (1876): Top crust (made earth) about 2 feet; black boggy earth, wet at bottom, about 4 feet; and then sand.

In June 1882, the works for the Felixstow Docks, at the mouth of the Orwell, opposite Harwich, gave the following section, at the S.W. part:—

Brown alluvial clay; a few feet (a little grey clay at the bottom in a hollow).

Shingle, rising up westward to the surface: clayey at first, but where bare of the usual sandy character.

From Mr. S. V. Wood, who saw the section a few months later, I hear that he was told that there was clay under the shingle, and then more shingle below again at one part.

There are some small local deposits, too small to be shown on the map, that may be described here.

Just W. of Gusford Hall a deep drain, cut (in 1875) to the little side-stream, showed an alluvial deposit of silt (partly with freshwater shells), sand, peat, and gravel. The stream passes under the cart-track and then flows as a little cascade, over an encrusting mass of calcareous tufa, the carbonate of lime of which must have been derived from the Crag at the spring head. W.W.

In a field sloping gently to a small brook, about N. of Well House, and seven-eighths of a mile S.E. of Mount Bures, a little below the edge of the Glacial gravel, there is a peaty and sandy soil, full of friable shells in the upper part, and lower down coarse sand and white marl, some of which last is hard and pierced by irregular tubes, such as rootlets would leave. All the shells are terrestrial, and one species, *Cyclostoma elegans*, does not occur in the district now. W.H.D.

Coast Deposits.

1. *Shingle.*

The state of the coast from Harwich to Orfordness, the accumulations of shingle along it and their shiftings, have been described in detail by Mr. J. B. Redman.* The ridges, or "fulls," of shingle are the results of successive beach-accumulation, and they show the way in which the mass has been added to. The general course of the shingle being south-westward, there is a tendency for it to pile up in that direction, and to form spits projecting from the eastern sides of the river-mouths.

At the joint mouth of the Stour and the Orwell this process has resulted in the formation of a shingle-spit, from the western end of the Felixstow cliffs for two miles, to Langer or Landguard Point, narrow at first, but afterwards broadening at Langer Common. About a quarter of a mile N.E. of the fort I saw a pit 9 feet deep in bedded shingle and sand, which had been worked 2½ feet deeper close by.

On either side of Bawdsey Haven, the mouth of the Deben, there is a smaller mass of shingle. On the western side of the river, near the ferry, at the western edge of the northern point, I saw a section showing the shingle beneath alluvial clay, from 0 to 2 feet thick.

From Martello Tower X., for nearly three miles northward, is the long strip of Bawdsey Beach and Shingle Street.

It is, however, on the left side of the Ore, or Alde, that we have one of the finest spreads of shingle in the kingdom, reaching north-eastward to Aldborough, and which tends to increase in

---
* *Proc. Inst. Civ. Eng.*, vol. xxiii., pp. 191–204, plate 2. (1865.)

length by the deposit of more shingle at its south-western end. MR. REDMAN, in his paper referred to above, tells us that a Chart of the time of Henry the Eighth shows distinctly that the mouth of Orford Haven was then opposite Orford Castle (which would be somewhere about the part marked "Crouch Harbour" on the Ordnance Map); whilst a chart of the time of Elizabeth shows a considerable south-westerly progression. When the Ordnance Map was made (published 1838), North Weir Point, as the end of the spit is called, was about east of Hollesley. W. W.

The development of this beach, however, has not been invariably progressive, breaches made by storms having sometimes given a temporary exit for the waters of the Ore and of the Butley River at the Upper Narrows, when the part of the channel to the south would be partially closed.

The Ordnance Map of 1838 shows irregular separate knolls of shingle for a mile southwards from North Weir Point. The point no longer exists as there shown, the knolls having been united into a continuous bank, as marked on the Geological Survey Map, which has been corrected from a later survey.

It is improbable that the beach will ever reach further than the northern end of Bawdsey Cliff, or some two miles further than now. The erection of piers, or large groins, at Aldborough, by checking the southerly passage of shingle, or rather by diverting it seaward, might result in the re-opening of the original mouth of the river at Aldborough, and the ultimate obliteration of the present 10 miles of useless estuary. The Butley River would be so small as hardly to need a channel through the shingle, and a large area, now between tide-marks, would become available pasture, if not truly dry land.

The alluvial islands of Havergate and Dove Marshes, in the tidal channel of the Ore, are united by a bank of shingle.

W. H. D.

Some years ago Mr. Redman showed me some samples of the shingle and it may be of interest to note their composition. That from the offing consisted almost wholly of flints and flint-pebbles, with a few pebbles of quartz and quartzite, some pieces of chert, grit, sandstone, ironstone, and ferruginous grit, a few pieces of shells, some pieces of cinder (from a steamer), and a pebble of hard trap. The beach shingle likewise was almost wholly of flints and flint pebbles; but with pebbles of quartz and quartzite (mostly small) and small pieces of grit and chert.

2. *Blown Sand.*

Of this, the result of the action of wind along a dry sandy shore, there is but little in our district, and that little of no very marked character. The chief mass is a strip for about 1½ miles from the south-western end of Felixstow Cliff towards Landguard, for the greater part dividing the shingle and the marsh, but at last being over the broad part of the shingle flat. Other patches occur on the south of Landguard Port, and on either side of Bawdsey Haven. W. W.

CHAPTER X.—MISCELLANEOUS.

DISTURBANCES.

As is the case in the greater part of the London Basin, the beds are very even, or free from local disturbance; but here, on the northern side of that tract, they are subject to a slight southerly dip, so that the Chalk, which crops out on the N.W., sinks some way below the sea-level on the south and also on the east, the slight easterly tendency of the dip seeming to increase in that direction.

We have, however, evidence, in the deep boring at Harwich, of that earlier disturbance which brought up a ridge of various older rocks before the Cretaceous beds were deposited. Here the lowest beds proved are of Carboniferous age, but below the Coal Measures. It becomes a question, therefore, whether we may not expect to find the Coal Measures deep underground in parts of East Anglia, and also in what directions, from Harwich, they are most likely to occur? These important questions can only be settled by deep borings, and as yet that above noted is the only one in our eastern counties that has pierced through the Secondary beds, the other deep borings at Combs (Stowmarket), at Yarmouth, at Norwich, and at Holkham, ending in Cretaceous, or possibly in the last case, in Jurassic beds.

Of more local disturbance there is, however, some evidence in our district, both in the lowest part of the Brett Valley, and also in the Valley of the Orwell. Of the former district MR. BENNETT notes that "at Waterhouse Farm, Layham, Chalk is said to have been reached at a depth of only 15 feet, and further south, close to Shelly Church, at only 6 feet. I was told, too, that Chalk was dug years ago at the latter place." This agrees with the section published by MR. CLARKE, and reproduced at p. 10, and we have, therefore, evidence, invisible though it be, of a rise of the beds here, bringing up the Chalk close to the surface.

At Ipswich, however, we have not to depend on such hidden evidence, for the mapping of the district shows a rise of the beds south of the town, as may be seen from the account of the various sections (pp. 5, 10–12). It is possible that this rise may be continuous with that of Shelly, the Drift-covered plateau between shutting off all proof, and even that it may run much further south-westward beyond our district, to Wickham Bishop near Witham, where a well-section proves a remarkably sudden folding, perhaps with faulting.

Again, from the fact of the Chalk having been found at a depth of only 115 feet at East Mersea (see p. 109), whilst it is rather deeper at Colchester, whereas one would have expected, from the general southerly dip, that the surface of the Chalk would be at a higher level near Colchester than at Mersea, we have evidence (got since the publication of the Memoir on that district) of a rise between those places.

Economics.

Building Materials, etc.

At the eastern edge of our district we touch the large pits of Sudbury, where the Chalk is burnt for lime, and at Bramford, on our northern edge, the same is the case. Our Chalk, consisting of the top part only, is too soft for use in building; but its flints have formed the material for most of the old church towers. Indeed, Suffolk and Norfolk are noted for the dressed flint-work of their old buildings. Rough flints, too, are naturally much used in building.

The septaria, or cement-stones, which are so plentiful in some parts of our London Clay, were once used as a building-stone, as may be seen at Wrabness Church, the thick Norman walls of which consist chiefly of these stones, with a few flints, and at Chelmondiston Church, which is built of septaria, flints, and pebbles. Beyond our district other examples may be seen, as at Frinton, where the remains of a small church on the top of the cliff may be seen to be made of stones from the beach, chiefly septaria, and in the Norman church of Clacton, the stones of which have probably been brought in from the beach. The keep of Orford Castle, however, (just north of our district) is perhaps the best specimen of London Clay masonry, the walls being chiefly built of septaria, with cornering etc. of firmer stone. An analysis of London clay cement-stone has been inserted in page 133.

The upper part of the Coralline Crag sometimes forms a fair building-stone, for which purpose it has been worked at Sutton.

Where the Drift gravels contain large stones these have naturally been used for building, and anyone wishing to see a great variety of such stones should go to Wherstead, where the church walls form a good rock-collection, with many varieties of granite and of gneiss, greenstone, flint, quartzite, sandstone, Red Chalk?, and other Cretaceous and older rocks, besides greywether-sandstone and septaria.

The clays of the Reading Series and the London Clay are worked for tiles and draining-pipes, and the London Clay forms a good brickearth in its more sandy state, as near Hadleigh and at Ipswich, where the lower beds are worked. The Drift brickearths, as a rule, are of little importance; but they are worked at and near Boxford, on the east of Ipswich, and at Trimley. The Boulder Clay, too, is used for brickmaking, after getting rid of the stones by washing.

The cement-works of Dovercourt and Waldringfield are chiefly supplied by imported materials (from the Medway, &c.); but I believe that the local river-mud is also used. The once extensive trade in the cement-stones of the London Clay, which gave employment to a fleet of small vessels (engaged in dredging up the stone along the coast), is now quite a thing of the past, the manufacture of Portland Cement having abolished that of Roman Cement, in which these stones were used.

Mineral Manures.

It is a common Suffolk custom to cover manure-heaps with Crag sand, which acts as an absorbent; but the shelly Crag is not without a value of its own, probably from containing a certain amount of phosphate, as well as from the carbonate of lime of the shells.

The earliest notice of the employment of Crag as a fertiliser that I have seen is in a note by the Rev. R. Pickering, dated 1744,[*] from which the following remarks are taken: "At Woodbridge in Suffolk, ... there are some Pits . . . . consisting of several *Strata* of Shells from the Bottom to within about nine Feet of the Surface, where the natural Soil of Gravel and Sand begins . . . . The Farmer, in whose Ground these Shells are, has, as I am informed, laid the Foundation of an ample Fortune from them. The Man contented himself in the old beaten Track of the Farmers, ... till an happy Accident forced him upon a bold Improvement. He used to mend his Cartways . . . . . with these Shells; in which Business his Cart one Day broke down, and threw the Shells out of the Cart

---

[*] *Phil. Trans.*, vol. xliii. no. 474, pp. 191, 192. (1745.)

Track into the cultivated Part of the Field. This Spot produced so remarkable a Crop next Year, that he put some Loads upon a particular Piece, kept the Secret to himself, and waited the Event. This Trial answering Expectation, he directly took a Lease of a large Quantity of poor Land, at about five Shillings the Acre; and having manur'd it heartily with these Shells, in about three Years it turned to so good an Account, that he had 15 Shillings the Acre proffer'd to take the Lease out of his Hands."

The chief mineral industry of our district is the getting of the phosphatic nodules at the base of the Crag, for the manufacture of artificial manure. To a great extent this nodule-bed has been already worked out; but there are yet "coprolite-works" going on in our district. The way in which these are carried on is as follows:—

The pit, through overlying Crag and Drift, is made in successive steps, each 3 feet deep, except those at top and at bottom, which of course vary according to the surface of the ground and to the lie of the nodule-bed. The sand, etc. is separated from the stones and nodules by screening, the larger contents of the bed thus left are carried to the surface, and the unprofitable stones are picked out from the phosphatic nodules, bones, etc., which are carted off and taken to the distant manufactory. In this way a large area is sometimes worked over, the part first dug out being filled up with the material from that next attacked, and so on, the whole field in in the end being levelled and returned to cultivation.

Many analyses of the Crag nodules have been made, and it may be useful to reproduce some of these.

Mr. T. J. Herapath has given the following analyses of Crag phosphates, both nodules, or, as he calls them (after Buckland), "pseudo-coprolites," and fossil bones[*]:—

Pseudo-Coprolites from the neighbourhood of Sutton.
Densities respectively 2·7216 and 2·7891.

Water and organic matters	7·200	9·210
Cloride of sodium and sulphate of soda	traces.	traces.
Carbonate of lime	18·514	5·176
Carbonate of magnesia	0·855	2·016
Sulphate of lime	some.	1·161
Phosphate of lime	51·018	45·815
Phosphate of magnesia	traces.	some.
Perphosphate of iron	8·902	12·476
Phosphate of alumina	2·700	6·397
Oxide of manganese	0·057	0·267
Fluoride of calcium	3·161	2·688
Silicic acid and loss	7·593	14·804
	100·	100·
Nitrogen, per cent.	0·0289	0·01989

Three other specimens, received at different times from other parts, contained—

		Per cent.	
Earthy and other phosphates	64·056	79·545	67·176
Fluoride of calcium	0·311	2·554	2·768
Nitrogen	Traces.	0·0314	Undetermined.

Fossil Bones.

"The majority of these bones which I have examined were obtained from . . . . the neighbourhood of Sutton. . . ."

"The sample . . . . evidently consisted principally of bones of extinct cetaceans; and the fossils could readily be divided into two

---

[*] *Journ. R. Agric. Soc.*, vol. xii., pp. 98, 100, 101. (1851.)

classes, according to the appearance they presented. The bones of the first class (α) were very frangible, and possessed a somewhat porous or spongy texture, caused by the existence of numerous minute cavities or air-tubes in the substance of the bone; whilst those of the second class (β), on the contrary, were very solid, and possessed a fibrous structure. They were much harder than the former, and readily took a fine polish. The air-cells in the latter were invisible to the unassisted eye, and could only be detected by examining thin sections of the bone under the microscope."

Analyses of both kinds are given:—

Analyses of Fossil Bones (α).	1	2	Mean.
Water driven off at 300° to 350° Fahr.	3·361	2·912	3·1360
Water and organic matters expelled at a red heat	4·351	3·361	3·8560
Carbonate of lime	27·400	23·800	25·6000
Carbonate of magnesia	0·371	0·286	0·3285
Sulphate of lime	0·514	Traces.	0·2570
Phosphate of lime, with some phosphate of magnesia	49·632	56·966	52·8490
Perphosphate of iron	6·600	4·800	5·7000
Phosphate of alumina	3·400	4·638	4·0190
Fluoride of calcium	3·657	Undetermined	3·6570(?)
Silicic acid	0·626	0·098	0·3620
	99·912	—	99·7645
Nitrogen, per cent.	0·1244	Undetermined.	

Analyses of Fossil Bones (β).				
Specific gravity	2·644	2·874	2·907	Mean.
Water driven off at 300° or 350° Fahr.	2·000	2·760	1·976	2·2453
Water and organic matters expelled at a red heat	4·786	5·321	4·679	4·9287
Carbonate of lime	21·000	16·400	17·600	18·3333
Carbonate of magnesia	1·089	0·252	Some.	0·4470(?)
Sulphate of lime	0·298	A little.	0·896	0·3980
Phosphate of lime / Phosphate of magnesia	58·781	61·175	62·721	60·8923
Perphosphate of iron	6·600	9·400	5·200	7·0660
Phosphate of alumina	1·200	0·400	2·416	1·3350
Fluoride of calcium	Undetermined.	Undetermined.	4·167	4·1670(?)
Silicic acid	0·120	0·261	0·200	0·1700
	—	—	89·855	99·9825
Nitrogen, per cent.	Undetermined.	0·838	0·0482	—

Dr. A. Voelcker, in his work on Phosphatic Manures[*] treats of the Suffolk Phosphates, and remarks that "in commercial phraseology, we

[*] On the Chemical Composition and Commercial Value of Norwegian Apatite, Spanish Phosphorite, Coprolites and other Phosphatic Materials used in England for Agricultural Purposes. *London*, 1861, pp. 11, 12. Reprinted from *Journ. R. Agric. Soc.*, vol. xxi., pp. 359, 360. (1860).

have to understand by Suffolk-coprolites, or Crag-coprolites, or pseudo-coprolites, the mixed fossil bones, fish-teeth, and phosphatic pebbles which occur in the Suffolk Crag. These phosphatic matters are distinguished from the grey coloured Chalk-coprolites by a brownish, ferruginous colour, and a smoother appearance. They are very hard, and yield on grinding a yellowish-red powder. Analysed in the manner usually adopted in commercial analyses, the composition of several samples of ground Suffolk coprolites may be illustrated by the following tabulated results:—"

General Composition of Suffolk Coprolites.

	No. 1.	No. 2.	No. 3.	No. 4.	No. 5.
Moisture and a little organic matter	4·61	3·80	4·11	6·28	4·74
Phosphates	56·52	60·21	61·15	60·99	44·20
Carbonate of lime, magnesia, fluorine, &c. (determined by difference)	25·95	21·77	22·39	21·74	20·92
Insoluble siliceous matter	12·92	14·22	12·35	10·99	30·14
	100·00	100·00	100·00	100·00	100·00

"In good samples of Suffolk coprolites the amount of insoluble siliceous matter varies from 10 to 14 per cent.; No. 5, therefore, appears to be a very inferior specimen."

"Besides fluoride of calcium, they contain a good deal of oxide of iron and alumina, which partially, at least, are thrown down with the phosphates when the latter are determined by precipitation with ammonia, as is usual in commercial analyses. In this case the amount of phosphates will be stated in excess. The true value of these pseudo-coprolites, therefore, can only be correctly estimated if the phosphoric acid which they contain is accurately determined. This has been done in the subjoined analyses which at the same time represent their detailed composition";—

Detailed Composition of Suffolk Coprolites.

	No. 1.	No. 2.
Moisture and water of combination with a trace of organic matter	5·76	2·53
Lime	40·70	38·20
Magnesia	·34	1·34
a Phosphoric acid	28·32	24·24
Oxide of iron / Alumina	} 4·87	{ 4·81 / 3·72
b Carbonic acid	5·08	5·37
Sulphuric acid	·87	1·40
Potash	·78	·56
Soda	·25	1·18
Chlorine	traces.	·07
Fluorine and loss	3·02	4·31
Insoluble siliceous matter	10·01	12·27
	100·00	100·00
(a) Equal to tribasic phosphate of lime (bone-earth)	61·30	52·52
(b) Equal to carbonate of lime	11·64	12·20

"No. 1, it will be seen, is a very superior sample: No. 2 represents a good average sample of Suffolk coprolites. In two other samples, in which the amount of insoluble matter and phosphoric acid alone was determined, I find:—"

	No. 1.	No. 2.
Insoluble silicious matter	12·56	11·05
Phosphoric acid	23·48	24·26
Corresponding to bone-earth	50·87	52·56

It should be remembered that phosphates have been worked not only at the base of the Red Crag, though PROF. PRESTWICH says, that "it was only at one small pit [at Sutton], and there for a short time, that the bed of phosphatic nodules at the base of the Coralline Crag was worked." He also tells us that "the condition . . . of the bones at the base of this Crag is precisely of the same character as that of those at the base of the Red Crag."*

Water.

The Crag and the Glacial sand and gravel together form so large a part of the surface of our district, especially in the eastern half, that they receive a large amount of the rainfall. Moreover, as these porous beds are nearly everywhere underlain by the London Clay, a large quantity of water is stored in them, the overflow escaping in the many streamlets along the sides of the valleys. It is not surprising, therefore, that these beds should be the general source of water-supply, and the less so from the rural character of the district. It is only where no supply is thus to be got, as at Harwich, and where, though present, it is not enough, as at Ipswich, that public supplies have been got by wells through the Tertiary beds into the Chalk.

From Appendix A., however, it will be seen that private enterprise has often got deeper-seated water, by sinking either to the sandy beds beneath the London Clay, or still further to the Chalk.

The Ipswich Waterworks get their supply from two sources. The springs at the base of the porous Drift and Crag are tapped in many places on the north and east of the town, the water being led away in pipes; but a larger amount is got from a well (originally sunk for a paper-mill abandoned some time ago), the possession of which enables the Waterworks Company to give a constant supply of good water.

The large amount of good water that has been found in the Chalk at Ipswich is in striking contrast with the yield at Harwich, and thence for some way south-westward along the Essex coast. In this latter district the efforts of engineers have as yet mostly yielded water of a brackish kind. The cause of this is not clear; but there must be something to prevent the natural flow of fresh water through the Chalk from the northwest; perhaps the disturbance alluded to (p. 100) as probably running westward from Ipswich may have something to do with it.

---

* *Quart. Journ. Geol. Soc.*, vol. xxvii., p. 133. (1871.)

APPENDIX A.—WELL-SECTIONS.

I. ESSEX.

For accounts of other wells in that part of Essex included in Sheet 48, N.E. (Dovercourt and Harwich), see "The Geology of the Eastern End of Essex (Walton Naze and Harwich)," *Geological Survey Memoir*, 1877.

DEDHAM. Mr. Downes', near the Lamb Inn.
REV. W. B. CLARKE, *Trans. Geol. Soc.*, ser. 2, vol. v., p. 372 (1840.)

		FEET
Earth [soil]		1½
[Post Glacial (River) Drift]	Gravel	1
	Brown clay	5
	Gravel	1
	Red sand	1½
	Dark grey sand	¼
	Gravel	¼
Blue London Clay		10
		20¼

DEDHAM, Pig Lane.
Same authority.
Surface beds from 16 to 60 feet.
London Clay ,, 28 ,, 37 ,,

MISTLEY. Mr. Free's, Malting. 1883. Boring.
Communicated by MR. P. BRUFF, C.E.
About 37 feet above Ordnance Datum.

Water rose to 32½ feet below the surface (14 inches higher at high tide): supply abundant (over 6,000 gallons an hour), and quality good.

		FEET
Made ground		2¾
Mould		¾
Gravel		4
[London Clay, 36¼ feet.]	Brown clay, with 15 inch rock (septaria) 2 feet above the bottom	15¾
	Dark sandy loam	2
	Clay	10¼
	Fine light-coloured sand (water) [? basement-bed]	8¼
[Reading Beds, 58 feet.]	Mottled clay	16¾
	Fine light-coloured sand (water)	3½
	Green loamy sand	10
	Mottled clay	2
	Coarse grey sand	½
	Green clay	1
	Coarse grey sand	2¼
	Green clay	7
	Blue silty clay, bottom foot brown	12
	Streaky loam, top 9 inches dark, the rest grey	2¼
	Green-coated flints	¼
	To Chalk	101¾
Chalk; at first rather soft, then in small cuboidal pieces, with much water; few flints met with		130¼
		232

WELL-SECTIONS. 107

RAMSEY. New Farm House (after 1870)? S.W. of Copperas Wood.
Communicated by MR. E. W. GARLAND.

Through London Clay to a bed of marl with plenty of water, which, however, is unfit for drinking or for cooking-purposes, being very unwholesome; about 90 feet.

RAMSEY RAY, West of Harwich. N.E. end of the island. 1880? Trial-boring.

Communicated by MR. J. B. CRAWFORD.

18 feet above Ordnance Datum.
Water brackish; stands at 2 feet 4 inches above Ordnance Datum.

		FEET
[London Clay, 36½ feet.]	Yellow clay	9
	Blue clay	27½
[Reading Beds, 50 feet.]	Dark grey sand	1¼
	Brown clay	15
	Light-coloured sand	6½
	Dark loamy sand	4½
	Dark hard clay	4¾
	Grey sand	2¼
	Brown clay	8
	Green sand	¼
	Brown clay	4½
	Green sand	2¼
	To Chalk	86½
Chalk		110
		196½

The accounts of the following Essex wells, in the southern divisions of Sheet 48 of the Geological Survey Map, are here inserted, as supplementary to the Memoirs on 48, S.W. and S.E.

BRAMBLE ISLAND. Enclosed Land westward of Pewit Island. 1880.
Sunk and communicated by MR. T. TILLEY.
Water rises to the surface. Large yield, but brackish.

		FT.	IN.
[? Alluvium and London Clay.]	Dark clay	13	10
	Blue clay	17	8
	Clayey sand	3	6
	Blue clay	16	6
	Brown clay	18	6
	Brown sandy clay	8	0
[Reading Beds, 37¼ feet.]	Coloured clay	15	0
	Loamy sand	5	0
	Coloured sandy clay	5	0
	Mottled clay	12	0
	Flints	0	3
	To Chalk	115	3
Chalk and flints		48	3
		163	6

E 14651. H

CLACTON-ON-SEA. Waterworks.

Since the publication of the Colchester Memoir these waterworks have been completed, and additional information has been given by Mr. J. Church, C.E. His account of the well differs somewhat from the one already published (which may be only of a trial-boring), and as it will be useful to compare this account of the first well (1880, 81) with that of the new one (1883), I give the two side by side, all the information being from Mr. Church.

The shaft of the older well has been carried down to 120 feet, and the water level is 45 feet down. The two wells are 16 feet apart.

The first sand-spring occurred at a depth of 157 feet, the second at 202. A good supply is being got at 210 feet, although charged with sand.

In the older well the water was brackish at 203 feet; but after deepening the bore to 405 feet good water rose.

The yield has been tested as far as the pumps allow, up to 100 gallons a minute. Analysis shows the water to be of good quality, with only 4·9 grains of chlorides to a gallon.

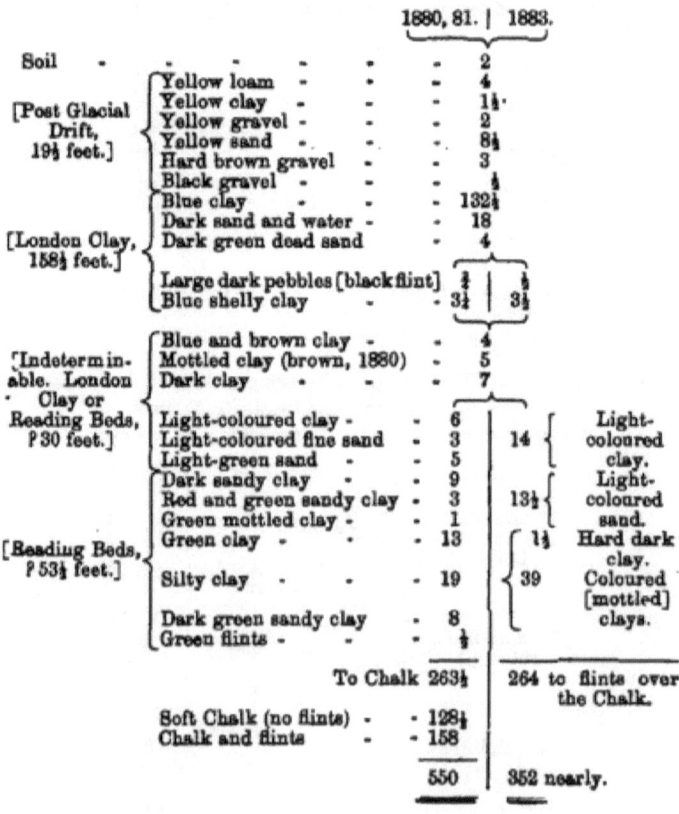

		1880, 81.	1883.
Soil			2
[Post Glacial Drift, 19½ feet.]	Yellow loam		4
	Yellow clay		1½
	Yellow gravel		2
	Yellow sand		8½
	Hard brown gravel		3
	Black gravel		½
[London Clay, 158½ feet.]	Blue clay		132½
	Dark sand and water		18
	Dark green dead sand		4
	Large dark pebbles [black flint]	⅔	⅔
	Blue shelly clay	3½	3½
[Indeterminable. London Clay or Reading Beds, ? 30 feet.]	Blue and brown clay		4
	Mottled clay (brown, 1880)		5
	Dark clay		7
	Light-coloured clay		6 } 14 { Light-coloured clay.
	Light-coloured fine sand		3
	Light-green sand		5
[Reading Beds, ? 53½ feet.]	Dark sandy clay		9 } 13½ { Light-coloured sand.
	Red and green sandy clay		3
	Green mottled clay		1
	Green clay		13 } 1½ Hard dark clay.
	Silty clay		19 } 39 Coloured [mottled] clays.
	Dark green sandy clay		8
	Green flints		½
	To Chalk	263½	264 to flints over the Chalk.
	Soft Chalk (no flints)	128½	
	Chalk and flints	158	
		550	352 nearly.

WELL-SECTIONS.

COLCHESTER. Waterworks, new well. 1881.
Communicated by MR. T. TILLEY (to W. H. D.).
Shaft 43 feet, the rest bored. Water-level 19½ feet below the surface.

		FEET.
Made ground		14
Blue [London] Clay		79
[Reading Beds, 51 feet.]	Mottled clay	30
	Running sand	1½
	Mottled clay	7½
	Green sand	3
	Plastic clay	8
	Flints	1
	To Chalk	144
Chalk and flints	about	234½
		378½

EAST MERSEA. 1883.
Bored and communicated by MR. T. TILLEY.
Good supply, but the water rather salt.
Pipes carried 7 feet into the Chalk.

		FEET.
[Alluvium, 37 feet.]	Red Clay	15
	Black silt	22
[? Gravel]	Stone, with brackish water	1½
	Pebbles, "supposed old beach"	1½
[London Clay?]	Red clay	15
[Reading Beds, 60 feet.]	Green sand, very hard	30
	Black clay	30
	To Chalk	115
Chalk		225
		340

FRINTON. For Walton water-supply, 1879. About half a mile N.W. of the church.
Communicated by MR. P. BRUFF, C.E.
38 feet above low water.
Shaft 51 feet 4 inches, the rest bored. Water brackish.

		FT.	IN.
[Drift? 13 feet.]	Brickearth	6	0
	Sand	1	6
	Sandy brickearth	3	0
	Sand	2	6
[London Clay, 98 feet.]	Light-coloured clay	34	0
	Dark clay, with two layers of stone [septaria] 6 and 16 inches thick, in lower half	64	4
[Reading Beds, 81 feet.]	Sand with pebbles*	15	0
	Red clay with sandy veins	10	0
	Plastic clay	20	0
	Black sand	1	0
	Light-coloured sand	1	0
	Plastic clay	10	0
	Red clay	2	0
	Green sand	6	0
	Clayey greensand	15	6
	Flints	0	6
	To Chalk	192	4
Chalk. Two flint layers passed through		254	0
		446	4

Boring said to have been continued to a depth of about 500 feet.

* This bed may be the basement-bed of the London Clay, or it may belong to the Oldhaven Beds.

WALTON-ON-NAZE. At the back of East Terrace, 1882.

About 3 feet above high water of spring tides.

Communicated by Messrs. J. WARNER AND SONS.

Old shaft 20 feet, the rest bored.

Water first got at 60 feet, and it rose to 4 feet in the shaft. At 140 feet the supply was somewhat increased, and rose another foot. The water-level varies about 3 feet, with the tide. The chalk, to the depth of about 20 feet, very soft and saturated with water, and it yielded water more or less throughout.

		FEET.
Brickearth (and soil)		? 8 (or less ?)
[London Clay, ? 99 feet.]	Dark clay, a foot shingly at 25 feet	27
	Light-coloured sandy clay	1
	Dark clay, with layer of septaria and layer of cement-stone	24
	Grey sand with water (saltish, rose 4 feet in well)	3
	Dark clay, with a foot layer of flint pebbles at 70 feet, fragment of bivalve at 80 feet	44
[Reading Beds,] 23 feet.]	Light-coloured mottled clay	2
	Light-coloured loamy clay	6
	Light-coloured mottled clay	3
	Dark brown sandy clay	4
	Greenish sandy clay	1
	Dark brown mottled clay	2
	Dark brown clay	1
	Greenish mottled clay	4
	To Chalk	130
Chalk, 240 feet	Grey discoloured chalk with layers of flints	2
	Soft white chalk with occasional flints	238
		370

The following MS. note, by the late JOHN BROWN (of Stanway), may refer to the well made for the late Mr. Warner, of which Messrs. Warner have no account, except that it was 350 feet deep, and in the garden of No. 1, East Terrace. On a drawing of the coast-section, which this note accompanied, it is stated that the Chalk "had been reached by boring at 130 feet." For note and drawing I am indebted to my colleague MR. H. B. WOODWARD.

		FEET.
[? Alluvium and Brickearth, 26 feet.]	Blue clay, with vegetables and remains of goat	4
	Oysters, *Buccinum undatum*, *Trochi*, *Mytilus* [a bed of shells]	2
	Till with fossil mammalia	20
London Clay [including Reading Beds]		100
	To Upper Chalk, with Foraminifera	126

2. SUFFOLK.

Assington. Vicarage.

Sunk and communicated by Mr. Kingsbury, of Boxford, as also were the other Assington wells (from memory).—F. J. B.

Gravelly soil	10 Feet.
Stony yellow [Boulder] Clay, no water	50 ,,

Another well, S. of the above :—

Stony yellow clay	40 Feet.
Pebbles and blowing sand to water	3 ,,

Assington. Dillack's Farm.

Water rose to surface.

Stony yellow clay	18 Feet.
Sandy clay	1 ,,

Assington. Lane Farm.

Chalky [Boulder] clay	30 Feet.
Sandy clay	10 ,,
Blowing sand and pebbles	1 ,,
To water	41 ,,

Assington Street.

Yellow clay	30 Feet.
Shingle, to water	2 ,,

Belstead.

Rev. W. B. Clarke, *Trans. Geol. Soc.*, ser. 2., vol. v., p. 380.

Stiff loam	15 Feet.
Crag [?]	35 ,,

Bentley Hall. Same authority, p. 381.

Sand	20 Feet.
Crag	10 ,,

Boxford. West of Church (Mr. Kingsbury's House).

Sunk and communicated (from memory) by Mr. Kingsbury, as also the other Boxford wells.—F. J. B.

Chalky clay, not bottomed, no water - 75 feet.

Boxford (Dr. Gurdon's), 50 yards S. of the Church.

Chalky [Boulder] clay, auger dropped and water rose to surface, 40 Feet.

Boxford (E. of Rectory, between road and stream).

Boggy soil, to chalk, no water - 35 Feet.

Boxford Brewery.

Gravel	16 Feet.
? Boulder clay	2 ,,
Blue and green clay	30 ,,
To Chalk	48 ,,
Chalk	6 ,,
	54 ,,

Boxford Brewery.

Another account or another well.

	Feet
Gravel	12
Sand	7
Light-colored clay	7
Reddish-brown clay	3
Dark greenish sandy clay	3
Blue clay	3
To Chalk	35
Chalk	10
	45

Capel St. Mary.

Rev. W. B. Clarke, *Trans. Geol. Soc.*, ser. 2, vol. v., p. 381.

Diluvial [Boulder] clay	45 Feet.
Crag sand	40 ,,

Copdock.

Rev. W. B. Clarke, *Trans. Geol. Soc.*, ser. 2, vol. v., p. 380.

Diluvial [Boulder] clay	15 Feet.
Sand	45 ,,

Cotts Tye Kiln (S.W. of Kersey).—F. J. B.

Stiff loam	30 Feet.
Blue clay	30 ,,

Another account divides the upper bed into yellow loam, 15 Feet, and chalky clay (? white clay), 15 Feet.

Dorking Tye, S.W. of Assington.

Sunk and communicated (from memory) by Mr. Kingsbury.—F. J. B.

Boulder clay	60 Feet.
Blowing sand and pebbles	2 ,,

East Bergholt. The Rectory.

Rev. W. B. Clarke, *Trans. Geol. Soc.*, ser. 2, vol. v., p. 371.

	Feet.
Earth [soil]	2
Red gravel	4
London Clay { Yellow clay growing darker [lower down ?]	20
{ Blue clay with selenite	97
Black earth	3
(a) Chalk	50
(a) Upper green sand, greenish sand, and blackish earth	4
	180

(a) ? Can these two beds belong to the Reading Series. "Chalk" being marly clay, and the "green sand" bottom-bed; it cannot of course be Upper Greensand.—W. W.

EAST BERGHOLT, Arnold's.

REV. W. B. CLARKE, *Trans. Geol. Soc.*, ser. 2, vol. v., p. 371.

Gravel	3 FEET.
Loam, gravel, and sand	11 ,,
Clay	½ ,,
To sand and water	14½ ,,

EDWARDSTON HALL.

Sunk and communicated (from memory) by MR. TRICKER, as also were the two following.—F. J. B.

Loam	10 FEET.
Black clay	40 ,,
Sand and gravel	14 ,,

EDWARDSTON LODGE. Same as the above.

EDWARDSTON, Quick's Farm.

Chalky [Boulder] clay	20 FEET.
Black clay	40 ,,
Sand and gravel	4 ,,
	64 ,,

EDWARDSTON, Mill Green, east of the church.

Sunk and communicated (from memory) by MR. KINGSBURY of Boxford.—F. J. B.

Boulder clay	20 FEET.
Sand and gravel	24 ,,

ELMSETT.

Sunk and communicated by MESSRS. BENNETT, of Ipswich.

Old well	60 FEET.
Clay and marl	24 ,,
Fine sand	47½ ,,
Loam and flints	1½ ,,
To Chalk	133 ,,
Chalk	59 ,,
	192 ,,

ELMSETT.

REV. W. B. CLARKE, *Trans. Geol. Soc.*, ser. 2, vol. v., p. 380.

Diluvial [Boulder] clay	10 FEET.
Sand	46 ,,

ELMSETT GREEN, half a mile W. of, at Poplar Hall.

Sunk and communicated (from memory) by MR. TRICKER of Edwardston.—F. J. B.

Chalky [Boulder] clay	30 FEET.
Chalk	49 ,,

FELIXSTOW. Opposite the Railway Station. 1883?
Borings made and communicated by MESSRS. BENNETT, of Ipswich.
No. 1. No water got.

		FEET
Topsoil, mould, &c.		10
[London Clay] {	Clay	18
	Dark loam	2
	Clay	6
	Dark loam	1
	Septaria	over 1
	Clay [? partly clay of the Reading Beds]	31
[Reading Beds] {	Dark sandy loam	1½
	Light-coloured clay	3½
	Mottled clay	9½
	Light-coloured sandy loam	8½
		92

No. 2.—Not more than 50 yards from No. 1. Water got from the sand, enough to supply a 4-inch pump, with 2-inch iron suction-pipe, which was kept at work for some hours.

		FEET
Top soil		7
London Clay [and clay of the Reading Beds]		55
[Reading Beds] {	Dark sandy loam	3½
	Mottled clay	2½
	Light-coloured sand	1
		69

FLOWTON.

REV. W. B. CLARKE, *Trans. Geol. Soc.*, ser. 2, vol. v., p. 380.

Diluvial clay - 90 FEET.
Chalk - 4 ,,

"At Flowton Hall, clay 94 feet."

GREAT WALDINGFIELD.

Communicated by DR. J. S. HOLDEN, of Sudbury. (1877.)

	FEET
Boulder clay	25
Sand	½
Shell-mud, with *Bithinia tentaculata, Cyclas, Limnæa peregra, Planorbis albus*, and other shells, besides fragments of wood; plenty of water	10
	35½

There is some doubt as to the clay being Boulder Clay, from the occurrence beneath of a freshwater bed unlike anything known to occur beneath that clay in the district, but like what might be found above it. Perhaps there may have been some mistake in the information given to Dr. Holden.
(W. W.)

Another well, 400 or 500 yards off, is in Chalk at a depth of 35 feet.

GROTON PLACE.

Sunk and communicated (from memory) by MR. TRICKER, of Edwardston;
F. J. B.

Boulder clay - 30 FEET.
Sand and gravel 12 ,,

GROTON. CASTLINGS HEATH.

Sunk and communicated by MR. KINGSBURY, of Boxford.—F. J. B.

Boulder clay - 100 feet.
Chalk, to water 20 ,,

GROTON. Gosling Green.

Sunk and communicated (from memory) by MR. TRICKER, as also the next.—F.J.B.

Boulder clay	20 FEET.
Black clay	20 ,,
Sand and gravel	24 ,,
	64

GROTON. Gosling's (? Castling's) Heath or Gosling Green?.

Stiff yellow loam	40 FEET.
Red sand	10 ,,
White sand	10 ,,
Pebbly sand, with water	6 ,,
	66 ,,

HADLEIGH. 1827. (Two wells.)

REV. W. B. CLARKE, *Trans. Geol. Soc.*, ser. 2, vol. v., p. 372.

	A. On a Level with the River.	B.
	FEET.	FEET.
Gravel	12	—
Blue clay	90	70
Chalk	28	30
	130	100

HADLEIGH. Railway Station.

Sunk and communicated (from memory) by MR. PETTIT, of Hadleigh, as also are the next two sections.—F.J.B.

Water rose 4 feet.

Sandy loam	12 FEET.
Boulder clay	8 ,,
Dark green clayey sand	13 ,,
Blowing sand and pebbles	4 ,,
	37 ,,

HADLEIGH. Frog Hall, E. of the town.

Boulder clay	14 FEET.
Sand and gravel	8 ,,
Fine white sand (not bottomed)	32 ,,
	54 ,,

HADLEIGH. Coram Street, about a mile westward of the town.

Boulder clay	35 FEET.
Sand	12 ,,
To black pebbles and water	47 ,,

HADLEIGH. Pond Hall, in straw-yard, 1¼ miles S. of E. of the Railway Station.—F.J.B.

Gravel, to water, always tepid - 16 FEET.

HAVERGATE ISLAND. Marshes E. of Boyton.

REV. W. B. CLARKE, *Trans. Geol. Soc.*, ser. 2, vol. v., p. 383.

		FEET.
London Clay	{ Blue clay, with the usual rocky concretions [septaria]	80
	Rock, 2 inches [Basement-bed].	
Sand [Reading Beds]		20

HEMLEY.

(Same Authority.)

Loamy soil	-	6 FEET.
Crag	-	44 ,,

HIGHAM HILL, Mr. Harris'.

REV. W. B. CLARKE, *Trans. Geol. Soc.*, ser. 2, vol. v., p. 373.

		FEET.
[Drift and ? Crag.]	{ Gravel	10
	Sand	20
London Clay		10
To sand, with water strongly impregnated with sulphur, and useless		40

HINTLESHAM.

(Same Authority p. 380.)

Diluvial [Boulder] clay	15 FEET.
Sand with gravel	21 ,,

HOLTON.

(Same Authority, p. 373.)

		FEET.
1. The Hall.	Diluvial [Boulder] clay and chalk stones	40
2. Rectory.	,, ,, ,,	42

IPSWICH. Cliff Brewery, Messrs. Cobbold's.
Sunk and communicated by Messrs. BENNETT, of Ipswich.
Water rises to nearly 13 feet below the surface at high water. Supply 2 barrels a minute.

	FEET.
Depth of old boring, just on to the Chalk	{ 27 7
? To Chalk	34
Chalk. No flints met with. At a depth of about 175 feet loose chalk, full of small nodules, was found, and a few feet lower a tougher chalk, like pipe-clay	166
	200

IPSWICH. Henley Road (highest part of Ipswich) for Mr. T. N. Fonnereau.
Sunk and communicated by Messrs. BENNETT, of Ipswich.
Water-level, 125 feet down.

		FEET.
Depth of well [Drift, Crag, and London Clay, probably]		70
[London Clay]	London Clay	21
	Brown loam	8
[Reading Beds, 37½ feet.]	Loamy sand [? Oldhaven Beds]	6
	Dry red sand	6
	Running sand	19
	*Dark greenish clay	5½
	*Dark green clay, and flints	1
	To Chalk	136½
Chalk		113½
		250

* In this, and other sections, the green beds above the Chalk may belong to the Thanet Beds.

IPSWICH. Orwell Works. Ransome, Sims, & Co.
Sunk and communicated by MESSRS. BENNETT.
5 feet cylinders for 30 feet, the rest bored.
Water rose to within 11 feet of the surface. Good supply.

Made earth [? including alluvium or gravel]	about 30 FEET.
Chalk	,, 143 ,,
	173 ,,

IPSWICH. St. Peter's Iron Works (Messrs. Turner), by the water-side.
Sunk and communicated by MESSRS. BENNETT, of Ipswich.
Water rises to within 9 feet of the surface. Supply good.

		FEET.
Depth of well [made ground and alluvium probably]		15
River Drift, shingle and sand		17¾
[? Drift over 37 feet.]	Blue loamy sand	11¼
	Sharp sand	4
	Sand and marl or chalk-stone	16
	Clay	6
	To Chalk	70
Chalk		62
		132

IPSWICH. St. Peter's Quay, New Mill (Messrs. Cranfield's), just E. of the last. 1883.

Sunk and communicated by MESSRS. BENNETT, of Ipswich.

Shaft 11 feet, the rest bored.

An excellent supply of water, rising to about 8 feet from the surface.

		Ft.	Ins.
Mixed soil [made ground, &c.]		11	0
	Clean shingle	4	9
	Coarse loam and chalk-stones	1	7
	Loam	1	6
	Stiff light-coloured clay	6	0
	Red loam	1	6
	Very fine white loam	5	6
	Dark loam	10	3
	Clay	2	6
	Loam	13	3
[These beds seem to be Drift, which must fill a deep hollow in the Chalk here, that rock coming to a much higher level on all sides.]	Fine loamy sand	12	6
	Clay	1	4
	Loamy sand, coarse for top 1½ feet, the rest finer	8	6
	Clay	1	0
	Dark loamy sand	18	10
	Boulder clay, stiff, of a light-slate-colour, full of chalk-stones and large flints	3	0
	Coarse light-coloured sand, and shells	4	6
	Fine light-coloured sand	3	6
	Shingle and sand	3	0
	Light-coloured loam	4	0
	Broken-up septaria (6 inches) and boulder clay (as above)	4	0
	Red loamy sand	1	0
	Light-coloured running sand	4	0
	To Chalk	127	0
Chalk		81	0
		208	0

IPSWICH. The Union (Stoke).

Sunk and communicated by MESSRS. BENNETT.

Water salt.

To Chalk - about 60 feet.
In   „   -   „   300   „
                      ———
                      360

IPSWICH. Waterworks (St. Clement's).

Well, 17 feet, then a 12-inch bore. Supply abundant.

To Chalk - 27 feet.

KERSEY.

REV. W. B. CLARKE, *Trans. Geol. Soc.* ser. 2, vol. v., p. 374.

Diluvial clay, sandy [? at bottom] - 75 feet.

WELL-SECTIONS. 119

KIRTON. Rectory, 1876.

About 66 feet above Ordnance Datum.
Sunk and communicated by MESSRS. BENNETT, of Ipswich.
Good supply of pure water to within 64 feet of the surface.

		Ft.	Ins.
[London Clay, 110½ feet.]	Depth of well, in brown clay (the rest bored)	16	0
	Brown clay	52	0
	Rock [septaria]	1	1
	Clay	14	11
	Rock [septaria]	1	1
	Clay - nearly	5	11
	Rock [septaria]	1	6
	Clay [a specimen of rock, marked 98 feet]	13	0
	Dark loam [a specimen of brown clay, marked 110 feet, *i.e.* just below this]	5	0
[Reading Beds, 44½ feet.]	[Basement-bed?] stones and loamy gravel	1	0
	Fine loamy sand	2	0
	Mixed clay, light-coloured and dark [a specimen of brown mottled clay, marked 115 feet]	5	0
	Soft rock or marl	0	6
	Blue clay, streaked with red [specimens of brown mottled clay, grey and red mottled sandy clay, grey mottled sandy clay, and red and grey mottled clay, marked 120, 133, 135, and 137 feet]	20	6
	Red loam [specimens of red and grey mottled clay, and brown clay, marked 139 and 147 feet]	12	6
	Green clay streaked with grey [specimens of green sandy clay and green sandy clay mottled brown (2), marked 151, 153, and 155 feet]	4	0
	To Chalk	155	0
Chalk		48	0
		203	0

LANDGUARD OR LANGER FORT. 1881–1884.

11·14 feet above Ordnance Datum.
From a drawing and specimens, communicated by Lieut.-Col. B. BRINE, R.E.

Cylinders to 58 feet, the rest bored.

Very salt water at 227½ feet, suddenly rose to 9 feet below the surface of the ground.

	Ft.	Ins.
Sand and shingle. Pieces of septaria at over 36½, and over 46½ feet. Piece of calcareous tufa? at nearly 44 feet. Pieces of calcareous sandstone at over 46½, and at 48 feet. Firm irony sand at 47 feet	47	8
Clay, shingle and pieces of stone [cement-stones from the London Clay]	2	3
Hard sandstone (cement-stones, partly reddish and sandy)	1	9

120   GEOLOGY OF IPSWICH, ETC.

	Ft.	Ins.
Loamy clay, intermixed with sandstone. Specimens of brown clay, sandy clay, clayey sand, and sand ? partly hardened, and calcareous. Hard calcareous sandy stone at 54 feet	2	8
Stiff clay. Specimen of calcareous sandy stone at 54½ feet (just at the top), the others brown and grey clay	2	1
Loam, with some pieces of stone. Specimen of brown and grey clay just at top, and of brown sandy clay at over 61 feet	4	10
Stiff clay. Specimens; at 64¼ and 67 feet, dark brown and reddish clay; at 78 feet blackish and grey clay, slightly mottled brown; at 86 feet green, red, and purple clayey sand; at 86½ feet green, clayey sand, partly brownish; at 87½ feet red, and green clayey sand or sandy clay; at 88½ feet purple and greenish sandy clay; at 91 feet green sandy clay, with small green-coated flints	30	0
Flints. Specimens large and green-coated	1	3
To Chalk	92	6
Soft [? from water] white chalk with flints	115	0
Hard blocky white chalk with flints	228	0
Soft white chalk with flints	76	6
Knotty (? concretionary) white chalk, with flints } Hard white chalk, with flints	82	0
Chalk [specimen of grey flaky chalk, probably from a marly layer, at 801 feet, and of white chalk at 805-9 feet]	215	0
	809	0

It seems as if the London Clay ends with the loam, at 61¼ feet, the Reading Beds beginning with the stiff clay below, and being therefore 31¼ feet thick.

An earlier attempt (1877) at a distance of over 50 feet gave a slightly different section, and brackish water was then got at 109 feet, rose to about 9 feet below the surface, and was inexhaustible. The information, additional to the above, given by this well was as follows —

	Feet.
Shingle and sand, with fresh water	44½
London Clay. Specimens of rather sandy brown clay at 73 and 80 feet. Dark brown sandy clay at bottom	38½
Reading Beds. Specimens ; brown sandy clay with a tinge of green at 83½ and 84½ feet; brown greenish and reddish sandy clay at 85; greenish and reddish sandy clay at 87; the like, stiffer, at 88; green and brown (or red) sandy clay at 89 -	10
To Chalk	93
Chalk, with broken flints (some green-coated) at the top -	93 (?more).

Judging by the later well, from which better specimens were got, the division between the London Clay and the Reading Beds should be higher.

LEADENHEATH. The Hare and Hounds.

Sunk and communicated (from memory) by Mr. KINGSBURY, of Boxford.— F. J. B.

Loam	6 Feet.
Sand and gravel	40 ,,

MILDEN. W. of the church.

Sunk and communicated (from memory) by MR. KINGSBURY.—F. J. B.

```
         Boulder clay  -  12 FEET.
         Sand    -     -  12  ,,
                          ____
                To Chalk  24  ,,
         Chalk   -     -  80  ,,
```

MONKS ELEIGH [probably on the higher ground].
REV. W. B. CLARKE, *Trans. Geol. Soc.*, ser. 2, vol. v., p. 374.

Diluvial [Boulder] clay to chalk - 62 FEET.

NEWTON. Rogers' Farm, a mile N.E. of the village.
Sunk and communicated by MR. KINGSBURY.—F. J. B.

```
         Chalky clay       -  40 FEET.
         Sand and gravel   -  15  ,,
```

ORFORD MARSHES. About 250 yards N.W. of High Light Bridge. Just beyond the edge of Sheet 48, N.E. For Lord Rendlesham, 1879. About 6 feet above Ordnance Datum.

Sunk and communicated by MESSRS. BENNETT, of Ipswich.

A good supply of water (brackish) rises 14 inches above the surface.

		FT.	INS.
[Alluvium, 20 feet.]	{ Light [coloured] Ooze	19	0
	{ Brown Ooze	1	0
White [bluish shelly deoxidised Red] Crag		10	0
[London Clay, 106¾ feet.]	{ Clay	67	9
	{ Septaria	1	0
	{ Clay	25	0
	{ Brown clay	10	0
	{ Loamy sand [? Basement-bed]	3	0
[Reading Beds 42½ feet].	{ Mottled sand	14	0
	{ Green sand and loam	12	0
	{ Dark clay, hard and dry	12	0
	{ Mottled red and green clay	3	2
	{ Green clay and brown flints	1	3
	To Chalk	179	2
Chalk		55	10
		235	0

POLSTEAD. Burnt House Farm, 1½ miles E. of the village.

Sunk and communicated (from memory) by MR. KINGSBURY, as also was the following section.—F. J. B.

```
         Chalky clay      -  10 FEET.
         Sand and gravel  -  45  ,,
```

POLSTEAD HEATH. The Shoulder of Mutton.

```
         Stony loam -      -   15 FEET.
         Chalky clay -     -   25  ,,
         Fine buff sand, to water -  30  ,,
                                     ____
                                     70  ,,
```

RAYDON WOODHOUSE.

Sunk and communicated (from memory) by MR. WELLUM, of Raydon.—F. J. B.

  Chalky clay - - - 30 FEET.
  Red Sand (? Crag) to water - 12 ,,

RUSHMERE.

REV. W. B. CLARKE, *Trans. Geol. Soc.*, ser. 2, vol. v., p. 382.

  Loam - 14 FEET.
  Crag sand - 52 ,,

SEMER. Rectory.

Sunk and communicated by MR. PETTIT, of Hadleigh.—F. J. B.

  Chalky clay - 10 FEET.
  Sand and gravel - 10 ,,
  To Chalk - - 20 ,,
  Chalk - - 10 ,,

The REV. W. B. CLARKE notes a well at Semer as gravel 50 feet, and chalk 22 feet. (*Trans. Geol. Soc.*, ser. 2, vol. v., p. 374.)

SHOTLEY. Fison's Brickyard. 1883.

Made and communicated by MESSRS. BENNETT, of Ipswich.

Well 17 feet, the rest bored.

Water rises to within 15¼ feet of the surface, not quite pure in quality.

			FEET.
[Red Crag?]	Loose sand		17
	Dark loam		2
[London Clay,] 8 feet.	Clay		1
	[? Basement-bed] (or ? trace of Oldhaven beds.)	Light coloured blowing sand	3½
		Small pebbles	1½
[Reading Beds, 45 feet.]	Blowing sand		12½
	Dark blue clay		1½
	Light-blue clay		2
	Light-coloured loamy sand		3½
	Mottled clay		4½
	Blue clay		2
	Mottled clay		6
	Grey loam		1
	Light-coloured sand		½
	Green loamy sand		1½
	Dark brown loam		1
	Bright yellow sand		1½
	Mottled sand or loam		2
	Mottled clay		2
	Green clay		2
	Green clay and brown flints		1½

               To Chalk 70
Chalk - - - - - - - - 30
                  100

STOKE-BY-NAYLAND. In the village.

Sunk and communicated (from memory) by MR. KINGSBURY.—F. J. B.

  Brick earth - 5 FEET.
  Sand and gravel - 64 ,,

WALDRINGFIELD. Cement Works, by the River Deben, just N. of the Bush Inn. 1881.

About 8 feet above Ordnance Datum.

Sunk and communicated by Messrs. BENNETT, of Ipswich.

An excellent supply of good water, rising to within 7 feet of the surface.

		FEET.
[? Alluvium.]	Depth of [old] well	9
[London Clay?]	Light [-coloured] loam	2
	Brown clay	18
[Reading Beds]	Dark loam	2
	Blue clay	9
	Mottled clay	2
	Green sand	6
	Clay	8
	Light [-coloured] loamy sand	1
	Clay	5
	Green clay and brown flints	1
	To Chalk	63
Chalk		62
		125

It is difficult to make out the division between the London Clay and the Reading Beds.

WALTON. Garrison Springs.

Communicated by LIEUT.-COL. B. BRINE, R.E.

Water-level 18 inches above H. W. M. Good supply. Water good, but hard.

	FEET.
London Clay, with hard septaria at 36½ feet (13 inches) and at 51¼ feet (12 inches)	70
Dark loam [? Basement-bed]	1½
Running sand [? Reading Beds]	1½
	73

WESTERFIELD. Brewery.

Sunk and communicated by Messrs. BENNETT, of Ipswich.

Water-level about 105 feet down. Supply good.

		FEET.
[Drift.]	Clay and marl [? Boulder Clay]	9
	Stone and coarse sand	6
[Drift and Crag?]	Clean coarse sand	12
	Fine sand	7
	Fine grey sand	3
	Fine sand	2
	Fine loamy sand	½
	Fine running sand	1½
	Red running sand	11
[London Clay?]	Brown clay	1
	London Clay	24
[Reading Beds, 30 feet.]	Mottled red clay	8
	Light [-coloured] clay	9
	Light [-coloured] loamy sand	8
	Green clay and brown flints	5
	To Chalk	107
Chalk		80
		187

E 14651.

WHATFIELD. The Hall.

Sunk and communicated (from memory) by MR. PETTIT, of Hadleigh.—
F. J. B.

Chalky [Boulder] Clay - 60 FEET.
Chalk - - - 41 ,,

A well here is noted by the REV. W. B. CLARKE (*Trans. Geol. Soc.*, ser. 2 vol. v., p. 374) as through 40 feet of the Clay and 66 of Chalk.

WHERSTEAD.

REV. W. B. CLARKE, *Trans. Geol. Soc.*, ser. 2, vol. v., p. 382.

Gravel - 3 FEET.
Clay - 6 ,,
Crag - 40 ,,

WHITTON. Sparrow's Nest, 2 miles N. of Ipswich. 1875.

Sunk and communicated by MESSRS. BENNETT, of Ipswich.

Water rose to within 105 feet of the surface.

		FEET.
	Depth of old well -	48
	Clay (blue) -	24
	Sand (fine) -	1
[Drift and ? trace of Reading Beds.]	Blue clay -	21½
	Coarse sand -	8
	Blue clay -	4
	Hard rocky substance -	½

To Chalk 107
Chalk - - - - - 293

400

WILLIAMS TYE GREEN, S.W. of KERSEY.

Sunk and communicated (from memory) by MR. KINGSBURY, of Boxford, and from observation.—F. J. B.

	FEET.
Stony yellow clay - - - - - -	15
Very dark Boulder Clay, containing a piece of wood very little altered - - - - - -	29
Tough, green, sandy clay - - - - -	2
Shingle - - - - - - -	5
Boulder Clay - - - - - -	10
Brown sand, to water - - - - -	2
	63

WILLIAMS TYE GREEN. Marsh Farm, close by the above.

Sunk and communicated (from memory) by MR. KINGSBURY, of Boxford.—F. J. B.

Stiff yellow stony clay - 45 FEET.
Sand - - - 10 ,,
Pebbly sand, to water - 6 ,,
---
61 ,,

WOOLVERSTONE.

Rev. W. B. CLARKE, *Trans. Geol. Soc.*, ser. 2, vol. v., p. 381.

Soil	1 Feet.
Clay, with water	30 ,,
To London Clay	31 ,,

The following borings, just north of our district, were made after the publication of the Memoir descriptive of that neighbourhood (Sheet 50, S.W. of the Geological Survey Map), and an account of them is therefore given here.

LAVENHAM. Bolton and Partners, Limited (between the Railway Station and the Town). 1884.

Communicated by COL. SIR F. BOLTON, R.E.

Level of the ground 40 feet below that of the rails at the Station.
Shaft about 7 feet, the rest bored (with 18-inch cylinders 7 feet into the Chalk).
Water-level in the Gravel 16 feet down, and at the same level in the tube [from Chalk].

		FEET.
[Glacial Drift.]	Sand and gravel	60
	Flint drift	17
	To Chalk	77
Chalk, 211 feet	Soft chalk (water-bearing fissure at a depth of 174 feet)	159
	Hard chalk	
	Very hard chalk, with water at a depth of 258 feet, and with a flint-bed just below	52
		288

STOWMARKET. Messrs. Cobbold's Malting, about 100 yards W. of the Railway Station. 1884.

Bored and communicated by MESSRS. BENNETT, of Ipswich.

Water rose to within 1 foot 9 inches of the surface, several feet above the level of the river, near by.

Tubes driven 15½ feet into the Chalk.

		FEET.
Depth of well [? old]		17
[Drift and Crag ?]	Light-coloured clay	15
	Light-coloured running sand	9
	Light-coloured clay	2
	Running sand	1½
	Light-coloured loam	1½
	Very light-coloured Crag	1½
	Septaria	½
	Crag and sand	9
	Green-coated flints	½
	To Chalk	57½
Chalk		52½
		110

APPENDIX B.—TRIAL-BORINGS. (SUFFOLK.)

CAPEL. Trial-boring, in a field near to and N.W. of the Railway Station. 1876.

Made and communicated by Messrs. BENNETT, of Ipswich.

		FEET.
Subsoil		1½
[Glacial Drift?] { [Boulder] clay		22
Loam		5
White sand		2
		30½

IPSWICH. Dock Commission. Borings made at the Site of intended new Entrance Lock to the Dock (at its S.W. corner). 1878.

Communicated by MR. T. MILLER, C.E.

These borings, all within a small area, serve to show the varying character of the beds below the river, and the varying depth to the Chalk. The accompanying plan, Fig. 27, shows the positions of each boring, which could not be well expressed in words; but it should be remembered that it also shows a former state of things, the new entrance having been since made.

FIG. 27.

Plan of Borings at the Southern End of Ipswich Dock.

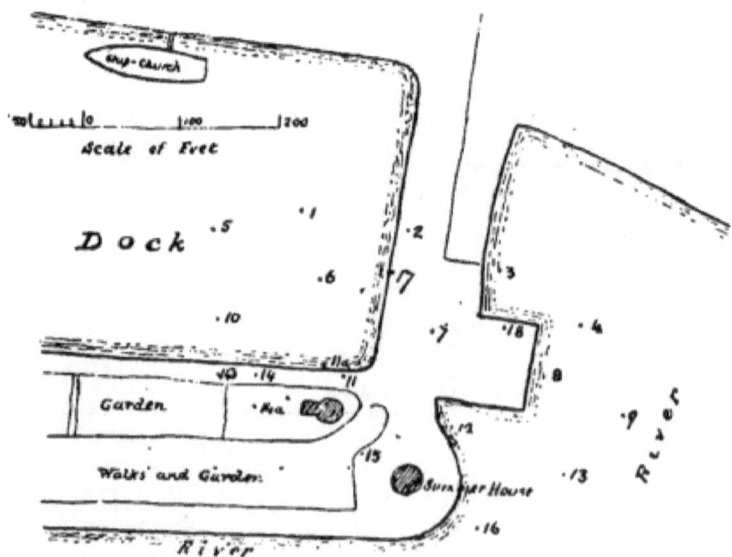

BORINGS.

1. About 1½ feet below Ordnance Datum.

	FEET.
Ooze and gravel	4½
Sand and gravel	10
Sharp sand	6
Chalk and sand	2
To Chalk	22½

2. About 13¾ feet above Ordnance Datum.

	FEET.
Made ground and mixed gravel	13½
Peat	1½
Fine gravel, with dark sand at bottom	6
Dark brown clay	3
Dark brown loam	5½
Dark sand	2½
Sand and gravel, chalky at bottom	8½
To Chalk	40½

3. About 4½ feet above Ordnance Datum.

	FEET.
Made ground and mixed gravel	10½
Ooze and gravel	2
Coarse gravel	4
Gravel and ooze	3
Fine gravel	3
Sand	2½
To Chalk, nearly	25

4. About 3 feet below Ordnance Datum.

	FEET.
River mud, with gravel mixed in lower half	8
Gravel	2
To Chalk	10

5. Over 7 feet below Ordnance Datum.

	FEET.
Ooze and gravel	2
Sand and gravel	7
To Chalk	9

6. Over 2 feet below Ordnance Datum.

	FEET.
Ooze	3
Peat	1
Gravel and sand	17
To Chalk	21

7. 13¼ feet above Ordnance Datum.

	FEET.
Made ground	9
Ooze and fine gravel	7¾
Gravel, with sand at lower part	12¼
To Chalk nearly	29

8. Nearly 1½ feet above Ordnance Datum.
>   Mixed ooze and gravel - 5¾ Feet.
>   Sand and gravel - nearly 8½ ,,
>
>   To Chalk about 14¼ ,,

9. Over 3 feet below Ordnance Datum.
>   River sand - 6 Feet.
>   Coarse gravel - 3¼ ,,
>
>   To Chalk 9¼ ,,

10. Over 3 feet below Ordnance Datum.
>   Ooze and gravel - 3 Feet.
>   Sand and gravel - 8 ,,
>
>   To Chalk 11 ,,

11. 8 feet above Ordnance Datum.
>   Abandoned after 23½ feet in sand and gravel, in which boulders of sandstone were found.

11A. 6¾ feet above Ordnance Datum.
>   Feet.
>   Ooze - 9
>   Gravel, top, 17 feet, coarse, the rest fine - 42
>   Sand - 1½
>   Sand and chalk - 2¾
>
>   To Chalk 55

12. About 9½ feet above Ordnance Datum.
>   Feet.
>   Ooze, sand, and gravel - 11½
>   Fine sand, with shingle in the upper part 9
>
>   To Chalk 20½

13. 3½ feet below Ordnance Datum.
>   Feet.
>   Mud and gravel - 2
>   Peat, the lower half with gravel - 2
>   Gravel (upper half coarse) and sand - 4
>   Fine loamy sand, bottom foot sharp sand - 7
>   Chalk and sand - 2
>
>   To Chalk 17

14 and 14A. (13¾ and over 14 feet above Ordnance Datum) did not reach Chalk, but after going through ooze and gravel, were stopped by boulders at 22 and 43 feet respectively.

14.B 13¾ feet above Ordnance Datum.
>   Feet.
>   Soil - 9
>   Ooze and gravel - 5¼
>   Dark loam - 3¾
>   Gravel, upper half coarse, lower fine - 4
>   Sand - 5
>
>   To Chalk and brown flints 27

BORINGS.

15. About 14½ feet above Ordnance Datum.

	FEET
Soil . . . . about	9½
Ooze and gravel	7
Gravel, coarse and fine . . .	48
Coarse sand	6
Pipe-clay, the lower half with coarse sand .	2
Chalk and black clay . . .	3
To Chalk	75½

16. 3½ feet above Ordnance Datum.

	FEET
Beach	1
Peat	1
Gravel [? chiefly mixed with clay] . .	4
Sand, loamy, then fine, then coarse .	12
Gravel, with sand at top part, loamy at bottom part . . .	12
To Chalk	30

17. 12 feet above Ordnance Datum.

	FEET
Made ground, mixed, chiefly gravel	13
Clean gravel	18
Soft chalk	8
	39

18. 7½ feet above Ordnance Datum.

	FEET
Made ground, mixed, chiefly gravel about	13
Gravel . . . . . "	11
Stiff chalk . . . . . "	18
	42

IPSWICH. Borings along the line of the Intercepting Sewer, from the Gasworks to the end of the London Hardway (along the left side of the Orwell).

Communicated by MR. P. BAUFF, C.E.

20. S.E. of Gasworks, and N. of Myrtle Street; and 19, S. of Myrtle Street.

Made ground (gravelly)	11	FEET.
Gravel . . .	3½ and 2½	,,

18. Junction of Clifton Road and Mile End Road.

	FEET
Made ground (gravelly) .	4
Mud [alluvium] . .	3½
Gravel . . .	5
Clay	½

17. Fork of roads north of the Cliff Brewery—

	FT.	INS.
Soil and made ground . .	4	8
Sand (18 inches) and gravel .	5	2
Black clay (? alluvial) . .	0	4

16. Road just North of the Cliff Brewery.

	Ft.	Ins.
Road material	4	0
Sand, with a foot of gravel at bottom	4	0
Fine sand	6	2
Clay (chalky)	0	5

[These last two may be Reading Beds.]

15. Close to the central part of the Cliff Brewery.

	Ft.	Ins.
Road material	2	9
Gravel, dry sand, wet sand, and gravel	7	3
Clay	0	5

14. South of the Cliff Brewery and Shipyard, at edge of shore.

	Ft.	Ins.
Road material	3	8
Black mud, with stones [alluvial]	1	7
Sand (6 inches) and hard clay [Reading Beds]	4	5

13. Below high-water mark, 5 chains southward of 14.

	Ft.	Ins.
Soft clay [? alluvial]	8	4
Chalk	0	5

12. Below high-water mark, about 4 chains S.S.W. of 13 (opposite gap).

	Ft.	Ins.
Sand and then gravel	6	8

11. Below high-water mark, 5 chains S.W. of 12.

	Ft.	Ins.
Coarse gravel, sand, and fine gravel	7	2
Blue clay [Reading Beds]	1	6

10. Below high-water mark, 11 chains from 11, by Hog Island.

	Feet.
Mud (18 inches) and soft clay [alluvium]	5½
Chalk	7½

9. Below high-water mark, 7 chains from 10, by Hog Island.

	Feet.
Mud	2
Sand	2¼
Hard clay [Reading Beds]	3¼

8. Below high-water mark, about 5 chains from 9, by S. end of Hog Island.

	Ft.	Ins.
[? Alluvium] Soft clay, sand (8 inches) and clay	5	7
[? River Drift] Sand with gravel at bottom (6 inches)	2	1

7. Below high-water mark, about 6½ chains from 8.

	Ft.	Ins.
Sand	7	0
Brown [? London] clay	2	5

6. Below high-water mark, 6 chains from 7.

	Ft.	Ins.
Sand	6	10
Gravel	1	10

5. Below high-water mark, about 6 chains from 6.

	Ft.	Ins.
Mud [alluvial]	1	0
Loam and gravel	5	2
Loamy clay and hard clay (18 inches) [? London Clay]	4	6

BORINGS.	131

4. Below high-water mark, 5 chains from 5 [? included in the Sewerage Outfall Works].

	FEET.
Loam with a little gravel	5
Soft clay	1½
Gravel	1
[? London Clay] Soft clay, wet clay (6 inches), and hard clay	3½

3. On the London Hardway, below high-water mark [? included in the Sewerage Outfall Works], about 6 chains from 4.

	FEET.
Gravel [pathway of the "hard"]	1½
Mud [alluvial]	4
Hard brown [? London] clay	2½

2. On the London Hardway, about 5½ chains above low-water mark

	FT.	INS.
Gravel [pathway of the "hard"]	2	8
[Alluvium] { Mud	9	0
Dark soft peat	2	3
Dark gravel	0	6

1. On the London Hardway, less than 3 chains above low-water mark.

	FT.	INS.
Gravel [pathway of the "hard"]	3	0
Mud [alluvial]	6	0
Gravel, top foot fine, light-coloured and with shells, the rest dark	1	10

IPSWICH. Viaduct of the Felixstow Railway, Spring Road. Four trial borings, for N. and S. piers and abutments. 1876?

Communicated by MR. H. JONES, C.E.

Level of road at viaduct about 46 feet.

Soil	about 2 FEET.
London Clay	about 20 to 22 ,,
Hard sand and gravel	12 or 13 ,,

ORWELL RIVER. Three borings at Butterman's Bay, about 2 miles below Pin Mill.

Communicated by MR. T. MILLER, Engineer to the Ipswich Dock Commission.

At the bottom of the river, 22 feet below low water.

Gravel, not bottomed - 8 FEET.

WALTON BATTERY, northern end. 1872.

Communicated by LIEUT.-COLONEL B. BRINE, R.E.

	FEET.
Mud and shingle	5
Clean shingle	5
Stiff blue clay	2½
Shell and sand	8
Hard matter, like sandstone	½

21

APPENDIX C.

SUPPLEMENTARY NOTES TO OTHER MEMOIRS.

1. SECTIONS AT SUDBURY. (SHEET 47.)

In 1879, the year after the publication of the Memoir on Sheet 47, I had occasion to re-visit Sudbury, and then got some additional information of sections in that town, only just west of the border of the district described in the present Memoir. It will be well, therefore, to give this information here, as it will probably be a long time before a second edition of the Memoir on Sheet 47 is called for. It may be noted that in that Memoir some Sudbury sections that are just within the margin of Sheet 48 N.W. are described.

The new Victoria Brickyard, a little N. of Ballingdon Windmill, showed the following beds:—

Post-Glacial Drift. { Brown-bedded brickearth, at the lower part, with irregular beddings of sand; up to 10 feet.
Gravel and sand; several feet.

The beds were seen to rise S.W. at as much as 15° (with only a little gravel below the brickearth generally), and then Thanet Sand (pink sand and clayey green sand), was shown, up to about 5 feet thick, but much disturbed, with the Chalk rising up very irregularly. Just S., alongside the lane, the Thanet Sand was cut into at the surface.

FIG. 28.
Section in the Chalk Pit at Sudbury Waterworks. 1879.

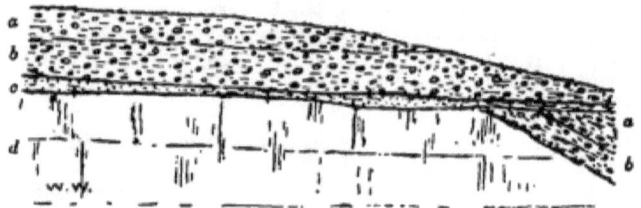

a. Pinkish Boulder Clay.
b. Pale grey   „   „
c. Green sand: base of Thanet Beds, up to more than 2 feet in parts of the pit.
d. Chalk.

The pit close to, and southward of, the Waterworks (see p. 52 of Memoir), was more open, and the interesting section shown in Fig. 28 was shown.

It will be seen that at the lower end (towards the valley), the green base-bed of the Thanet Sand has been washed, or dragged, over the Drift (that forms part of the mass that plunges down to the bottom of the pit), in such a way as to be perfectly even and continuous with that part of the bed which is in place; so that it is impossible to mark where the re-constructed part begins.

At the more easterly of the brickyards on the hill N.E. of Sudbury (p. 53 of Memoir), the pit, having been cut further back, showed a cap of pale Boulder Clay, up to 6 feet thick, lying evenly on the brickearth, at the highest (central) part of the section.

The gap between the two pits at the N.E. edge of the town, by the road to Waldingfield (Fig. 15, p. 54 of Memoir), had been reduced by a half. This extension (of the N.E. pit), justified the broken lines in the figure, which were introduced to show the probable connection of the beds in the two pits. In the Victoria Pit, then cut further back, I saw a layer of Boulder Clay, up to more than 2 feet thick, near the bottom of the gravel No. 3 at one part.

The pit eastward of the Cemetery (pp. 55, 56, and Fig. 17 of Memoir), had been carried down to the Chalk, so that the bottom part of the section was as follows:—

Thanet Beds. { 6. Fine soft sand, the upper half grey, the lower pinkish; about 9½ feet.
7. Clayey greensand; about 1¼ feet.

8. Chalk.

Moreover, the Crag sand (4), reached up to a thickness of 15 feet, at the western end, with a little Boulder Clay on it.

At the Grove, the great brickyard at Balingdon (pp. 57, 58, of Memoir), the Boulder Clay No. 4 was seen to be split into two, by a wedge-shaped mass of gravel (with intercalated Boulder Clay), up to 10 feet thick, there being but little Boulder Clay below this. The upper part of the clay was then mostly darker.

Probably there have been many further improvements in the sections here, perhaps about the finest in any inland spot in East Anglia, showing not only the Glacial Drift, in great complexity; but also a trace of Red Crag, Eocene beds, and the top part of the Chalk.   W.W.

2. ANALYSES OF SEPTARIA FROM COLCHESTER. (SHEET 48, S.W.)

The following analyses of Septaria from the London Clay of Colchester,* in the tract to the south, may be of interest. They were not seen in time to be inserted in the Memoir on 48 S.W.

Carbonate of lime		67·50		68·70
Silicate of Alumina	14·40 } 22·10	{ 12·80	21·40
Alumina Silica	7·70		8·60	
Carbonate of iron		4·60		
Uncombined alumina		1·10		1·30
Bitumen and water		0·20		0·40
Manganese carbonate				0·71
Magnesia carbonate				2·41
		95·5		94·92

Traces of potash and titanic acid were found in both, but no calcic phosphate.

The author remarks that FUCHS has found titanic acid in clay from the London district, but no reference is given.   W.H.D.

* C. M. KERSTEN.—Untersuchung zweier Abänderungen hydraulischen Kalksteines aus der Nähe von Colchester (Essex) in England. *Journ. prakt. Chem.* bd. xxv., pp. 317–319 [1842].

APPENDIX D.—LIST OF WORKS ON THE GEOLOGY AND PALÆONTOLOGY OF SUFFOLK.

The following List (with 345 entries of works by 122 authors) refers to the whole of the county and not merely to that part of it described in this Memoir:—

1. INDEX OF AUTHORS, WITH THE NUMBERS AFFIXED TO THEIR WORKS.

Accum, F., 31.
Alexander, Capt. H., 59, 68, 75, 83, 84.
Allman, Prof. G. J., 231.
Anon., 28, 43, 168, 222, 261, 283, 312, 313.

Bayne, A. D., 232.
Bell, A., 200, 201, 213, 223-225, 233, 234.
Bell, R. [G.], 168, 225, 234, 307.
Belt, T., 262, 272.
Bennett, F. J., 2, 6, 8, 10, 11, 18, 20a.
Blake, J. H., 5, 6, 10, 13, 14, 14a, 18, 20b, 273, 284, 296.
Bowerbank, J. S., 111.
Brady, H. B., 172.
Brown, J., 60, 134.
Bruff, P., 135.
Buckland, Prof. W., 103.
Bunbury, Sir H., 35.
Burrows, H. A., 258.
Busk, Prof. G., 132.

Carpenter, Dr. P., 160.
Charlesworth, E., 46-48, 51, 53-58, 61, 69, 92, 192, 192a, 235, 235a, 283.
Chester, G. F., 121.
Clarke, Rev. W. B., 62-64, 76, 109.
Conybeare, Rev. W. D., 34.
Coode, Sir J., 259.
Crisp, Dr. H., 202.
Crowfoot, W. M., 192b, 287.
Cullum, Sir J., 23.

Dalton, W. H., 3, 4, 7, 9, 290, 297, 311.
Darwin, C., 122.
Davidson, T., 112.
Dawkins, Prof. W. B., 193, 236, 285, 291.
De Luc, J. A., 27.
Dennis, Rev. J. B. P., 126.
De Rance, C. E., 260.
Desnoyers, —, 65.
Dowson, E. T., 192b, 288.
Duncan, Prof. P. M., 226, 237, 246.

Evans, J., 136, 143, 194, 238.

Falconer, Dr. H., 127, 161.
Fisher, Rev. O., 169, 170, 175, 203, 204, 292.
Fitch, R., 49.
Flower, J. W., 176, 205.

Flower, Prof. W. H., 249, 263, 274.
Forbes, Prof. E., 113, 114.
Frere, J., 26.

Geikie, Prof. J., 250.
Gillingwater, E., 24.
Glyde, J., 128.
Godwin-Austen, R. A. C., 171, 195.
? Gowing, —, 310.
Gunn, Rev. J., 130a, 177-179, 196-196b, 206, 214, 214a, 226a, 247, 251, 264, 298, 314.

Haime, J., 106.
Harmer, F. W., 180, 199, 206a, 230, 243, 252, 275, 281, 282.
Harrison, W. J., 299.
Hele, N. F., 215.
Henslow, Prof. J. S., 93, 94, 97-99.
Henslow, Prof., 276.
Herapath, T. J., 110.
Hughes, Prof. T. McK., 239, 285a.
Hull, Prof. E., 180a.
Hurwood, E., 140.
Huxley, Prof. H. T., 151.

Jecks, C., 206b, 216.
Jeffreys, Dr. J. G., 143a.
Jenyns, Rev. L., 181.
Jones, Rev. H., 207.
Jones, Prof. T. R., 129, 152, 172, 240.

Kendall, P. F., 305.
King, Rev. S. W., 182.
Knights, —, 261.

Lankester, Prof. E. R., 147, 153, 154, 162, 163, 183, 184, 197, 208-210, 217, 218, 277, 293.
Loume, B. T., 148.
Lubbock, Sir J., 164.
Lyell, Sir C., 42, 44, 66, 70, 71, 77-85, 115, 116, 149.

Mackie, S. J., 144.
Maw, G., 155, 185-188, 198, 211.
Mitchell, Dr. J., 67.
Milne-Edwards, Prof. A., 106.

Nall, J. G., 173.
Newton, E. T., 20, 294, 306.
Norton, H., 265.

Owen, Sir R., 80, 86, 89, 90, 93, 124, 145, 219.

Palmer, C. J., 241.
Parker, W. K., 152, 172, 240.
Pattison, S. R., 150.
Penning, W. H., 1, 16, 266.
Phear, Sir J. B., 125.
Phillips, Prof. J., 117.
Phillips, W., 34.
Pickering, Rev. R., 22.
Prestwich, Prof. J., 104, 107, 119, 141, 142, 156, 165, 227, 300, 301.
Prigg, H., 189, 212, 302, 308.

Raynbird, H., 100.
Redman, J. B., 157.
Reid, C., 12, 19.
Reid, W. C., 267.
Ringler, Thomson, T. G., 105.
Robberds, J. W., 37.
Rose, C. B., 96, 137, 146.

Scott, G., 242.
Seekamp, N., 28.
Skertchly, S. B. J., 11, 15, 17, 285b, 289.
Smith, W., 29, 32, 33.
Sowerby, J., 27a, 30, 33a, 34a, 36a.

Sowerby, J. D., 36a, 37a, 82a.
Symonds, Rev. W. S., 268.

Taylor, J. E., 212a, 222, 228, 248, 253-255, 269, 278, 278a.
Taylor, R. C., 36, 38-41.
Trimmer, J., 131.

Voelcker, Dr. A., 138.

Wake, Dr. R., 87.
Walcott, Rev. M. E. C., 139.
Whitaker, W., 1-6, 9, 16, 18, 256, 279, 309, 310.
White, W., 123.
Wiggins, J., 101.
Wood, S. V., 45, 72-74, 81, 82, 88, 91, 102, 108, 118, 120, 130, 133, 174, 243, 244, 257, 281, 289a, 303.
Wood, S. V., Junr., 158-159a, 166, 174, 190-191a, 199, 220, 221, 230, 243, 245, 270, 280-282, 295, 303.
Woodward, B. B., 296a.
Woodward, Dr. H., 167.
Woodward, H. B., 19, 271, 286, 304.
Woodward, S., 50, 52.
Wright, T., 21.

Young, A., 25.

2. GEOLOGICAL SURVEY PUBLICATIONS.

Maps.

1. Sheet 47 (small part on N.E. Clare, Long Melford, Sudbury). By W. WHITAKER and W. H. PENNING. 1881. Drift Edition, 1884.
2. Sheet 48, N.W. (all but S. part: Hadleigh, Ipswich, Nayland). By W. WHITAKER and F. J. BENNETT (chiefly). 1882.
3. Sheet 48, N.E. (all but S.W. part: Felixstow, Ipswich). By W. WHITAKER and W. H. DALTON. 1882.
4. Sheet 49, S. (Aldborough). By W. WHITAKER and W. H. DALTON (chief part). 1883.
5. Sheet 49, N. (Southwold). By W. WHITAKER and J. H. BLAKE. 1883.
6. Sheet 50, S.W. (Bildeston, Lavenham, Mendlesham, Needham Market, Stowmarket). By W. WHITAKER, F. J. BENNETT, and J. H. BLAKE (chiefly). 1881.
7. Sheet 50, S.E. (Debenham, Framlingham, Saxmundham, Woodbridge). By W. H. DALTON. 1883.
8. Sheet 50, N.W. (all but N. part: Botesdale, Eye, Ixworth). By F. J. BENNETT. 1883.
9. Sheet 50, N.E. (all but N.W. corner: Halesworth). By W. WHITAKER, W. H. DALTON (chiefly), and F. J. BENNETT. 1884.
10. Sheet 51, S.E. (all but W. part: Bury St. Edmunds). By F. J. BENNETT and J. H. BLAKE. 1882.
11. Sheet 51, N.E. (all but W. part: Mildenhall, Thetford). By F. J. BENNETT and S. B. J. SKERTCHLY. 1883.
12. Sheet 66, S.E. (small part on S.E. Beccles, Bungay). By C. REID. 1881.
13. Sheet 67, S. (greater part: Lowestoft). By J. H. BLAKE. 1882.
14. Sheet 67, N. (small part on S.). By J. H. BLAKE. 1881.

Horizontal Section.

14A. Sheet 128. Section of the Suffolk Cliffs at Kessingland and Pakefield, and at Corton. By J. H. BLAKE. 1884.

Memoirs.

15. The Geology of the Fenland. By S. B. J. SKERTCHLY. 1877.
16. The Geology of the N.W. part of Essex, and the N.E. part of Herts, with Parts of Cambridgeshire and Suffolk (Sheet 47). 1878. (Part). By W. WHITAKER and W. H. PENNING.

17. On the Manufacture of Gun-flints, the Methods of Excavating for Flint, the Age of Palæolithic Man, etc., by S. B. J. SKERTCHLY. 1879.
18. The Geology of the Neighbourhood of Stowmarket (Sheet 50, S.W.). By W. WHITAKER, F. J. BENNETT, and J. H. BLAKE. 1881.
19. The Geology of the Country around Norwich (Part: includes 66, S.E.), by H. B. WOODWARD and C. REID. 1881.
20. NEWTON, E. T.—The Vertebrata of the Forest Bed Series of Norfolk and Suffolk, 1882.
20A. The Geology of the Country around Diss. (Sheet 50 N.W.) By F. J. BENNETT. 1884.
20B. Explanation of Horizontal Sections, Sheet 128 [See 14A]. By J. H. BLAKE. 1885.

3. LIST OF BOOKS, PAPERS, ETC. CHRONOLOGICALLY ARRANGED.

Some general works entered in Appendix I. of The Geology of the London Basin, Part 1. (*Geological Survey Memoirs*, vol. iv., 1872) may refer to Suffolk.

1668.

21. WRIGHT, T.—A curious and exact Relation of a Sand-flood, which hath lately overwhelmed a great tract of Land in County of Suffolk. *Phil. Trans*, vol. iii., no. 37, p. 722.

1745.

22. PICKERING, REV. R.—A Letter concerning the Manuring of Land with fossil shells [Woodbridge]. *Phil. Trans.*, vol. xliii., no. 474, p. 191.

1784.

23. CULLUM, SIR J.—The History and Antiquities of Hawstead in the County of Suffolk. [Note of Soils, and Account of Well at Hardwick, p. 230.] 4to. London. Ed. 2 in 1813.

1790.

24. GILLINGWATER, E.—An Historical Account of the Ancient Town of Lowestoft, in the County of Suffolk, &c. [Changes of the Coast &c. noticed, pp. 23-32, 44-49.] 4to. London.

1794.

25. YOUNG, A.—General View of the Agriculture of the County of Suffolk [Map and Account of Soils]. 4to. London. Another Ed. in 8vo. n 1797.

1800.

26. FRERE, J.—Account of Flint-Weapons discovered at Hoxne in Suffolk. *Archæologia*, vol. xiii., p. 204. Reprinted by PRESTWICH, 1861 (No. 141).

1811.

27. DE LUC, J. A.—Geological Travels. Translated from the French MS. 8vo. London. Vol. ii., pp. 2–8, 16–18 (refers to waste of coast).

1812–15.

27a. SOWERBY, J.—The Mineral Conchology of Great Britain, vol. i.

1814.

28. ANON.—Inquirenda about Ipswich Spa Waters [mostly quotation from an old book]. *The East Anglian*, p. 60. Reply by H. SZEKAMP, p. 110.

1816.

29. SMITH, W.—Strata identified by organized Fossils. 4to. Lond. (Suffolk, pp. 2, 5).
30. SOWERBY, J.—The Mineral Conchology of Great Britain, vol. ii., pp. 13?, 16–18?.

1819.

31. ACCUM, F.—Guide to the Chalybeate Spring of Thetford. 8vo. London. (Analysis of the water in *Phil. Mag.*, vol. liii., p. 359.) [Norfolk or Suffolk.]

32. SMITH, W.—Geological View and Section through Suffolk to Ely [from Bawdsey].

33. ———.—Geological Map of Suffolk.

1819–22.

33a. SOWERBY, J.—The Mineral Conchology of Great Britain, vol. iii.

1822.

34. CONYBEARE, REV. W. D., and W. PHILLIPS.—Outlines of the Geology of England and Wales. 8vo. London.

1822, 23.

34a. SOWERBY, J.—The Mineral Conchology of Great Britain, vol. iv.

1824.

35. BUNBURY, SIR H.—On the Strata observed in boring at Mildenhall in Suffolk. *Trans. Geol. Soc.*, ser. 2, vol. i., p. 379.

36. TAYLOR, R. [C. ?]—On the Alluvial Strata and on the Chalk of of Norfolk and Suffolk. *Ibid.*, p. 374.

1824, 25.

36a. SOWERBY, J. and J. D.—The Mineral Conchology of Great Britain, vol. v.

1826.

37. ROBBERDS, J. W.—Geological and Historical Observations on the Eastern Vallies of Norfolk. 8vo. *London* and *Norwich*. (Refers also to Lothingland, in Suffolk.)

1826–29.

37a. SOWERBY, J. and J. D.—The Mineral Conchology of Great Britain, vol. vi.

1827.

38. TAYLOR, R. C.—On the Geology of East Norfolk . . . [refers to Suffolk]. *Phil. Mag.*, ser. 3, vol. i., pp. 277, 346. Reprinted, with additions, in a separate form, with the following two.

39. ———.—On the Natural Embankments formed against the German Ocean, on the Norfolk and Suffolk Coast, and the Silting up of some of its Æstuaries. *Phil. Mag.*, ser. 3, vol. i., p. 295.

40. ———.—On the Geological Features of the Eastern Coast of England . . . *Ibid.*, p. 327.

1828.

41. TAYLOR, R. C.—Review of Martin's 'Geological Memoir on Western Sussex' and Buckland's 'Formation of the Valley of Kingsclere, &c.' [Refers to Suffolk.] *Mag. Nat. Hist.*, vol. i., p. 249.

1830.

42. LYELL, [SIR] C.—Principles of Geology, vol. i. 8vo. London. (Waste of coast, pp. 271–275.) (Many later editions.)

1831.

43. ANON. (G. M.)—A Black Mineral Substance found in Clay [Section near Lowestoft]. *Mag. Nat. Hist.*, vol. iv., p. 191.

1833.

44. LYELL [SIR] C.—Principles of Geology, vol. iii. (Crag, pp. 171–182.) 8vo. London. Many later editions.

1834.

45. WOOD, S. V.—[On Lacustrine Formations, Suffolk.] *Mag. Nat. Hist.*, vol. vii., p. 274. (Refers to Stutton.)

1835.

46. CHARLESWORTH, E.—On the Crag of part of Essex and Suffolk. *Proc. Geol. Soc.*, vol. ii., no. 41, p. 195.

47. ———.—Observations on the Crag-formation and its Organic Remains: with a View to establish a Division of the Tertiary Strata overlying the London Clay in Suffolk. *Phil. Mag.*, ser. 3, vol. vii., p. 81.

48. ———.—Reply to Mr. Woodward's Remarks on the Coralline Crag; with Observations on certain Errors which may affect the determination of the Age of Tertiary Deposits. *Ibid.*, p. 464.

49. FITCH. R.—On the Coralline Crag of Ramsholt and Orford. *Ibid.*, p. 463.

50. WOODWARD, S.—Some Remarks upon the Crag Formation of Norfolk and Suffolk. *Ibid.*, p. 353.

1836.

51. CHARLESWORTH, E.—On the Crag of Suffolk, and on the Fallacies connected with the Method now usually employed for ascertaining the relative Age of Tertiary Deposits. *Phil. Mag.*, ser. 3, vol. viii., p. 529. See also (under different title), *Edin. New Phil. Journ.*, vol. xxii., p. 110, *Rep. Brit. Assoc.* for 1836, *Mag. Nat. Hist.*, vol. ix., p. 537. (Abstract. ? in full in *Records of General Science*, vol. iv., p. 465.)

52. WOODWARD, S.—On the Crag Formation; in answer to Mr. Charlesworth's "Reply." *Phil. Mag.*, ser. 3, vol. viii., p. 138.

1837.

53. CHARLESWORTH, E.—A Notice of the Remains of Vertebrated Animals found in the Tertiary Beds of Norfolk and Suffolk. *Rep. Brit. Assoc.* for 1836, *Sections*, p. 84 (in full in 1838, *see* 61).

54. ———.—Observations on the Crag, and on the Fallacies involved in the present System of Classification of Tertiary Deposits. *Phil. Mag.*, ser. 3, vol. x, p. 1.

55. ———.—Notice of the Occurrence of Voluta Lamberti on the Suffolk Coast; with Observations upon its Claim to rank with existing Species. *Mag. Nat. Hist.*, ser. 2, vol. i., p. 35.

56. ———.—Observations upon Voluta Lamberti, with a Description of a gigantic Species of Terebratula from the Coralline Crag. *Ibid.*, p. 90.

57. ———.—Notice of a new Fossil Shell from the Coast of Suffolk. *Ibid.*, p. 218.

58. ———.—Notice of the Teeth of Carcharias megalodon occurring in the Red Crag of Suffolk. *Ibid.*, p. 225.

1838.

59. ALEXANDER, CAPT. [H.]—Letter explanatory of casts of portions of Mastodon teeth from the crag, and on the occurrence of a particular bed containing Echini in the coralline crag at Sudbourne. *Proc. Geol. Soc.*, vol. iii., no. 59, p. 10.

60. BROWN, J.—Bones of Mammalia in the Crag. *Mag. Nat. Hist.*, ser. 2, vol. ii., p. 346.

61. CHARLESWORTH, E.—A Notice of the Remains of Vertebrated Animals occurring in the Tertiary Beds of Norfolk and Suffolk. *Ibid.*, p. 40.

62. CLARKE, REV. W. B.—Note on the Crag Beds of Suffolk and Essex. *Ibid.*, p. 162.

63. ———.—Letter in reference to the alleged occurrence of the bones of terrestrial Mammalia in the red and coralline Crag of Suffolk. *Ibid.*, p. 224.

64. ———.—Letter on the Non-identity of Suffolk Diluvium and Crag. *Ibid.*, p. 285.

65. DESNOYERS, —.—Considerations upon the position in the Tertiary System to which the Faluns of the Loire and the Crag of England ought to be referred; and upon the difficulty of determining their relative age solely by the law of the proportional number of fossil species analogous to species now in existence. *Ibid.*, p. 111. Translated from *Bull. Soc. Géol. France*, t. viii., p. 203 (1837).

66. LYELL, [SIR] C.—Outline of the Geology. Pp. xx., xxi. of J. Gage's "History and Antiquities of Suffolk. Thingoe Hundred." Fol. *London*.
67. MITCHELL, DR. J.—On the Drift from the Chalk and the Strata below the Chalk in the counties of Norfolk, Suffolk, etc. . . . *Proc. Geol. Soc.*, vol. iii., no. i., p. 3.

1839.

68. ALEXANDER, (CAPT.) H.—Teeth of the Mastodon. *Mag. Nat. Hist.*, ser. 2, vol. iii., p. 466.
69. CHARLESWORTH, E. — Illustrated Geological Notices. 1. On the discovery of a Portion of an Opossum's Jaw in the London Clay near Woodbridge, Suffolk. 2. On some Fossil Teeth of the Genus Lamna from the same Deposit. *Mag. Nat. Hist.*, ser. 2, vol. iii., p. 448.
70. LYELL, [SIR] C.—[Letter on the Crag.] *Bull. Soc. Géol. France*, t. x., p. 321.
71. ———.—On the Relative Ages of the Tertiary Deposits commonly called "Crag," in the Counties of Norfolk and Suffolk. *Mag. Nat. Hist.*, ser. 2, vol. iii., p. 213. Long abstract in *Proc. Geol. Soc.*, vol. iii., no. 63, p. 126.
72. WOOD, S. V.—Descriptions of the Species of the Genus Lima, from the Coralline Crag, in his Cabinet. *Mag. Nat. Hist.*, ser. 2, vol. iii., p. 323.
73. ———.—Letter announcing the discovery of Fossil Quadrumanous Remains near Woodbridge, Suffolk. *Ibid.*, p. 444. With a Description of the Fossil mentioned in the preceding Letter, by [SIR] R. OWEN, p. 446.
74. ———.—On the Fossil Shells of the Crag. *Ibid.*, p. 460.

1840.

75. ALEXANDER, CAPT. H.—The Soils of East Suffolk considered Geologically. 8vo. *Woodbridge*.
76. CLARKE, REV. W. B.—On the Geological Structure and Phænomena of the County of Suffolk, and its Physical Relations with Norfolk and Essex. *Trans. Geol. Soc.*, ser. 2, vol. v., p. 359.
77. LYELL, [SIR] C.—On Remains of Mammalia in the Crag and London Clay of Suffolk. *Rep. Brit. Assoc.* for 1839, *Sections*, p. 69.
78. ———.—On the discovery of Fossil Teeth of a Leopard Bear and other animals in a Crag Pit at Newbourn in Suffolk. *Ann. Nat. Hist.*, vol. iv., p. 186.
79. ———.—On the occurrence of Fossil Quadrumanous Marsupial and other Mammalia in the London Clay near Woodbridge in Suffolk. *Ibid.*, p. 189.
80. OWEN, [SIR] R.—Description of the Mammalian Remains found at Kyson in Suffolk . . . . *Ibid.*, p. 191.
81. WOOD, S. V.—On the Fossil Shells of the Crag (continued). *Mag. Nat. Hist.*, ser. 2, vol. iv., pp. 230, 294.
82. ———.—A Catalogue of Shells from the Crag. *Ann. Nat. Hist.*, vol. vi., p. 243.

1840-46.

82a. SOWERBY, J. and J. D. ?—The Mineral Conchology of Great Britain, vol. vii.

1841.

83. ALEXANDER, CAPT. [H.]—On the Annual Destruction of Land at Easton Bavent Cliff, near Southwold. *Proc. Geol. Soc.*, vol. iii., no. 79, p. 445.
84. ———.—Treatise on the nature and properties of the Soils of Norfolk, Suffolk, and Essex, chemically and geologically considered, in relation to agricultural purposes: including the Prize Essay upon the nature and properties of the Soils of East Suffolk (see 1840). 8vo. *London* and *Woodbridge*.
85. LYELL, [SIR] C.—On the Faluns of the Loire, &c. . . . . . . and on the relative age of the Faluns and Crag of Suffolk. *Proc. Geol. Soc.*, vol. iii., no. 79, p. 437.

86. OWEN, [SIR] R.—Description of some Molar Teeth from the Eocene Sand at Kyson in Suffolk, indicative of a new Species of Hyracotherium. *Ann. Nat. Hist.*, vol. viii., p. 1.

1842.

87. WAKE, DR. B.—Southwold and its Vicinity, Ancient and Modern. (Chap. x., pp. 211-217, Geology and Fossils.) 8vo. *London*.

88. WOOD, S. V.—A Catalogue of Shells from the Crag (continued). *Ann. Nat. Hist.*, vol. ix., pp. 455, 527.

1843.

89. OWEN, [SIR] R.—Report on the British Fossil Mammalia. *Rep. Brit. Assoc.* for 1842, p. 54.

1844.

90. OWEN, [SIR] R.—Report on the British Fossil Mammalia (continued). *Rep. Brit. Assoc.* for 1843, p. 208.

91. WOOD, S. V.—Descriptive Catalogue of the Zoophytes from the Crag. *Ann. Nat. Hist.*, vol. xiii., p. 10.

1845.

92. CHARLESWORTH, E.—On the Occurrence of the Genus Physeter (or Sperm Whale) in the Red Crag of Felixstow. *Proc. Geol. Soc.*, vol. iv., no. 99, p. 286, and *Quart. Journ. Geol. Soc.*, vol. i., p. 40.

93. HENSLOW, PROF. J. S.—On Concretions in the Red Crag at Felixstow, Suffolk. With an Appendix consisting of a description of the Fossil Tympanic Bones referable to four distinct species of Balæna, by [SIR] R. OWEN. *Proc. Geol. Soc.*, vol. iv., no. 99, p. 281, and *Quart. Journ. Geol. Soc.*, vol. i., p. 35.

1846.

94. HENSLOW, PROF. J. S.—On Nodules, apparently Coprolitic, from the Red Crag, etc. *Rep. Brit. Assoc.* for 1845, *Sections*, p. 51.

95. OWEN, [SIR] R.—A History of British Fossil Mammals and Birds, 8vo. *London*.

96. ROSE, C. B.—On the Occurrence of a Fossil Petro-tympanic Bone of a Whale from the Crag near Ipswich. *Quart. Journ. Geol. Soc.*, vol. ii., p. 32.

1848.

97. HENSLOW, REV. PROF. J. S.—On Detritus derived from the London Clay and deposited in the Red Crag. *Rep. Brit. Assoc.* for 1847, *Sections*, p. 64.

98. ———.—On Fossil Phosphates. *Gardeners' Chronicle*, p. 180.

99. ———.—On the Phosphate Nodules of Felixstow in Suffolk. *Ibid.*, p. 764.

100. RAYNBIRD, H.—On the Farming of Suffolk [with Remarks on the Soils, &c. and Map]. *Journ. R. Agric. Soc.*, vol. viii., p. 261.

101. WIGGINS, J.—On Fossil Bones found in the Crag of Suffolk. *Quart. Journ. Geol. Soc.*, vol. iv., p. 294.

102. WOOD, S. V.—The Crag Mollusca, or, Description of Shells from the Middle and Upper Tertiaries of the East of England. Part 1. Univalves. *Palæontograph. Soc.*

1849.

103. BUCKLAND, REV. PROF. W.—On the Causes of the general Presence of Phosphates in the Strata of the Earth and in all fertile soils; with Observations on Pseudo-Coprolites. (Brit. Assoc.) *Journ. R. Agric. Soc.*, vol. x., p. 520.

104. PRESTWICH, [PROF.] J.—On some Fossiliferous Beds overlying the Red Crag at Chillesford, near Orford, Suffolk. *Quart. Journ. Geol. Soc.*, vol. v., p. 345.

105. RINGLER-THOMSON, T. G.—On the Position in which Shells are found in the Red Crag. *Ibid.*, p. 345.

1850.

106. MILNE-EDWARDS, PROF. A., and J. HAIME.—A Monograph of British Fossil Corals. Part I. (Tertiary and Cretaceous.) *Palæontograph. Soc.*

107. PRESTWICH, [PROF.] J.—On the Structure of the Strata between the London Clay and the Chalk. Part I. The Basement-bed of the London Clay. *Quart. Journ. Geol. Soc.*, vol. vi., p. 252. (Suffolk, pp. 271-273.)

108. WOOD, S. V.—A Monograph of the Crag Mollusca, ... Part II. Bivalves (No. 1, pp. 1-150, pls. i.-xii.) *Palæontograph. Soc.* [? Not really published until 1851.]

1851

109. CLARKE, REV. W. B.—A few Remarks upon the Crag of Suffolk. *Ann. Nat. Hist.*, ser. 2, vol. viii., p. 205.

110. HERAPATH, T. J.—Some Observations on the Chemical Composition and Agricultural Value of the Fossil Bones and Pseudo-Coprolites of the Crag. *Journ. R. Agric. Soc.*, vol. xii., p. 91.

1852.

111. BOWERBANK, J. S.—On the probable Dimensions of Carcharodon Magalodon from the Crag. *Ann. Nat. Hist.*, ser. 2, vol. ix., p. 120.

112. DAVIDSON, T.—A Monograph of British Tertiary Brachiopoda. *Palæontograph. Soc.*

113. FORBES, PROF. E.—Monograph of the Echinodermata of the British Tertiaries. *Ibid.*

114. ———.—On the Echinodermata of the Crag (abstract). *Rep. Brit. Assoc.* for 1851, *Sections*, p. 58.

115. LYELL, SIR C.—On the Tertiary Strata of Belgium and French Flanders. *Quart. Journ. Geol. Soc.*, vol. viii., p. 277. (Refers to Suffolk.)

116. ———.—On the Occurrence of a Stratum of Stones covered with Barnacles in the Red Crag at Wherstead, near Ipswich. *Rep. Brit. Assoc.* for 1851, *Sections*, p. 65.

117. PHILLIPS, PROF. J.—On the Structure of the Crag. *Ibid.*, p. 67.

1853.

118. WOOD, S. V.—A Monograph of the Crag Mollusca, ... Continuation of Bivalves. (Part 2. No. 2. Pp. 151-216, Pls. xiii.-xx.) *Palæontograph. Soc.*

1854.

119. PRESTWICH, [PROF.] J.—On the Structure of the Strata between the London Clay and the Chalk in the London and Hampshire Tertiary Systems. Part II. The Woolwich and Reading Series. *Quart. Journ. Geol. Soc.*, vol. x., p. 75. (Suffolk, pp. 92, 93.)

120. WOOD, S. V.—On some Tubular Cavities in the Coralline Crag at Sudbourn and Gedgrave near Orford. *Phil. Mag.*, ser. 4, vol. vii., p. 320.

1855.

121. CHESTER, G. F.—A Brief Sketch of the Antiquities of the Valleys of the Waveney and Yare. (Refers to implements from Hoxne.) *Norf. Arch.*, vol. iv., p. 310.

122. DARWIN, C.—A Monograph on the Fossil Balanidæ and Verrucidæ of Great Britain. *Palæontograph. Soc.*

123. WHITE, W.—History Gazetteer and Directory of Suffolk (Soils, pp. 43, 44). 8vo. *Sheffield.*

1856.

124. OWEN, [SIR] R.—Description of some Mammalian Fossils from the Red Crag of Suffolk. *Quart. Journ. Geol. Soc.*, vol. xii., p. 217.

125. PHEAR, [SIR] J. B.—On the Geology of some parts of Suffolk, particularly of the Valley of the Gipping. *Trans. Cambridge Phil. Soc.*, vol. ix., pt. iv., p. 431.

1857.

126. DENNIS, REV. J. B. P.—On the Microscopical Characters of certain so-called Cetacean Bones associated with Cetolites in the Detrital Bed of the Red Crag at Felixstow, Suffolk. *Quart. Journ. Micr. Sci.*, vol. v., p. 191.

127. FALCONER, DR. H.—On the Species of Mastodon and Elephant occurring in the fossil state in Great Britain. Part I. Mastodon. *Quart. Journ. Geol. Soc.*, vol xiii., p. 307.

128. GLYDE, J.—Suffolk in the Nineteenth Century. (Physical Features, Soils, pp. 2-18.) 8vo. *London.*

129. JONES, PROF. T. R.—A Monograph of the Tertiary Entomostraces of England. *Palæontograph. Soc.*

130. WOOD, S. V.—A Monograph of the Mollusca of the Crag, with Descriptions of Shells from the Upper Tertiaries of the British Isles. Vol. ii. Bivalves. [=Part ii., No. 3, pp. 217-342, pls. xxi.-xxxi.] *Palæontograph. Soc.*

1858.

130a. GUNN, J.—On the Hoxne Brick-pits (*Norfolk Archæol. Soc.*). Report in local newspaper.

131. TRIMMER, J.—On the Upper and Lower Boulder-clays of the Gorleston Cliffs in Norfolk. [Gorleston Cliffs are in Suffolk.] *Quart. Journ. Geol. Soc.*, vol. xiv., p. 171.

1859.

132. BUSK, PROF. G.—A Monograph of the Fossil Polyzoa of the Crag. *Palæontograph. Soc.*

133. WOOD, S. V.—On the Extraneous Fossils of the Reg Crag. *Quart. Journ. Geol. Soc.*, vol. xv., p. 32.

1860.

134. BROWN, J.—On Some Fossil Remains of Mammalia lately discovered in Essex; with Remarks on the Position of the Beds of Drift in that County and in the County of Suffolk. *Proc. Geol. Assoc.*, vol. i., no. 4, p. 29.

135. BRUFF, P.—[On a Well at Combs, &c.] In the discussion on a paper by C. E. Amos. *Proc. Inst. Civ. Eng.*, vol. xix., p. 38.

136. EVANS, J.—Flint implements in the Drift (refers to Hoxne). *Archæologia*, vol. xxxviii., p. 280.

137. ROSE, C. B.—On the Divisions of the Drift in Norfolk and Suffolk. *Geologist*, vol. iii., pp. 137, 317.

138. VOELCKER, DR. A.—On the Chemical Composition and Commercial Value of . . . . . Coprolites and other Phosphatic Materials used in England for Agricultural Purposes. (Analyses of Suffolk "coprolites," pp. 359, 360.) *Journ. R. Agric. Soc.*, vol. xxi., p. 350.

139. WALCOTT, REV. M. E. C.—A Guide to the Coasts of Essex, Suffolk, and Norfolk. (Remarks on Geology scattered throughout). 8vo. *London.*

1861.

140. HURWOOD, G.—On the River Orwell and the Port of Ipswich. *Proc. Inst. Civ. Eng.*, vol. xx., p. 4.

141. PRESTWICH, [PROF.] J.—On the Occurrence of Flint-implements, associated with the Remains of Animals of Extinct Species in Beds of a late Geological Period, in France at Amiens and Abbeville, and in England at Hoxne. *Phil. Trans.*, vol. cl., pt. 2, p. 277.

142. ———.—Notes on some further Discoveries of Flint Implements in Beds of Post-Pliocene Gravel and Clay. *Quart. Journ. Geol. Soc.*, vol. xvii., p. 362.

1862.

143. EVANS, J.—Flint Implements in the Drift; being an Account of Further Discoveries . . . (short reference to Suffolk). *Archæologia*, vol. xxxix., p. 57.

143a. JEFFREYS [DR.] J. G.—British Conchology, vol. i. Land and Freshwater Shells. (Crag, pp. lxxxix.-xcviii.)
144. MACKIE, S. J.—Bos frontosus (Bawdsey Bog, Suffolk). *Geologist*, vol. v., p. 441.
145. OWEN, [SIR] R.—On the Hyracotherian Character of the Lower Molars of the supposed Macacus from the Eocene Sand of Kyson, Suffolk. *Ann. Nat. Hist.*, ser. 3, vol. x., p. 240.
146. ROSE, C. B.—On Two Beds of Re-deposited Crag Shells in the Vicinity of Yarmouth, Norfolk. [Refers to Suffolk, not Norfolk.] *Proc. Geol. Assoc.*, vol. i., no. 8, p. 192.

1863.

147. LANKESTER, [PROF.] E. R.—New Species of Fish from the Crag. *Geologist*, vol. vi., p. 110.
148. LOOME, B. T.—Popular Natural History of Great Yarmouth and its Neighbourhood including a Description of the District, its Fauna, Geology and Flora. 8vo.
149. LYELL, SIR C.—The Geological Evidences of the Antiquity of Man with an Outline of Glacial and Post-Tertiary Geology. Eds. 2 and 3 in the same year, Ed. 4 in 1873.
150. PATTISON, S. R.—Description of a Land Surface underneath the Drift on the Coast of Suffolk. *Geologist*, vol. vi., p. 207.

1864.

151. HUXLEY, PROF. T. H.—On the Cetacean Fossils termed "Ziphius," by Cuvier, with a Notice of a new Species (Belemnoziphius compressus) from the Red Crag. *Quart. Journ. Geol. Soc.*, vol. xx., p. 388.
152. JONES, PROF. T. R., and W. K. PARKER.—On the Foraminifera of the Crag. *Ann. Nat. Hist.*, ser. 3, vol. xiii., p. 64.
153. LANKESTER, [PROF.] E. R.—On a new Species of Hyæna from the Red Crag of Suffolk. *Ibid.*, p. 56.
154. ———.—On New Mammalia from the Red Crag. *Ibid.*, vol. xiv., p. 353.
155. MAW, G.—Præglacial and Glacial Drift. *Geol. Mag.*, vol. i., p. 294.
156. PRESTWICH, [PROF.] J.—Theoretical Considerations on the Conditions under which the (Drift) Deposits containing the Remains of Extinct Mammalia and Flint Implements were accumulated, and on their Geological Age. *Phil. Trans.*, vol. cliv., pt. 2, p. 247. (Refers to the Valleys of the Waveney and Lark, pp. 252-254, 265-267, &c.)
157. REDMAN, J. B.—The East Coast between the Thames and the Wash Estuaries. *Proc. Inst. Civ. Eng.*, vol. xxiii., p. 186.
158. WOOD, S. V., JUNR.—On the Formation of the River-and other Valleys of the East of England. *Phil. Mag.*, ser. 4, vol. xxvii., p. 180.
159. ———.—On the Red Crag and its relation to the Fluviomarine Crag, and on the Drift of the Eastern Counties. *Ann. Nat. Hist.* ser. 3, vol. xiii., p. 185.
159a. ———.—On the Belgian Equivalents of the Upper and Lower Drift of the Eastern Counties. *Ibid*, p. 393.

1865.

160. CARPENTER, DR. P.—On the Connection between the Crag Formations and the Recent North Pacific Faunas. (Brit. Assoc.) *Geol. Mag.*, vol. ii., p. 152.
161. FALCONER, DR. H.—On the Species of Mastodon and Elephant occurring in the Fossil State in Great Britain. Part 2 (Elephant). *Quart. Journ. Geol. Soc.*, vol. xxi., p. 253 (Suffolk, pp. 303, 307). Reprinted in "Palæontological Memoirs, etc. of the late H. Falconer," vol. ii., p. 76. 8vo. *London.*
162. LANKESTER, [PROF.] E. R.—On the Sources of the Mammalian Fossils of the Red Crag, and on the Discovery of a new Mammal in that Deposit, allied to the Walrus. *Quart. Journ. Geol. Soc.*, vol. xxi., p. 221.
163. ———.—On the Crags of Suffolk and Antwerp. *Geol. Mag.*, vol. ii., pp. 103, 149.

164. LUBBOCK, [SIR] J.—Prehistoric Times. . . . . 8vo. *London*. Chap. ix. On the Antiquity of Man (Suffolk, &c.).
165. PRESTWICH, [PROF.] J.—Part of the South-eastern Sheet of the Greenough Map. *Geol. Soc.*
166. WOOD, S. V., JUNR.—A Map of the Upper Tertiaries in the Counties of Norfolk, Suffolk, etc. . . . . (with Sections, and Remarks in Explanation, in 8vo.) *Privately printed*. Abstract in *Quart. Journ. Geol. Soc.*, vol. xxi., p. 141.
167. WOODWARD, [DR.] H.—An Excursion to the Crag District. *Intellectual Observer*, vol. viii., p. 33.

1866.

168. ANON. (R. B[ELL?]).—Crag. *Naturalists Circular*, no. 3, p. 17; No. 4, p. 27.
169. FISHER, REV. O.—On the Relation of the Norwich or Fluvio-marine Crag to the Chillesford Clay or Loam. *Quart. Journ. Geol. Soc.*, vol. xxii., p. 19.
170. ————.—On the Warp (of Mr. Trimmer)—its Age and probable Connexion with the Last Geological Events. *Ibid.*, p. 553.
171. GODWIN-AUSTEN, R. A. C.—On the Kainozoic Formations of Belgium. *Ibid.*, p. 228.
172. JONES, PROF. T. R., W. K. PARKER, and H. B. BRADY.—A Monograph of the Foraminifera of the Crag. Part I. containing Pp. i.-v., 1-72. Appendices i. & ii., Plates i.-iv. *Palæontograph. Soc.*
173. NALL, J. G.—Great Yarmouth and Lowestoft. Geology of the District, pp. 233-239. 8vo. *London*.
174. WOOD, S. V.—On the Structure of the Red Crag. Explanation of the Diagram-section by S. V. WOOD, JUNR. *Quart. Journ. Geol. Soc.*, vol. xxii., p. 538.

1867.

175. FISHER, REV. O.—Further Remarks upon the Relation of the Chillesford Beds to the Fluviomarine Crag (abstract). *Quart. Journ. Geol. Soc.*, vol. xiii., p. 175.
176. FLOWER, J. W.—On some Flint Implements lately found in the Valley of the Little Ouse River at Thetford, Norfolk [partly Suffolk]. *Quart. Journ. Geol. Soc.*, vol. xxiii., p. 45.
177. GUNN, REV. J.—The Order of Succession of the Pre-Glacial, Glacial, and Post-Glacial Strata in the Coast Sections of Norfolk and Suffolk. (*Norwich Geol. Soc.*) *Geol. Mag.*, vol. iv., p. 371, and *Norwich Mercury*, May 11.
178. ————.—On an Excursion to Corton and Hopton. (*Norwich Geol. Soc.*), *Geol. Mag.*, vol. iv., p. 561.
179. ————.—On the Anglo-Belgian Basin of the Forest-bed of Norfolk and Suffolk, and the Union of England with the Continent during the Glacial Period. (*Brit. Assoc.*) *Geol. Nat. Hist. Repertory*, vol. i., p. 339.
180. HARMER, F. W.—Drift of the Eastern Counties. *Geol. Mag.*, vol. iv., p. 374.
180a. HULL [PROF.] E.—On the Parallelism of the Drift Deposits in Lancashire and the Eastern Counties. *Ibid.*, p. 183.
181. JENYNS, REV. L.—A Lecture on the Phosphatic Nodules obtained in the Eastern Counties, and used in Agriculture. *Proc. Bath Field Club*, vol. i., No. 1, p. 9.
182. KING, REV. S. W.—[Crag Shells.] *Geol. Mag.*, vol. iv., p. 330.
183. LANKESTER, [PROF.] E. R.—Are the Coralline Crag of Suffolk and the Black Crag of Belgium contemporaneous Deposits. *Geol. Mag.*, vol. iv., p. 91.
184. ————.—On the Structure of the Tooth in Ziphius Sowerbiensis . . . and on some Fossil Cetacean Teeth. *Trans. Microsc. Soc.*, ser. 2, vol. xv., p. 55.
185. MAW, G.—On the Occurrence of Consolidated Blocks in the Drift of Suffolk. *Quart. Journ. Geol. Soc.*, vol. xxiii., p. 110.

186. ———.—On the relative Ages of the Coast Boulder-clay of the Eastern Counties and that on the Higher Ground. *Geol. Mag.*, vol. iv., p. 97.
187. ———.—The Drift Deposits of the Eastern Counties. *Ibid.*, p. 276.
188. ———.—On the Sequence of the Drifts in the Eastern Counties. *Ibid.*, p. 426.
189. PRIGG, H. (wrongly given as Brigg).—On the occurrence of Flint Implements in the Gravel of the Little Ouse Valley at Thetford and elsewhere. *Rep. Brit. Assoc.* for 1866, *Sections*, p. 50.
190. WOOD, S. V., JUNR.—Age and Position of the Drift Deposits of the Eastern Counties. *Geol. Mag.*, vol. iv., p. 159.
191. ———.—Boulder Clay and Drift of Norfolk and Suffolk . . . . . *Ibid.*, p. 470.
191a. ———.—A Memoir in Explanation of the Structure of the Glacial and Post-Glacial beds mapped in a Geological Survey of the Ordnance Sheets Nos. 1 and 2 . . . . . . incorporated with which is an Essay upon the General Structure of the Post-glacial System over the E. . . . . . of England. Large fol. MS. and Maps, in the Library of the Geological Society.

1868.

192. CHARLESWORTH, E.—On the Prospective Annihilation of the Suffolk Red Crag Phosphatic Stones, "Coprolite" (Norwich Geol. Soc.). *Geol. Mag.*, vol. v., p. 577.
192a. ———.—The Large Fossil Tooth in the Pakefield Cliff. *Land and Water*, March 14.
192b. CROWFOOT, W. M. and E. T. DOWSON.—[Letter relative to the Beds at Kessingland]. *Norwich Mercury*, Oct. 10.
193. DAWKINS, [PROF.] W. B.—On the Dentition of Rhinoceros Etruscus, Falc. *Quart. Journ. Geol. Soc.*, vol. xxiv., p. 207.
194. EVANS, J.—On some Cavities in the Gravel of the Valley of the Little Ouse, in Norfolk [in Suffolk also]. *Geol. Mag.*, vol. v., p. 443.
195. GODWIN-AUSTEN, R. A. C.—Address to the Geological Section of the British Association, Norwich, August 19, 1868. *Geol. Mag.* vol. v., p. 469, [contains 2 paragraphs not in *Rep. Brit. Assoc.*] and *Rep. Brit. Assoc.* for 1868 (published 1869), and *Geol. Nat. Hist. Repertory*, vol. ii., p. 229.
196. GUNN, REV. J.—On the Alternate Elevations and Subsidings of the Land, and the Order of Succession of the Strata in Suffolk and Norfolk. *Geol. Nat. Hist. Repertory*, vol. ii., p. 237, ?and, under a different title, in *Norwich Mercury* and *Norfolk News*.
196a. ———.—On an Excursion to Chillesford. *Norwich Mercury*, April 11.
196b. ———.—Notes on the Chillesford Clay at Kessingland. *Ibid*, December 9.
197. LANKESTER, [PROF.] E. R.—The Suffolk Bone-bed and the Diestian or Black Crag in England. *Geol. Mag.*, vol. v., p. 254.
198. MAW, G.—On the Disposition of Iron in variegated Strata. *Quart. Journ. Geol. Soc.*, vol. xxiv., p. 351. (Suffolk, pp. 356, 375–377.)
199. WOOD, S. V. JUNR., and F. W. HARMER.—Abstract of a Paper on "The Glacial and Post-Glacial Structure of Norfolk and Suffolk." *Geol. Mag.*, vol. v., p. 452, *Geol. Nat. Hist. Repertory*, vol. ii., p. 241, and (in 1869) *Rep. Brit. Assoc.* for 1868, *Sections*, p. 80.

1869.

200. BELL, A.—On the Molluscan Fauna of the Red Crag. *Rep. Brit. Assoc.* for 1868, *Sections*, p. 59.
201. ———.—Sussex and Suffolk Tertiaries. *Geol. Mag.*, vol. vi., p. 41.
202. CRISP, DR. H.—On the Fossil Whale recently found on the East Coast of Suffolk. *Rep. Brit. Assoc.* for 1868, *Sections*, p. 61.
203. FISHER, REV. O.—On Denudation and the Crags. *Geol. Mag.*, vol. vi., p. 141.
204. ———.—"Middle Drift" Gravel at Lopham Ford. *Ibid.*, pp. 189, 288.

205. FLOWER, J. [W.]—On the Distribution of Flint Implements in the Drift, with reference to some recent Discoveries in Norfolk and Suffolk. *Quart. Journ. Geol. Soc.*, vol. xxv., p. 449.

206. GUNN, REV. J.—Elephas Meridionalis in the Red Crag. *Geol. Mag.*, vol. vi., p. 143.

206a. HARMER, F. W.—The result of the Geological Survey of the Eastern Counties, by Mr. S. V. Wood, Junr., and himself. *Eastern Daily News*, April 11.

206B. JECKS, C.—The [Norwich] Geological Society's Excursion to Ipswich and Bentley. *Norfolk News* (July).

207. JONES, [REV.] H.—On the Discovery of some Supposed Vestiges of a Pile Dwelling in Barton Mere, near Bury St. Edmunds [note of beds]. *Quart. Journ. Suff. Inst.*, vol. i., no. ii., p. 31.

208. LANKESTER, [PROF.] E. R.—On the Oldest Beds of the Crags. *Rep. Brit. Assoc.* for 1868, *Sections*, p. 70.

209. ———.—The Mammalia of the Crag. *Geol. Mag.*, vol. vi., p. 47.

210. ———.—Note on a New Trilophodont Crag Mastodon (from the Suffolk Bone-bed). *Ibid.*, p. 355.

211. MAW, G.—On the Sequence of the Deposits in Norfolk and Suffolk superior to the Red Crag. *Rep. Brit. Assoc.* for 1868, *Sections*, p. 73.

212. PRIGG, H.—The discovery of associated works of Man, and the Elephant, &c., in the gravel near Thetford [? Norfolk or Suffolk]. *Quart. Journ. Suff. Inst.*, vol. i., no. i., p. 3.

212a. TAYLOR, J. E.—Excursion of the [Norwich] Geological Society to Aldborough. *Norfolk News, Norwich Mercury*, and *Ipswich Journal* (September).

1870.

213. BELL, A.—On some New or Little-known Shells, &c. of the Crag Formation. *Ann. Nat. Hist.*, ser. 4, vol. vi., p. 213.

214. GUNN, REV. J.—On the Relative Position of the Forest-bed and the Chillesford Clay in Norfolk and Suffolk, and on the real Position of the Forest-bed. *Quart. Journ. Geol. Soc.*, vol. xxvi., p. 551.

214a. ———.—Remarks on the Geology of the Eastern Coast. *Norfolk Chronicle*.

215. HELE, N. F.—Notes or Jottings about Aldeburgh, Suffolk . . . . . (Geology, pp. 15-32, and scattered notes.) 8vo. *London*.

216. JECKS, C.—On the Crag Formation [a few lines]. *Rep. Brit. Assoc.* for 1869, *Sections*, p. 91.

217. LANKESTER, [PROF.] E. R.—Contributions to a knowledge of the Newer Tertiaries of Suffolk and their Fauna. *Quart. Journ. Geol. Soc.*, vol. xxvi., p. 493.

218. ———.—On a New Large *Terebratula* occurring in East Anglia. *Geol. Mag.*, vol. vii., p. 410.

219. OWEN, [SIR] R.—Monograph on the British Fossil Cetacea from the Red Crag. No. 1, containing Genus Ziphius. *Palæontograph. Soc.*

220. WOOD, S. V., JUNR.—On the Relation of the Boulder-clay, without Chalk, of the North of England to the Great Chalky Boulder-clay of the South. *Quart. Journ. Geol. Soc.*, vol. xxvi., p. 90.

221. ———.—Observations on the Sequence of the Glacial Beds. *Geol. Mag.*, vol. vii., pp. 17, 61.

1871.

222. ANON. [J. E. TAYLOR].—A Guide to the Ipswich Museum. Pp. 64. 8vo. *Ipswich*.

223. BELL, A.—The Butley Crag Pits. *Geol. Mag.*, vol. viii., p. 450.

224. ———.—Contributions to the Crag Fauna. *Ann. Nat. Hist.*, ser. 4, vol. vii., p. 351.

225. BELL, A. and R.—The English Crags, and their Stratigraphical Divisions indicated by their Invertebrate Fauna. *Geol. Mag.*, vol. viii., p. 256.

226. DUNCAN, PROF. P. M.—On a New Species of Coral from the Red Crag of Waldringfield. *Quart. Journ. Geol. Soc.*, vol. xxvii., p. 369.

226a. GUNN, J.—Excursion to Ipswich, Foxall, and Falkenham. *Norfolk News* (June).
227. PRESTWICH, [PROF.] J.—On the Structure of the Crag-beds of Suffolk and Norfolk, with some Observations on their Organic Remains. Part I. The Coralline Crag of Suffolk. Part II. The Red Crag of Essex and Suffolk. Part III. The Norwich Crag and Westleton Beds. *Quart. Journ. Geol. Soc.*, vol. xxvii., pp. 115, 325, 452. Translated into French by MOURLON, in 1874.
228. TAYLOR, J. E.—The Relation of the Red to the Norwich Crag. *Geol. Mag.*, vol. viii., p. 314.
230. WOOD, S. V., [JUNR.], and F. W. HARMER.—On the Palæontological Aspects of the Middle Glacial Formation of the East of England, and on their bearing upon the Age of the Middle Sands of Lancashire. *Rep. Brit. Assoc.* for 1870, *Sections*, p. 90.

1872.

231. ALLMAN, PROF. G. J.—Notice of a Fossil Hydractinia from the Coralline Crag. *Geol. Mag.*, vol. ix., p. 337. Note thereon by S. V. WOOD, p. 431.
232. BAYNE, A. D.—Royal Illustrated History of Eastern England . . . . . . including a Survey of the Eastern Counties, Physical Features, Geology, &c. of . . . . . . Suffolk Vol. i. 8vo. *Yarmouth*.
233. BELL, A.—The Succession of the Crags. *Geol. Mag.*, vol. ix., p. 209.
234. BELL, A. and R.—On the English Crags and the Stratigraphical Divisions indicated by their Invertebrate Fauna. *Proc. Geol. Assoc.*, vol. ii. no. 5, p. 185. Supplement by A. BELL, no. 6, p. 270.
235. CHARLESWORTH, E.—[Exhibition and Description of Objects found in the Red Crag of Suffolk simulating Human Workmanship.] *Journ. Anthrop. Inst.*, vol. ii., no. 1, p. 91.
235A. ———.—On Perforated Stones from the Suffolk Crag. *Eastern Daily Press*, April 6.
236. DAWKINS, [PROF.] W. B.—On the Cervidæ of the Forest-bed of Norfolk and Suffolk. *Quart. Journ. Geol. Soc.*, vol. xxviii., p. 405.
237. DUNCAN, PROF. P. M.—On Trochocyathus anglicus, a new species of Madreporaria from the Red Crag. *Ibid.*, p. 447.
238. EVANS, J.—The Ancient Stone Implements, Weapons, and Ornaments of Great Britain. 8vo. *London*.
239. HUGHES, [PROF.] T. McK.—Man in the Crag. *Geol. Mag.*, vol. ix., p. 247.
240. JONES PROF. T R., and W. K. PARKER—On the Forminifera of the Family Rotalinæ (Carpenter) found in the Cretaceous Formations; with Notes on their Tertiary and Recent Representations. *Quart. Journ. Geol. Soc.*, vol. xxxviii., p. 103. (Suffolk Crag, p. 119.)
241. PALMER, C. J.—The Perlustration of Great Yarmouth, with Gorleston and Southtown. Vol. i. (Changes of coast, &c. noticed, pp. 1-5.) 4to. *Yarmouth*.
242. SCOTT, G.—On the Suffolk Tertiaries. 19 *Ann. Rep. Brighton Nat. Hist. Soc.*, p. 64.
243. WOOD, S. V.—Supplement to the Crag Mollusca, comprising Testacea from the Upper Tertiaries of the East of England. Part I. Univalves. With an Introductory Outline of the Geology of the Same District, and Map. By S. V. WOOD, JUNR., and F. W. HARMER. *Palæontograph. Soc.*
244. ———.—Coralline Crag Fossils. *Geol. Mag.*, vol. ix., p. 576.
245. WOOD, S. V., JUNR.—Reply to Mr. James Geikie's Correlation of the Scotch and English Glacial Beds. *Geol. Mag.*, vol. ix., p. 171.

1873.

246. DUNCAN, PROF. P. M.—On Caryophyllia Bredai, Milne-Edwards and Jules Haime, from the Red Crag of Woodbridge. *Quart. Journ. Geol. Soc.*, vol. xxix., p. 503.

247. GUNN, J.—On the Prospect of finding Productive Coal measures in Norfolk and Suffolk with Suggestions as to the place where an Experimental Boring should be made. *Rep. Brit. Assoc.* for 1872, *Sections*, p. 102.

247a. ———.—On the Discovery of Elephantine and Cervine Remains in the Forest Bed at Corton, in Suffolk. *Norwich Mercury* and *Norfolk News*, January 11

248. TAYLOR, J. E.—Descriptive Handbook of Ipswich and the neighbourhood, &c. (Geology, pp. 8-13, 79-83, &c.) 8vo.) *Ipswich*.

1874.

[The list from this year onward is, for the most part, the work of MR. W. H. DALTON.]

249. FLOWER, PROF. W. H.—Description of the Skull of a Species of Halitherium (H. Canhami) from the Red Crag of Suffolk. *Quart. Journ. Geol. Soc.*, vol. xxx., p. 1.

250. GEIKIE, [PROF.] J.—The Great Ice Age and its Relation to the Antiquity of Man. 8vo. London. Ed. 2 in 1877.

251. GUNN, J.—[Presidential Address to the Norwich Geological Society.] *Norwich Mercury*, No. 8445, p. 6. [Refers to Suffolk.]

252. HARMER, F. W.—The result of the Geological Survey of the Eastern Counties by Mr. S. V. Wood, Jun., and himself. (Norwich Geol. Soc.) *Eastern Daily Press*, April 11.

253. TAYLOR, J. E.—A Sketch of the Geology of Suffolk. From White's History, &c. of the County. 8vo. *Sheffield*.

254. ———.—A Submarine Forest in the Orwell. *Science Gossip*, No. 120, p. 278, (and newspapers). See 269.

255. ———.—On the Occurrence of Elephant Remains in the Basement Beds of the Red Crag. *Rep. Brit. Assoc.* for 1873, *Sections*, p. 91.

256. WHITAKER, W.—On the occurrence of Thanet Beds, and of Crag at Sudbury, Suffolk. *Quart. Journ. Geol. Soc.*, vol. xxx., p. 401.

257. WOOD, S. V.—Supplement to the Crag Mollusca, comprising Testacea from the Upper Tertiaries of the East of England. Part II. Bivalves, pp. 99-231. *Palæontograph. Soc.*

1875.

258. BURROWS, H. A.—A probable Origin of the Perforations in Sharks' Teeth from the Crag. *Proc. Geol. Assoc.*, vol., iv. no. 3, p. 164.

259. COODE, SIR J.—Report to the Board of Trade on the Coast-line at Landguard Common. *Parliamentary Papers*, Sess. 1875, no. 57. Fol. *London*.

260. DE RANCE, C. E.—On the Relative Age of some Valleys in the North and South of England, and of the various [Glacial] and Postglacial Deposits occurring in them. *Proc. Geol. Assoc.*, vol. iv., no. 4, p. 221.

1876.

261. ANON. [— KNIGHTS].—The Antiquity of Man. Account of a Geological Ramble around Brandon, and of a Discovery of Remains of Pre-historic Man. Reprinted from *Eastern Daily Press*, October.

262. BELT, T.—On the Geological Age of the Deposits containing Flint Implements, at Hoxne . . . and the Relation that Palæolithic Man bore to the Glacial Period. *Quart. Journ. Sci.*, n.s., vol. vi., p. 289.

263. FLOWER, PROF. W H.—Description of the Skull of a Species of Xiphodon, Cuvier. *Proc. Zool. Soc.*, p. 3. [*X. platyceps*, n. sp. Red Crag? Woodbridge.]

264. GUNN, J.—On the presence of the Forest-bed Series at Kessingland and Pakefield, in Suffolk, and its position beneath the Chillesford Clay. *Quart. Journ. Geol. Soc.*, vol. xxxii., p. 123.

265. NORTON, H.—A Report of three visits to Pakefield and Kessingland . . . 1875. Supplement to the *Norfolk Chronicle*, May 6.

266. PENNING, W. H.—Notes on the Physical Geology of East Anglia during the Glacial Period. *Quart. Journ. Geol. Soc.*, vol. xxxii., p. 191.

267. REID, W. C.—Mineral Phosphates and Superphosphate of Lime. *Chem. News*, vol. xxxiv., pp. 48, 55.

268. Symonds, Rev. W. S.—Among Glaciers Recent and Extinct. *Pop. Sci. Rev.*, vol. xv., p. 169.
269. Taylor, J. E.—Discovery of a Submerged Forest in the Estuary of the Orwell. *Rep. Brit. Assoc.* for 1875, *Sections*, p. 82. See 254.
270. Wood, S. V., Junr.—Physical Geology of East Anglia in the Glacial Epoch. *Geol. Mag.*, dec. ii., vol. iii., p. 284.
271. Woodward, H. B.—The Geology of England and Wales . . . 8vo. *London.*

1877.

272. Belt. T.—On the First Stages of the Glacial Period in Norfolk and Suffolk. *Geol. Mag.*, dec. ii., vol. iv., p. 156.
273. Blake, J. H.—On the Age of the Mammalian Rootlet-bed at Kessingland. *Geol. Mag.*, dec. ii., vol. iv., p. 298.
274. Flower, Prof. W. H.—Note on the Occurrence of *Hyænarctos* in the Red Crag of Suffolk. *Quart. Journ. Geol. Soc.*, vol. xxxiii., p. 534.
275. Harmer, F. W.—On the Kessingland Cliff-Section, and on the Relation of the Forest-Bed to the Chillesford Clay, with some Remarks on the so-called Terrestrial Surface at the base of the Norwich Crag. *Quart. Journ. Geol. Soc.*, vol. xxxiii., p. 134.
276. Henslow, Prof.—A Month at Felixstowe. The Fossils of the Red Crag. *Proc. W. Lond. Sci. Assoc.*, vol. i., pt. iv., p. 118.
277. Lankester, Prof. E. R.—The Crag Fossils in the Ipswich Museum. *Suffolk Chronicle*, Aug. 4. Reprinted by E. Charlesworth, with remarks on the prospective exhaustion of the phosphatic Crag stratum.
278. Taylor, J. E.—Excursion to the Crag District of Suffolk. *Proc. Geol. Assoc.*, vol. v., no. 3, p. 108.
278a. ――――.—The Brandon "Finds." *East Anglian Handbook*, p. 101. 8vo. *Norwich.*
279. Whitaker, W.—Note on the Red Crag. *Quart. Journ. Geol. Soc.*, vol. xxxiii., p. 122.
280. Wood, S. V., Junr.—American "Surface Geology" and its Relation to British, with some Remarks on Glacial Conditions in Britain . . . *Geol. Mag.*, dec. ii., vol. iv., pp. 481, 536.
281. Wood, S. V., Junr., and F. W. Harmer.—Observations on the Later Tertiary Geology of East Anglia. With a note by S. V. Wood on some New Occurrences of Species of Mollusca in the Crag and Beds superior to it. *Quart. Journ. Geol. Soc.*, vol. xxxiii., p. 74.
282. ――――.――――.—The Kessingland Freshwater Bed and Weybourne Sand. *Geol. Mag.*, dec. ii., vol. iv., p. 385.

1878.

283. Anon. [E. Charlesworth].—Fossil Exploration of Suffolk Crag (Orford Castle), and Hampshire Eocene Cliffs. Pp. 8. 8vo. *London.*
284. B[lake], J. H.—Excursion to Corton and Hopton. *Proc. Norwich Geol. Soc.*, pt. i., p. 37.
285. Dawkins, Prof. W. B.—Contributions to the History of the Deer of the European Miocene and Pliocene Strata. *Quart. Journ. Geol. Soc.*, vol. xxxiv., p. 402.
285a.—Hughes, Prof. T. McK.—On the Evidence afforded by the Gravels and Brick-earth [on the Antiquity of Man in the Eastern Counties]. *Journ. Anthrop. Inst.*, vol. vii., p. 162.
285b. Skertchly, S. B. J.—Chap. XV. Geology, in "The Fenland Past and Present," by Miller and Skertchly. 8vo. *Wisbech* and *Lond.*
286. Woodward, H. B.—Excursion to Mildenhall. *Proc. Norwich Geol. Soc.*, pt. i., p. 32.

1879.

287. Crowfoot, W. M.—On the Well-sections at Beccles. *Proc. Norwich Geol. Soc.*, vol. i., pt. iii., p. 76.
288. Dowson, E. T.—Note on the Crag at Dunwich. *Ibid*, p. 80.

289. SKERTCHLY, S. B. J.—Evidence of the Existence of Palæolithic Man during the Glacial Period in East Anglia. *Rep. Brit. Assoc.* for 1879, *Sections*, p. 379.

289a. WOOD, S. V.—Second Supplement to the Crag Mollusca . . . *Palæontograph. Soc.*

1880.

290. DALTON, W. H.—Note on the Range of the Lower Tertiaries of East Suffolk. *Rep. Brit. Assoc.* for 1880, p. 375.

291. DAWKINS, PROF. W. B.—Early Man in Britain and his Place in the Tertiary Period. 8vo. *London.*

292. FISHER, REV. O.—On the Implement-bearing Loams in Suffolk. *Proc. Camb. Phil. Soc.*, vol. iii., p. 285.

292a. HARMER, F. W.—Remarks on the Geology of Corton. *Trans. Norfolk Nat. Soc.*, vol. iii., p. 71.

293. LANKESTER, PROF. E. R.—On the Tusks of the fossil Walrus found in the Red Crag of Suffolk. *Trans. Linn. Soc.*, vol. xv., p. 144.

294. NEWTON, E. T.—Notes on the Vertebrata of the Pre-Glacial Forest-bed Series of the East of England. *Geol. Mag.*, dec. ii., vol. vii., pp. 152, 424, 447.

295. WOOD, S. V., JUNR.—The Newer Pliocene Period in England. Part I. *Quart. Journ. Geol. Soc.*, vol. xxxvi., p. 457.

1881.

296. BLAKE, J. H.—Address. On the Age and Relations of the so-called Forest Bed of the Norfolk and Suffolk Coast. *Proc. Norwich Geol. Soc.*, vol. i., pt. v., p. 137.

296a. WOODWARD, B. B.—The Crag. *Science for All*, pt. 46, p. 312.

1882.

297. DALTON, W. H.—The Surface-Metamorphism of the Eastern Counties. *Proc. Norwich Geol. Soc.*, vol. i., pt. vi., p. 166.

298. GUNN, J.—On the Rootlet-bed in relation to the Forest-bed Series of Norfolk and Suffolk. *Ibid.*, p. 161, and *Eastern Daily Press*, 14 December, 1880.

299. HARRISON, W. J.—Geology of the Counties of England . . . . 8vo. *London.*

300. PRESTWICH, PROF. J.—On the Strata between the Chillesford Beds and the Lower Boulder Clay, 'The Mundesley and Wesleton Beds.' *Rep. Brit. Assoc.* for 1881, p. 620.

301. ———.—On the Extension into Essex . . . . . of the Mundesley and Westleton Beds . . . . . *Ibid.*, and *Geol. Mag.*, dec. ii., vol. viii., p. 966 (1881).

302. PRIGG, H.—Notes on some Discoveries of Flint Implements in the Quaternary Deposits of the East of England. *Proc. Norwich Geol. Soc.*, vol. i., pt. vi., p. 162.

303. WOOD, S. V.—Third Supplement to the Crag Mollusca . . . . . Edited by S. V. Wood, Junr. *Palæontograph. Soc.*

304. WOODWARD, H. B.—Notes on the Bure Valley Beds and the Westleton Beds. *Geol. Mag.*, dec. ii., vol. ix., p. 452. (Abstract in *Rep. Brit. Assoc.* for 1882, p. 530.)

1883.

305. KENDALL, P. F.—On the Dissolution of Aragonite Shells in the Coralline Crag. *Geol. Mag.*, dec. ii., vol. x., p. 497.

306. NEWTON, E. T.—On the Occurrence of the Cave Hyæna in the "Forest Bed" at Corton Cliff, Suffolk. *Ibid.*, p. 433.

1884.

307. BELL, R. G.—Land Shells in the Red Crag. *Geol. Mag.*, dec. iii., vol. i., p. 262.

308. PRIGG, H.—On a portion of a Human Skull of supposed Palæolithic age from near Bury St. Edmunds. *Journ. Anthrop. Inst.*, vol. xiv., p. 51.

309. WHITAKER, W.—Some Geological Conditions affecting the Question of Water-supply from the Chalk (part of Presidential Address). *Proc. Norwich Geol. Soc.*, vol. i., pt. viii., p. 285, and *Geol. Mag.*, dec. iii., vol. i., p. 23.

310. ————.—On the Area of Chalk as a Source of Water Supply. *Journ. Soc. Arts*, and " The Health Exhibition Literature," vol. viii., pp. 364, 596. 8vo. *London*.

1885.

311. DALTON, W. H.—[On Specimens of *Voluta Lamberti* from the Coralline Crag.] *Quart. Journ. Geol. Soc.*, vol. xli., *Proc.*, p. 2.

No Date.

312. ANON.—Aldborough described, &c. (" A Descriptive List of those Minerals, Fossils, &c. which are to be found on the Shore," pp. 104–108). 12mo. *Ipswich*. (? about 1800.)

313. ANON. [? GOWING.]—Descriptive Handbook of Ipswich, the River Orwell, Harwich, Dovercourt, and Felixstow. [Geological information, pp. 97–99.] 12mo. *Ipswich*. (? 1869.)

314. GUNN, REV. J.—A Diagram of Coast and Inland Sections of Strata in Norfolk and Suffolk, with explanatory remarks. (2 pages.) Printed at the request of the Norfolk and Norwich Geol. Soc. 8vo. *Norwich* ?

POSTSCRIPT.

The following section was communicated by MR. P. BRUFF, just as I was sending off the revise, and therefore it could not be put in its proper place, in p. 106, without much disturbance of type, with consequent alterations in the index.   W. W.

BRADFIELD (Essex). In field 181 of the 25-inch Ordnance Map. 116 feet above Ordnance Datum. Trial-boring. 1885.

A little water found at a depth of 309 feet, and a little more at 403, which stands at 109 feet (or 11 feet above Low Water Level). Yielded only 11 gallons a minute.

			FEET.
Soil			1½
[Drift, 24¼ feet.]	Loamy sand		4
	Brown sand		13½
	Light [-coloured] sharp sand		6¼
	Gravel		¾
[London Clay, 111 feet.]	Brown clay		1
	Blue clay		97
	[Basement-bed.]	Hard grey sand, with small stones	9
		Hard green sand	4
[Reading Beds, 59 feet.]	Light-coloured clay		12
	Hard light [-coloured] brown sand		20
	Light-green clay		5
	Dark green clay, with sand		3
	Black clay		12
	Grey loamy sand, with a few green-coated flints at bottom		7
		To Chalk	196

Chalk: Flints about 2 feet down, and then none met with till 309 feet from the surface. From 375 to 425 feet flints were found every 2 or 3 feet. From 294 to 330 feet the chalk was soft and rubbly, the rest was tough and close, except at about 403 feet · · · · · · · 238

434

INDEX.

Names of places not in the district have * prefixed.

It should be noted that all pages from 135 to 151 refer only to the List of Works on Suffolk Geology. The names of authors in that List are not here indexed, having a special index therein.

*Akenham, 13.
*Aldborough, 2, 37, 39, 98, 99, 135, 146, 151.
Alde, River and Valley, see Ore.
Alderton, 66, 67, 70.
Aldham, 9, 10, 19, 20, 75.
Analyses of cement-stone, 133.
  „   „   phosphates (including fossil bones), 102-105.
*Ardleigh, 83.
Assington, 1, 18, 73, 83, 92, 111, 112.

Balanidæ, 141.
*Ballingdon, 132.
*Barton Mere, 146.
Bawdsey, 26, 40, 67, 69, 70, 98, 99, 137, 143.
Bawdsey Haven, 2, 98, 99.
Bealings, see Little Bealings.
Bealings Brook, 95.
*Beaumont, 42.
*Beccles, 135, 149.
Bell, A., 28, 41.
Bell, R., 41, 43.
Belstead, 2, 49, 77, 111.
Bennett, Messrs., 113, 114, 117-119, 121-126.
Bentley, 2, 22, 37, 41, 46, 47, 76, 84, 87, 111, 146.
*Bildeston, 135.
Black mass in chalk, 5.
Black mineral in clay, 137.
Bolton, Sir F., 125.
Bone-bed, see Phosphatic nodules.
Bones in Alluvium, 97.
  „   „   Valley Drift, 93-96.
*Botesdale, 135.
Boulder of Chalk, large, 88.
Boxford, 18, 19, 21, 74, 83, 88, 101, 111, 112.
Boxford River and Valley, 1, 18, 45, 73, 74, 83, 92.
Box-stones of Crag, 27, 30, 36, 38, 39, 42, 59.
Boyton, 26, 28, 70, 71, 82.
Bradfield, 152.
*Bramble Island, 107.
Bramford, 2, 5, 6, 14, 15, 25, 50, 78, 84, 88, 93, 101.
*Brandon, 148, 149.
Brantham, 46, 76.
Brett, River and Valley, 2, 9, 10, 19-22, 45, 74-76, 84, 92, 93, 100.
Brightwell, 83.
Brightwell Valley, 59-64.
Brine, Lieut.-Col. B., 119, 123, 131.
Brown, J., 110.
Bruff, P., 106, 109, 129, 152.
Bryozoa, see Polyzoa.

Buckham, E., 97.
Buckland, Prof. W., 85.
Bucklesham, 25, 60.
*Bungay, 135.
Bures, 1, 17.
Burstall, 22.
*Bury St. Edmunds, 135, 146, 150.
Butley, 36, 38, 41-43, 146.
Butley River, 2, 35, 99.

Capel, 2, 22, 46, 88, 112, 126.
Carpenter, Dr. P., 37.
Cavities in gravel, 145.
  „   tubular, in Coralline Crag, 141.
Cement-stones, or septaria, of London Clay, 17, 101, 106, 109, 110, 114, 116, 119, 121, 133.
Cetacea, remains of, 30, 34, 36, 38, 39, 102-105, 140, 142-146, 148.
Channel, deep, of Glacial Drift, 94.
Charlesworth, E., 27, 28, 32-34, 39, 42.
Chelmondiston, 48, 95, 101.
Chelsworth, 5, 93.
*Chillesford, 35, 37-39, 43, 140, 145.
Chillesford Beds, 35, 37-43, 61, 66, 85, 140, 144-146, 148, 149.
Chilton, 5, 8, 45, 73.
*Christchurch Bay, 36.
Church, J., 108.
*Clacton, 101, 108.
*Clare, 135.
Clarke, Rev. W. B., 9, 13, 21-23, 27, 34, 35, 44, 46, 77, 100, 106, 111-116, 118, 121, 122, 124, 125.
Cliffs, old, of Coralline Crag, 34, 47, 67, 68.
Coal Measures, prospect of finding, 148.
Coast, changes of, or waste of, 98, 99, 136, 137, 139, 143, 147, 148.
*Colchester, 100, 109, 133.
*Combs, 100, 142.
Consolidated blocks or masses in Drift, 77, 78, 81, 82, 89, 144.
Conybeare, Rev. W. D., 32.
Copdock, 49, 50, 76, 77, 84, 112.
Coprolites, see Phosphatic nodules.
Corals (Zoophytes), 140, 141, 147.
*Corton, 135, 144, 148-150.
Coyts Tye, 84, 112.
Crawford, J. B., 107.
Crowfoot, W., 30.

Dalton, W. H., 16.
Dawkins, Prof. W. B., 36.
Deben, River and Valley, 2, 25, 26, 38, 44, 58, 64, 65, 67-69, 80, 82, 85, 88, 90, 94, 95, 97, 98.
*Debenham, 135.

154 INDEX.

Decalcification of Crag, 29, 42, 43, 46, 47, 51, 57, 61-65, 67, 70, 71.
Dedham, 17, 18, 106.
Derivative Fauna of Red Crag, 30, 32-34, 36-39, 41-43, 142.
Desnoyers,—, 33, 34.
Disposition of iron in Strata, 40, 145.
*Diss, 136.
Distribution of Red Crag Mollusca, 31, 37.
Disturbance of beds, 9, 18, 21, 100, 105, 132.
Division of Crag, 138, 139, 143, 146, 147.
Divisions of Red Crag, 36-38, 40, 41.
*Dogger Bank, 41.
Dorking Tye, 112.
Dove Marshes, 99.
Dovercourt, 101, 106, 151.
*Dunwich, 149.

Earth-pillars, Miniature reversed, 64.
East Bergholt, 112, 113.
*East Mersea, 100, 109.
*Easton Bavent, 34, 139.
Echinodermata, 138, 141.
Edwardston, 83, 113.
Elevation of Land, 145.
Elmsett, 2, 77, 113.
*Ely, 137.
Entomostraca, 96, 142.
Erwarton, 48, 95.
*Eye, 135.

Falkenham, 58, 59, 94, 147.
Faults, in London Clay, 18.
Felixstow, 25, 43, 54-58, 69, 86, 94, 98, 99, 114, 135, 140, 149, 151.
*Fenland, 135, 149.
Finn, River and Valley, 2, 25, 26, 65-67, 78, 80-82, 90, 94, 95.
Fish, teeth of, 19, 21-23, 26, 27, 30, 33, 36-39, 45, 104, 138, 139, 141, 143, 148.
Fisher, Rev. O., 37-39.
Fitch, R., 96.
Flint implements, 136, 141-147, 150.
Flowton, 78, 114.
Fluviomarine Crag, see Norwich Crag.
Foraminifera, 110, 114, 144, 147.
Forest Bed, 136, 144, 146-150.
Foxhall, 61-63, 85, 147.
*Framlingham, 135.
Freshwater shells, scarcity of, in Red Crag, 43.
Freston, 48.
*Frinton, 101, 109.
Fuchs,—, 133.

Garland, E. W., 107.
Gedgrave, 26, 28, 71, 82, 141.
Geikie, Prof. J., 87.
Gipping, see Orwell.
Godwin-Austen, R. A. C., 37, 38.
*Gorleston, 142, 147.
*Grays, 37.
Great Horksley, 87.
Great Waldingfield, 1, 73, 92, 114.

Greywether-sandstone, 15, 16, 94.
Groton, 1, 18, 74, 113, 115.
Growth of beach, 99.
Gunn, J., 39.
Gusford Hall, 12, 50, 98.

Hadleigh, 1, 9, 19, 21, 45, 74-76, 84, 88, 93, 101, 115, 116, 135.
*Halesworth, 135.
Halton, 116.
*Hardwick, 136.
Hardy, W. E., 57.
Harkstead, 22, 48, 76.
Harmer, F. W., 41, 42, 78, 83.
Harwich, 1-3, 5, 17, 18, 34, 42, 44, 98, 100, 105, 106, 151.
Havergate, 99, 116.
Hemley, 2, 25, 64, 116.
Henslow, Prof. J. S., 34.
Herapath, T. J., 35, 102, 103.
Higham, 2, 22, 116.
Hintlesham, 77, 116.
Holbrook, 22, 46, 48, 76, 95.
Holden, Dr. J. S., 114.
*Holkham, 100.
Hollesley, 2, 36, 41, 70, 82, 91, 99.
*Hopton, 144, 149.
*Hoxne, 136, 141, 142, 148.
Hydractinia, 147.

Ipswich, 1-3, 5, 6, 10-13, 15, 16, 22, 23, 37, 50, 51, 78, 79, 84-89, 93, 94, 96, 97, 100, 101, 105, 117, 118, 126-131, 135, 136, 140, 142, 145, 147, 148, 151.
Ipswich Museum, 8, 31, 42, 93, 146, 149.
Iron in London Clay, 26.
  „   „ Red Crag, 29, 40, 44-46, 48, 49, 52, 58, 60, 62, 63, 67.
*Ixworth, 135.

Jecks, C., 39.
Jeffreys, Dr. J. G., 31, 41, 42.
Jenyns, Rev. L., 38.
Johnston, Prof., 35.
Jones, H., 131.
Jukes-Browne, A. J., 87.

*Kelsey, 37.
Kersey, 5, 9, 112, 118, 124.
Kersten, C. M., 133.
Kesgrave, 65, 60, 80, 85.
*Kessingland, 135, 145, 148, 149.
Kingsbury,— 111-114, 120, 121, 124.
Kingston or Kyson, 26, 52, 95, 139, 140, 143.
Kirton, 58-60, 85, 86, 119.

Lacustrine formations, 137.
La Marsh, 1, 17.
Land-surface underneath Drift, 143.
Langer or Landguard Common and Fort, 16, 98, 99, 119, 120.
Langham, 44.
Lankester, Prof. E. R., 30, 32, 37-39, 42, 54.
*Lark, Valley, 143.

INDEX.

*Lavenham, 125, 135.
Layham, 9, 21, 45, 84, 88, 100.
Leadenheath, 18, 86, 120.
*Lenham, 39.
Levington, 51, 52, 90, 95.
Little Bealings, 26, 66, 80, 82, 94.
Little Cornard, 73, 83.
Little Horksley, 73, 87.
*Little Ouse Valley, 144, 145.
Little Waldingfield, 1, 74.
Loam-horses, 59.
*Long Melford, 135.
*Lopham Ford, 145.
*Lothingland, 137.
*Lowestoft, 135–137, 144.
Lyell, Sir C., 26, 27, 33–35, 41, 49.

Mammalia, remains of, 26, 30, 34, 36–39, 54, 93, 95–97, 102–105, 110, 138–150.
Mammaliferous Crag, see Norwich Crag.
Manningtree, 1, 17.
Maps, Geological, 135, 144, 145, 147.
Martlesham, 2, 26, 65, 94, 95.
*Mendlesham, 135.
Milden, 121.
*Mildenhall, 135, 137, 149.
Miller, H., 93, 97.
Miller, T., 94, 97, 126–131.
Mineral Waters, 136, 137.
Mistley, 18, 44, 106.
Monks' Eleigh, 2, 5, 45, 75, 121.
Mount Bures, 87, 98.

Nacton, 25, 51, 79, 94.
Nayland, 1, 2, 45, 135.
*Needham Market, 135.
Newbourn, 63, 64, 80, 139.
Newton, 121.
Newton, E. T., 96.
Nodules, see Phosphatic.
Norfolk Crag, see Norwich Crag.
North Weir Point, 99.
*Norwich, 100, 136.
Norwich, or Fluviomarine, or Mammaliferous, or Norfolk, Crag, 32–42, 139, 143, 144, 147.

Ore, or Alde, River and Valley, 2, 26, 35, 67, 70, 71, 98, 99.
*Orford, 37, 99, 101, 138, 140, 141, 149.
Orford Haven, 99.
Orford Marshes, 121.
Orfordness, 98.
Orwell, or Gipping, River and Valley, 1, 2, 5, 6, 10–16, 22–25, 44, 48, 50–54, 58, 76, 78, 79, 83–85, 88, 93, 94, 97, 98, 100, 129–131, 141, 142, 148, 149, 151.
Owen, Sir R., 34.

*Pakefield, 135, 145, 148.
Palæolithic Man, 136, 144, 148, 150.
Parkinson, J., 32.
Passage of Boulder Clay into sand beneath, 81.

Penning, W. H., 87.
Pettit, —, 115, 122, 124.
Phillips, Prof. J., 35, 54.
Phillips, W., 32.
Phosphatic nodules of Crag, 27, 30, 34, 35, 37–39, 44, 45, 48, 50, 51, 53, 56, 57, 59–65, 67–71, 102–105, 140–142, 144, 145, 148.
Pickering, Rev. A., 101.
Pile-dwelling, 146.
Plant-remains in alluvium, 97.
   "   "   pyritized, in London Clay, 17, 56.
Playford, 66, 67, 82, 89, 90.
Polstead, 45, 83, 88, 121.
Polyzoa, or Bryozoa, 27, 28, 33, 142.
Position of shells in Crag, 35.
Prestwich, Prof. J., 8, 19, 23, 26–28, 31, 32, 35, 40, 41, 47, 48, 67–79, 93, 105.

Ramsey, 107.
Ramsholt, 26, 28, 67, 69, 82, 138.
Raydon, 45, 76, 88, 122.
Redman, J. B., 98, 99.
Ringler-Thomson, T. G., 35.
Ripple-marks, 40.
Rushmere, 66, 85, 122.

Sand-flood, 136.
*Saxmundham, 135.
Scott, G., 41.
Scrobicularia Crag, 31, 38, 41, 43.
Selenite, in London Clay, 112.
Semer, 6, 9, 74, 75, 88, 122.
Septaria, see Cement-stones.
Sharman, G., 93, 96.
Shells, freshwater, in Drift, 114.
  "   in Alluvium, 97.
  "   " Glacial sand, 80, 82.
  "   " London Clay, 11, 13, 19–21, 56, 108, 110.
  "   " Oldhaven Beds, 11.
  "   " Valley Drift, 93, 95, 96.
  "   of the Crag in Valley Drift, 94.
Shelly, 9, 10, 45, 74, 88, 100.
Shingle, composition of, 99.
Shingle Street, 70, 98.
Shotley, 48, 76, 95, 122.
Shottisham, 26, 67, 70, 82, 90, 91.
Silting-up of Estuaries, 137.
Sinking of land, 145.
*Southwold, 34, 135, 139, 140.
Sproughton, 10, 23.
Stoke-by-Nayland, 45, 122.
Stollery, —65.
Stones covered with Barnacles, in Crag, 30, 35, 46, 49, 141.
Stones, perforated, from Crag, 147.
Stour, River and Valley, 1, 2, 5, 8, 9, 17–19, 22, 38, 44–48, 73, 76, 83, 87, 88, 92, 95, 98.
*Stowmarket, 125, 135, 136.
Stratford St. Mary, 46.
Stutton, 2, 9, 46, 95, 96, 137.
Submerged Forest, 97, 148, 149.
*Sudbourne, 38, 138, 141.

*Sudbury, 6, 8, 21, 43, 132, 133, 135, 148.
Sutton, 2, 26-28, 38, 40, 67, 68, 90, 101, 102, 105.

Tattingstone, 22, 26, 27, 46-48, 95.
Taylor, Dr. J. E., 8, 18, 41, 42, 48, 97.
Taylor, R. C., 33.
*Thetford, 135, 137, 144-146.
Thingoe Hundred, 139.
Tilley, T., 107, 109.
Tricker, —113-115.
Trimley, 52-54, 58, 79, 85, 95, 101.
Tuddenham, 2, 15, 25, 67, 82, 89, 94.
Tufa, or white marl, 98.
Turtles, remains of, in London Clay, 17.

Valleys, formation of, 143.
Vanden Broeck, E., 29.
Vertebrata, 138. *See also* Fish, Mammalia.
Voelcker, Dr. A., 26, 103.

Waldringfield, 25, 64, 65, 94, 101, 123, 146.
Walton, 25, 54, 58, 131.
*Walton Naze, 31, 32, 36, 38, 39, 41-43, 110.

Warner, J., 110.
Washbrook Valley, 22, 49, 76-78.
Water, brackish, in wells, 105.
*Waveney Valley, 141, 143.
Westerfield, 78-80, 88, 89, 123.
Whatfield, 124.
Wherstead, 35, 49, 76, 101, 124, 141.
Whitaker, W., 42, 43.
Whitton, 13, 15, 23, 24, 78, 79, 124.
*Wickham Bishop, 100.
Williams Tye, 124.
Wood, S. V., 26, 31-34, 36, 37, 42, 43, 47, 96.
Wood, S. V., junr., 25, 32, 35-38, 40-43, 56, 57, 61, 63, 65, 72, 81-86, 98.
Woodbridge, 1, 2, 37, 67, 82, 87, 90, 94, 95, 101, 135, 136, 139, 147, 148.
Woodward, H. B., 110.
Woodward, S., 33.
Woolverstone, 48, 125.
Wormingford, 87.
Wrabness, 18, 95, 101.

*Yare Valley, 141.
*Yarmouth, 100, 143, 144, 147.

Zoophytes, *see* Corals.

The CARBONIFEROUS LIMESTONE, YOREDALE ROCKS and MILLSTONE GRIT of N. DERBYSHIRE. By A. H. GREEN, DR. C. LE NEVE FOSTER, and J. R. DAKYNS. (2nd Ed. in preparation.)
The BURNLEY COAL FIELD. By E. HULL, J. R. DAKYNS, R. H. TIDDEMAN, J. C. WARD, W. GUNN, and C. E. DE RANCE. 12s.
The YORKSHIRE COALFIELD. By A. H. GREEN, J. R. DAKYNS, J. C. WARD, C. FOX-STRANGWAYS, W. H. DALTON, R. RUSSELL, and T. V. HOLMES. 42s.
The EAST SOMERSET and BRISTOL COALFIELDS. By H. B. WOODWARD. 18s.
The SOUTH STAFFORDSHIRE COAL-FIELD. By J. B. JUKES. (3rd Edit.) (*Out of print.*) 3s. 6d.
The WARWICKSHIRE COAL-FIELD. By H. H. HOWELL. 1s. 6d.
The LEICESTERSHIRE COAL-FIELD. By EDWARD HULL. 3s.
HOLDERNESS, By C. REID.
BRITISH ORGANIC REMAINS. DECADES I. to XIII., with 10 Plates each. Price 4s. 6d. each 4to; 2s. 6d. each 8vo.
MONOGRAPH I. On the Genus PTERYGOTUS. By T. H. HUXLEY, and J. W. SALTER. 7s.
MONOGRAPH II. On the Structure of the BELEMNITIDÆ. By T. H. HUXLEY. 2s. 6d.
MONOGRAPH III. On the CROCODILIAN REMAINS found in the ELGIN SANDSTONES. By T. H. HUXLEY. 14s. 6d.
MONOGRAPH IV. On the CHIMÆROID FISHES of the British Cretaceous Rocks. By E. T. NEWTON. 5s.
The VERTEBRATA of the FOREST BED SERIES of NORFOLK and SUFFOLK. By E. T. NEWTON. 7s. 6d.
CATALOGUE of SPECIMENS in the Museum of Practical Geology, illustrative of British Pottery and Porcelain. By Sir H. DE LA BECHE and TRENHAM REEKS. 155 Woodcuts. 2nd Ed. by T. REEKS and F. W. RUDLER. 1s. 6d.; 2s. in boards.
A DESCRIPTIVE GUIDE to the MUSEUM of PRACTICAL GEOLOGY, with Notices of the Geological Survey, the School of Mines, and the Mining Record Office. By ROBERT HUNT and F. W. RUDLER. 6d. (3rd Ed.)
A DESCRIPTIVE CATALOGUE of the ROCK SPECIMENS in the MUSEUM of PRACTICAL GEOLOGY. By A. C. RAMSAY, H. W. BRISTOW, H. BAUERMAN, and A. GEIKIE. 1s. (3rd Edit.) (*Out of print.*) 4th Ed. in progress.
CATALOGUE of the FOSSILS in the MUSEUM of PRACTICAL GEOLOGY:
CAMBRIAN and SILURIAN, 2s. 6d.; CRETACEOUS, 2s. 9d.; TERTIARY and POST-TERTIARY, 1s. 8d.

SHEET MEMOIRS OF THE GEOLOGICAL SURVEY.

Those marked (O.P.) are Out of Print.

4	•	FOLKESTONE and RYE. By F. DREW. 1s.
7	•	PARTS of MIDDLESEX, &c. By W. WHITAKER. 2s. (O.P.)
10	•	TERTIARY FLUVIO-MARINE FORMATION of the ISLE of WIGHT. By EDWARD FORBES. 5s.
10	•	The ISLE of WIGHT. By H. W. BRISTOW. 6s. (O.P.)
12	•	S. BERKSHIRE and N. HAMPSHIRE. By H. W. BRISTOW and W. WHITAKER. 3s. (O.P.)
13	•	PARTS of OXFORDSHIRE and BERKSHIRE. By E. HULL and W. WHITAKER. 3s. (O.P.)
34	•	PARTS of WILTS. and GLOUCESTERSHIRE. By A. C. RAMSAY, W. T. AVELINE, and E. HULL. 8d.
44	•	CHELTENHAM. By E. HULL. 2s. 6d.
45	•	BANBURY, WOODSTOCK, and BUCKINGHAM. By A. H. GREEN. 2s.
45 SW		WOODSTOCK. By B. HULL. 1s.
47	•	N.W. ESSEX & N.E. HERTS. By W. WHITAKER, W. H. PENNING, W. H. DALTON, & F. J. BENNETT. 3s. 6d.
48 SW		COLCHESTER. By W. H. DALTON. 1s. 6d.
48 SE		EASTERN END of ESSEX (WALTON NAZE and HARWICH). By W. WHITAKER. 9d.
48 NW, NE.		IPSWICH, HADLEIGH, and FELIXSTOW. By W. WHITAKER, W. H. DALTON, and F. J. BENNETT.
50 SW		STOWMARKET. By W. WHITAKER, F. J. BENNETT, and J. H. BLAKE. 1s.
50 NW		DISS, EYE, &c. By F. J. BENNETT. 2s.
51 SW		CAMBRIDGE. By W. H. PENNING and A. J. JUKES-BROWN. 4s. 6d.
53 SE		PART of NORTHAMPTONSHIRE. By W. T. AVELINE and RICHARD TRENCH. 8d.
53 NE		PARTS of NORTHAMPTONSHIRE and WARWICKSHIRE. By W. T. AVELINE. 8d. (O.P.)
43 SE		PART of LEICESTERSHIRE. By W. TALBOT AVELINE, and H. H. HOWELL. 8d. (O.P.)
64	•	RUTLAND, &c. By J. W. JUDD. 12s. 6d.
66 NE, SE		NORWICH. By H. B. WOODWARD. 7s.
66 SW		ATTLEBOROUGH. By F. J. BENNETT. 1s. 6d.
68 E		CROMER. By C. REID. 6s.
68 NW, SW.		FAKENHAM, WELLS, &c. By H. B. WOODWARD. 2s.
70		SW PART of LINCOLNSHIRE, with PARTS of LEICESTERSHIRE and NOTTS. By A. J. JUKES-BROWN and W. H. DALTON.
71 NE		NOTTINGHAM. By W. T. AVELINE. (2nd Ed.) 1s.
80 NW		PRESCOT, LANCASHIRE. By E. HULL. (3rd Ed. With additions by A. STRAHAN.) 3s.
80 NE		ALTRINCHAM, CHESHIRE. By E. HULL. 8d. (O.P.)
80 SW		CHESTER. By A. STRAHAN. 2s.
81 NW, SW.		STOCKPORT, MACCLESFIELD, CONGLETON, &LEEK. By E. HULL and A. H. GREEN. 4s.
82 SE		PARTS of NOTTINGHAMSHIRE and DERBYSHIRE. By W. T. AVELINE. (2nd Ed.) 6d.
82 NE		PARTS of NOTTINGHAMSHIRE, YORKSHIRE, and DERBYSHIRE. By W. T. AVELINE. 8d.
87 NW		PARTS of NOTTS, YORKSHIRE, and DERBYSHIRE. (2nd Ed.) By W. T. AVELINE. 6d.
87 SW		BARNSLEY. By A. H. GREEN. 9d.
88 SW		OLDHAM. By E. HULL. 2s.
88 SE		PART of the YORKSHIRE COAL-FIELD. By A. H. GREEN, J. R. DAKYNS, and J. C. WARD. 1s.
88 NE	•	DEWSBURY, HUDDERSFIELD, and HALIFAX. By A. H. GREEN, J. R. DAKYNS, J. C. WARD, and R. RUSSELL. 6d.
89 SE		BOLTON, LANCASHIRE. By E. HULL. 6d.
89 SW		WIGAN. By EDWARD HULL (2nd Ed.) 1s. (O.P.)
90 SE		The COUNTRY between LIVERPOOL and SOUTHPORT. By C. E. DE RANCE. 3d. (O.P.)
90 NE		SOUTHPORT, LYTHAM, and SOUTH SHORE. By C. E. DE RANCE. 6d.
91 SW	•	The COUNTRY between BLACKPOOL and FLEETWOOD. By C. E. DE RANCE. 6d.
91 NW	•	SOUTHERN PART of the FURNESS DISTRICT in N. LANCASHIRE. By W. T. AVELINE. 6d.
92 SE		BRADFORD and SKIPTON. By J. R. DAKYNS, C. FOX-STRANGWAYS, R. RUSSELL, and W. H. DALTON. 6d.
93 NW		NORTH and EAST of HARROGATE. By C. FOX-STRANGWAYS. 6d.
93 NE		The COUNTRY between YORK and MALTON. By C. FOX-STRANGWAYS. 1s. 6d.

SHEET MEMOIRS OF THE GEOLOGICAL SURVEY—continued.

- 93 SW — CARBONIFEROUS ROCKS N. and E. of LEEDS, and the PERMIAN and TRIASSIC ROCKS a TADCASTER. By W. T. AVELINE, A. H. GREEN, J. R. DAKYNS, J. C. WARD, and R. RUSSELL. 6d. (
- 94 NE — BRIDLINGTON BAY. By J. R. DAKYNS and C. FOX-STRANGWAYS. 1s.
- 95 SW, SE — SCARBOROUGH and FLAMBOROUGH HEAD. By C. FOX-STRANGWAYS. 1s.
- 95 NW — WHITBY and SCARBOROUGH. By C. FOX-STRANGWAYS and G. BARROW. 1s. 6d.
- 96 SE — NEW MALTON, PICKERING, and HELMSLEY. By C. FOX-STRANGWAYS. 1s.
- 96 NE — ESKDALE, ROSEDALE, &c. By C. FOX-STRANGWAYS, C. REID, and G. BARROW. 1s. 6d.
- 98 SE — KIRKBY LONSDALE and KENDAL. By W. T. AVELINE, T. MC K. HUGHES, and R. H. TIDDEMAN.
- 98 NE — KENDAL, WINDERMERE, SEDBERGH, & TEBAY. By W. T. AVELINE & T. MC K. HUGHES. 6d. (C
- 101 SE — NORTHERN PART of the ENGLISH LAKE DISTRICT. By J. C. WARD. 9s.

THE MINERAL DISTRICTS OF ENGLAND AND WALES ARE ILLUSTRATE BY THE FOLLOWING PUBLISHED MAPS OF THE GEOLOGICAL SURVEY.

COAL-FIELDS OF ENGLAND AND WALES.

Scale, one inch to a mile.

Anglesey, 78 (SW).
Bristol and Somerset, 19, 35.
Coalbrook Dale, 61 (NE & SE).
Clee Hill, 53 (NE, NW).
Flintshire and Denbighshire, 74 (NE & SE), 79 (NE, SE).
Derby and Yorkshire, 71 (NW, NE, & SE), 82 (NW & SW), 81 (NE), 87 (NE, SE), 88 (SE).
Forest of Dean, 43 (SE & SW).
Forest of Wyre, 61 (SE), 55 (NE)
Lancashire, 80 (NW), 81 (NW), 89, 88 (SW, NW).
Leicestershire, 71 (SW), 83 (NW).
Northumberland & Durham, 103, 105, 106 (SE), 109 (SW, SE.)
N. Staffordshire, 72 (NW), 72 (SW),73(NE),80 (SE), 81(SW).
S. Staffordshire, 54 (NW), 62 (NW).
Shrewsbury, 60 (NE), 61 (NW & SW).
South Wales, 36, 37, 38, 40, 41, 42 (SE, SW).
Warwickshire, 62 (NE SE), 63 (NW SW), 54 (NE), 53 (NW).
Yorkshire, 88 (NE, SE), 87 (SW), 92 (SE), 93 (SW).

GEOLOGICAL MAPS.

Scale, six inches to a mile.

The Coal-fields and other mineral districts of the N. of England are published on a scale of six inches to a mile, at 4s. to 6s. each. MS. Coloured copies of other six-inch maps, not intended for publication, are deposited for reference in the Geological Survey Office, 28, Jermyn Street, London.

Lancashire.

Sheet.	Sheet.
15. Ireleth.	84. Ormskirk, St. Johns, &c.
16. Ulverstone.	85. Standish, &c.
17. Cartmel.	86. Adlington, Horwick, &c.
22. Aldingham.	87. Bolton-le-Moors.
47. Clitheroe.	88. Bury, Heywood.
48. Colne, Twiston Moor.	89. Rochdale, &c.
49. Laneshaw Bridge.	92. Bickerstaffe.
55. Whalley.	93. Wigan, Up Holland, &c.
56. Haggate.	94. West Houghton, Hindley.
57. Winewall.	95. Radcliffe, Peel Swinton.
61. Preston.	96. Middleton, Prestwich.
62. Balderstone, &c.	97. Oldham, &c.
63. Accrington.	100. Knowsley, Rainford, &c.
64. Burnley.	101. Billinge, Ashton, &c.
65. Stiperden Moor.	102. Leigh, Lowton.
69. Layland.	103. Ashley, Eccles.
70. Blackburn, &c.	104. Manchester, Salford, &c.
71. Haslingden.	105. Ashton-under-Lyne.
72. Cliviger, Bacup, &c.	106. Liverpool, &c.
73. Todmorden.	107. Prescott, Huyton, &c.
77. Chorley.	108. St. Helen's, Burton Wood.
78. Bolton-le-Moors.	109. Winwick, &c.
79. Entwistle.	111. Cheadle, Stockport, &c.
80. Tottington.	112. Stockport, &c.
81. Wardle.	113. Part of Liverpool, &c.

Durham.

1. Ryton.	5. Greenside.
2. Gateshead.	6. Winlaton.
3. Jarrow.	7. Washington.
4. S. Shields.	8. Sunderland.

Durham—continued.

Sheet.	Sheet.
9. ———	25. Wolsingham.
10. Edmondbyers.	28. Brancepeth.
11. Ebchester.	30. Benny Seat.
12. Tantoby.	32. White Kirkley.
15. Chester-le-Street.	33. Hamsterley.
16. Hunstanworth.	34. Whitworth.
17. Waskerley.	38. Maize Beck.
18. Muggleswick.	41. Cockfield.
19. Lanchester.	42. Bishop Auckland.
20. Hetton-le-Hole.	46. Hapksley Hill House.
21. Wear Head.	52. Barnard Castle.
23. Eastgate.	53. Winston.
24. Stanhope.	

Northumberland.

44. Rothbury.	80. Cramlington.	98. Walker.
45. Longframlington.	81. Earsdon.	101. Whitfield.
	82. NE. of Gilsland.	102. Allendale
46. Broomhill.	83. Condley Gate.	Town.
47. Coquet Island.	87. Heddon.	103. Slaley.
54. Longhorsley.	88. Long Benton.	105. Newlands.
55. Ulgham.	89. Tynemouth.	106. Blackpool Br.
58. Druridge Bay.	91. Greenhead.	107. Allendale.
63. Netherwitton.	92. Haltwhistle.	108. Blanchland.
64. Morpeth.	93. Haydon Bridge.	109. Shotleyfield.
65. Newbiggin.	94. Hexham.	110. Wellhope.
72. Bedlington.	95. Corbridge.	111. Allenheads.
75. Blyth.	96. Horsley.	112.
	97. Newcastle.	

Cumberland.

55. Searness.	69. Buttermere.
56. Skiddaw.	70. Grange.
63. Thackthwaite.	71. Helvellyn.
64. Keswick.	74. Wastwater.
65. Dockraye.	75. Stonethwaite Fell.

Westmorland.

2. Tees Head.	12. Patterdale.	25. Grasmere.
6. Dufton Fell.	18. Near Grasmere.	33. Kendal.

Yorkshire.

	110. Conistone	260. Honley.
7. Redcar.	Moor.	261. Kirkburton.
9. ———	133. Kirkby	262. Darton.
12. Bowes.	Malham.	263. Hemsworth.
15. Wycliffe.	184. Dale End.	264. Campsall.
20. Lythe.	155. Kildwick.	272. Holmfirth.
24. Kirkby Ravensworth.	190. Keighley.	273. Penistone.
	201. Bingley.	274. Barnsley.
25. Aldborough.	202. Calverley.	275. Darfield.
31. Whitby.	203. Seacroft.	276. Brodsworth.
33. ———	204. Aberford.	281. Laugsell.
38. Marske.	215. Peake Well.	282. Wortley.
39. Richmond.	216. Bradford.	283. Wath upon
40. ———	217. Calverley.	Dearne.
47. Robin Hood's	218. Leeds.	284. Conisborough.
Bay.	219. Kippax.	287. Low Bradford.
53. Downholme.	231. Halifax.	288. Ecclesfield.
68. Leybourne.	232. Birstal.	289. Rotherham.
83. Kidstones.	233. East Ardsley.	290. Braithwell.
84. E. Witton.	234. Castleford.	293. Hallam Moor.
97. Foxup.	246. Huddersfield.	295. Handsworth.
98. Kirk Gill.	247. Dewsbury.	296. Leighton - es-
99. Haden Carr.	248. Wakefield.	le-Morthen.
100. Lofthouse.	249. Pontefract.	299. ———
115. Arncliffe.	250. Darrington.	300. Harthill.

MINERAL STATISTICS.

Embracing the produce of Coals, Metallic Ores, and other Minerals. By R. HUNT. From 1853 to 1857, Inclusive 1s. 6d. each. 1858, Part I., 1s. 6d.; Part II., 5s. 1859, 1. 6d. 1860, 3s. 6d., 1861, 2s.; and Appendix, 1s. 1862, 2s. 6 1863, 2s. 6d., 1864, 2s. 1865, 2s. 6d., 1866 to 1881, 2s. each.
(These Statistics are now published by the Home Office, as parts of the Reports of the Inspectors of Mines.)

THE IRON ORES OF GREAT BRITAIN.

Part I. The North and North Midland Counties of England (Out of print). Part II. South Staffordshire. Price 1
Part III. South Wales. Price 1s. 3d. Part IV. The Shropshire Coal-field and North Staffordshire. 1s. 3d.

www.ingramcontent.com/pod-product-compliance
Lightning Source LLC
Chambersburg PA
CBHW030247170426
43202CB00009B/660